WITHDRAWN
UTSA Libraries

PALGRAVE Studies in Oral History

Series Editors: Linda Shopes and Bruce M. Stave

The Order Has Been Carried Out: History, Memory, and Meaning of a Nazi Massacre in Rome, by Alessandro Portelli (2003)

Sticking to the Union: An Oral History of the Life and Times of Julia Ruuttila, by Sandy Polishuk (2003)

To Wear the Dust of War: From Bialystok to Shanghai to the Promised Land, an Oral History, by Samuel Iwry, edited by L. J. H. Kelley (2004)

Education as My Agenda: Gertrude Williams, Race, and the Baltimore Public Schools, by Jo Ann Robinson (2005)

Remembering: Oral History Performance, edited by Della Pollock (2005)

Postmemories of Terror: A New Generation Copes with the Legacy of the "Dirty War," by Susana Kaiser (2005)

Growing Up in the People's Republic: Conversations between Two Daughters of China's Revolution, by Ye Weili and Ma Xiaodong (2005)

Life and Death in the Delta: African American Narratives of Violence, Resilience, and Social Change, by Kim Lacy Rogers (2006)

Creating Choice: A Community Responds to the Need for Abortion and Birth Control, 1961–1973, by David P. Cline (2006)

Voices from This Long Brown Land: Oral Recollections of Owens Valley Lives and Manzanar Pasts, by Jane Wehrey (2006)

Radicals, Rhetoric, and the War: The University of Nevada in the Wake of Kent State, by Brad E. Lucas (2006)

The Unquiet Nisei: An Oral History of the Life of Sue Kunitomi Embrey, by Diana Meyers Bahr (2007)

Sisters in the Brotherhoods: Working Women Organizing for Equality in New York City, by Jane LaTour (2008)

Iraq's Last Jews: Stories of Daily Life, Upheaval, and Escape from Modern Babylon, edited by Tamar Morad, Dennis Shasha, and Robert Shasha (2008)

Soldiers and Citizens: An Oral History of Operation Iraqi Freedom from the Battlefield to the Pentagon, by Carl Mirra (2008)

Overcoming Katrina: African American Voices from the Crescent City and Beyond, by D'Ann R. Penner and Keith C. Ferdinand (2009)

Bringing Desegregation Home: Memories of the Struggle toward School Integration in Rural North Carolina, by Kate Willink (2009)

I Saw it Coming: Worker Narratives of Plant Closings and Job Loss, by Tracy E. K'Meyer and Joy L. Hart (2010)

Speaking History: Oral Histories of the American Past, 1865–Present, by Sue Armitage and Laurie Mercier (2010)

Surviving Bhopal: Dancing Bodies, Written Texts, and Oral Testimonials of Women in the Wake of an Industrial Disaster, by Suroopa Mukherjee (2010)

Living with Jim Crow: African American Women and Memories of the Segregated South, by Anne Valk and Leslie Brown (2010)

Being Muslim in America, by Irum Shiekh (2010)

Stories from the Gulag, by Jehanne Gheith and Katherine Jolluck (2010)

Surviving Bhopal

Dancing Bodies, Written Texts, and Oral Testimonials of Women in the Wake of an Industrial Disaster

Suroopa Mukherjee

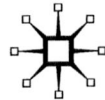

SURVIVING BHOPAL
Copyright © Suroopa Mukherjee, 2010.
All rights reserved.

First published in 2010 by
PALGRAVE MACMILLAN®
in the United States—a division of St. Martin's Press LLC,
175 Fifth Avenue, New York, NY 10010.

Where this book is distributed in the UK, Europe and the rest of the world, this is by Palgrave Macmillan, a division of Macmillan Publishers Limited, registered in England, company number 785998, of Houndmills, Basingstoke, Hampshire RG21 6XS.

Palgrave Macmillan is the global academic imprint of the above companies and has companies and representatives throughout the world.

Palgrave® and Macmillan® are registered trademarks in the United States, the United Kingdom, Europe and other countries.

ISBN: 978–0–230–60811–5

Library of Congress Cataloging-in-Publication Data

Mukherjee, Suroopa.
  Surviving Bhopal : dancing bodies, written texts, and oral testimonials of women in the wake of an industrial disaster / Suroopa Mukherjee.
    p. cm.
  Includes bibliographical references and index.
  ISBN 978–0–230–60811–5 (alk. paper)
    1. Bhopal Union Carbide Plant Disaster, Bhopal, India, 1984.
    2. Pesticides industry—Accidents—India—Bhopal—Political aspects.
    3. Methyl isocyanate—Environmental aspect—India—Bhopal. I. Title.

HD7269.C452I5266 2010
363.17'91—dc22   2009039977

A catalogue record of the book is available from the British Library.

Design by Newgen Imaging Systems (P) Ltd., Chennai, India.

First edition: April 2010

10 9 8 7 6 5 4 3 2 1

Printed in the United States of America.

Library
University of Texas
at San Antonio

For the wounded generation... the children of Bhopal survivors

Contents

Series Editors' Foreword	ix
Acknowledgments	xi
Introduction	1
CHAPTER 1	
The Killer Factory: A Disaster Waiting to Happen	17
CHAPTER 2	
Monstrous Memories: "Reliving" the Night of the Disaster	41
CHAPTER 3	
Bhopal Lives On: The Many Faces of the Continuing Disaster	61
CHAPTER 4	
Women as Bread Earners: Shattered Lives and the Relentless Struggle for Survival	81
CHAPTER 5	
"We Are Flames Not Flowers": The Inception of Activism	101
CHAPTER 6	
"No More Bhopals": Women's Right to Knowledge and Control of Their Bodies	131
CHAPTER 7	
"Dancing in the Streets": Protest, Celebration, and Modes of Self-Expression	159
Notes	185
Bibliography	197
Index	209

Series Editors' Foreword

If not for the events of December 3, 1984, modern Bhopal would be known to the world, if it was at all interested, as a provincial capital in India with a somewhat interesting history. But, when 42 tons of toxic gas escaped that December into the atmosphere from a Union Carbide plant, it marked that city as site of what many consider the world's worst industrial disaster. Without agreement on the final number of fatalities and lesser casualties, estimates range from the official estimate of 5,000 initially dead to 4 times that amount. More than 550,000 are thought to have suffered aftereffects, some dying from gas-related illnesses such as lung cancer, kidney failure, and liver disease, with others suffering birth defects as a result of genetic mutations in their parents' reproductive systems. The effect continued to resonate long after the event. In 2009, 25 years after it happened, a victims' group successfully persuaded an Indian magistrate to again order the arrest of the head of Union Carbide at the time of the accident, who left for the United States after an initial arrest in 1984. Although he now had safe harbor in the United States, his wife explained that Warren Anderson, 89 and in poor health, had "been haunted for many years" by what happened in Bhopal a quarter of a century earlier.[1]

The former corporate mogul was not the only one haunted. Thousands and thousands of victims, many of them women, suffered even more. It is their story that Suroopa Mukherjee, a literary scholar with an interest in oral history, brings to us. She employs oral history to probe beyond the often-obfuscating official record and reveals the special impact on women, often-illiterate women, who bore children with physical or mental defects, who lost spouses and faced uncertain economic futures, who were failed by a faulty medical and rehabilitation system, who were harried by bureaucracy, but who organized in action groups and unions in an effort to assert their agency. Mukherjee is fully engaged with her subject and places the narrative of Bhopal's women within a framework of global corporate development. Like those she studies, the author seeks that justice be done in the face of corporate greed.

This volume, our twentieth, not only adds environmental history to the subjects covered by the Palgrave Macmillan Studies in Oral History series, but

---

[1] Frank Eltman, Associated Press, "Warrant: 25 Years Later," *Hartford Courant*, August 2, 2009.

also enhances its international reach to include India along with studies that have focused on Italy, Argentina, China, and Iraq. Other books address various dimensions of U.S. history. All strive to place oral history in a broad historical and methodological context and give voice to those who live in interesting times.

Bruce M. Stave
University of Connecticut

Linda Shopes
Carlisle, PA

Acknowledgments

I wish to extend my thanks to: Hindu College, University of Delhi for granting me academic leave to pursue a Fellowship at Nehru Memorial Museum and Library (NMML) for three years.

To all the staff of the library at NMML, the office and the annexe building. This book would not have been possible without my stint at NMML.

To my students and members of *We for Bhopal* for being a constant source of inspiration.

To the Bhopalis for their hospitality, for sharing their thoughts and experience of life. It has changed the way I read, write, and teach.

To Anil Sadgopal, N. D. Jayprakash, Sadhna Karnick, and Alok Pratap Singh for giving their valuable time to educate me on various aspects of the social movement.

To group leaders Rashida Bi, Champa Devi Shukla, Jabbar Khan, B. Namdeo, Shahid Noor, Irfan Khan, and Nawab Khan for their insights and opinions.

To all the staff of Sambhavna Trust for allowing me to use the documentation center and for providing me with valuable data. There is a treasure trove of information that is available there for anybody who is interested in future research.

To Eurig, Dharmesh, and Tarunima saying thank you is not enough. They will discover how much of my writing owes to their valuable input.

To Rachna, Nity, Madhu, Sweta, Shalini, Gurpreet, Nimmi, Deena, Ravi, Vinuta, Nishant, Sheri, Terry, Bridget, Maud, Ryan, Gary, Indra, Ward, Tim, Aquene, and Shana—I salute your work.

To all my friends and colleagues—Brinda, Tapan, Rekha, Partho, Charu, Nonika for providing such a wonderful support system. To Prakash, special thanks, for lending books and shaping my thoughts over morning cups of coffee.

To my family—Gautam, Anasuya—for myriad things big and small. To my sister Suparna for her unstinted support for the Bhopal cause.

Finally, to Sathyu—his vision for justice in Bhopal goes way beyond Bhopal and therefore needs to be written about.

Introduction

The Bhopal gas tragedy—the world's worst manmade disaster—is much written and talked about, and yet surprisingly it has not generated enough academic interest in different disciplines. It is not a topic that is included in school and college curriculum. It is not part of the medical course or disaster management. It is taught as a case study in law schools at the undergraduate level and from what one gathers it has produced a few PhD degrees in Indian universities. What began as a failure of documentation and lack of authentic data on the cause and fallout of the disaster has over the years become a saga of neglect. At the same time, unknown to mainstream research, local efforts have gone into collecting indigenous material, which is then stored in the grassroot-level offices of survivors' organizations. Despite paucity of funds and limited expertise, a lot of meticulous care is taken to keep records of newspaper clippings, campaign material, and press releases on organizational activities. In recent years, student volunteers have come to Bhopal on short-term projects that are conceptualized and funded by bigger nongovernmental organizations (NGOs) in India and abroad. The findings of such research are freely circulated on Web sites and brought out as low-cost pamphlets that are meant for the layman and activists. The Bhopal gas tragedy has also created a plethora of visual images and creative writing in popular forms—including photographs, documentary films, video clippings, theater presentations, dance dramas, a novel short-listed for the Booker, an international bestseller, a children's book, a mainstream Bollywood film, a script for a forthcoming Hollywood production, and musical rendering—all of which have made Bhopal an integral part of the folklore. As the subtitle of this book *Dancing Bodies, Written Texts, and Oral Testimonials of Women in the Wake of an Industrial Disaster* indicates, what I seek is a middle ground between academic and popular writing that incorporates the gender perspective within a broader canvas that brings in image, text, and oral testimonials drawn from archival sources, fieldwork, and secondary material.

We all know that the disaster took place on the dawn of December 3, 1984. Sometime past midnight forty tons of lethal methyl isocyanate (MIC) and its various compounds escaped into the air, killing and injuring an entire population living in old Bhopal. What is less known is that the fallout of the event continues even today as an environmental, social, medical, economic, and political disaster. The most powerful media-generated images of the disaster are faces of men and women staring blankly at the uncertain future. There are other images, far more evocative and subversive, which have not gained sufficient attention. Bhopal has generated more controversies than proper analytical understanding of the various components that goes into defining it as an industrial disaster. As a result, the disaster has not encouraged mainstream research to probe into the areas of conflict and to arrive at a comprehensive understanding of the event, not simply as a catastrophe, but also as a modern-day phenomenon that is emblematic of the failure of the twentieth-century vision of a new world. *Surviving Bhopal* juxtaposes concepts of progress, technological innovation, and development that went into defining the vision, with the oral history of people who paid the price for its failure.

Who are these people and what is the relevance of recounting their history in the context of a neoliberal, globalized world order? Bhopal, the capital of Madhya Pradesh (MP), which is situated on a sandstone ridge, 1,652 ft above sea level, on the edge of two lakes, was built by Raja Bhoj, the Parmara ruler of Dhar in the eleventh century in what was then known as the town of Bhojpal. Modern Bhopal—derived from the word Bhupala that means "ruler of the land" was built on the site of this old town. In 1709 the Afghan chieftain Dost Muhammad made Bhopal his headquarters and became the first Nawab. From 1819 to 1901 Bhopal was ruled by a succession of women described by historians as "the rule of the Begums."[1] In 1984 the population of Bhopal was nearly one million, residing in three areas that formed the city. The old city that was established by the Nawabs lies in the northern part; the central part is the new city with government offices, ministers' bungalows, and the residential areas of the richer section of society; the south consists of the industrial township catering to government-run engineering industries. The poison gas from the Union Carbide India Limited (UCIL) factory affected the lives of people living in old Bhopal. A large section of this population consisted of first/second generation immigrants, who had come from villages in the neighboring districts, because the chances of earning their livelihood from the land was severely jeopardized by development schemes that introduced more mechanized forms of agriculture.[2] Most of these people earned their living in daily wages for hard, physical labor. The women who belonged to the minority community (Muslims formed 35 percent of the population) did piece-rate work from inside their homes and lived lives in purdah within the strict confinement of their families. It is this population that came in the path of the gas leak, creating a new category of people—"victims" of industrial disaster. Once the dead were buried, the "survivors" were left behind to carry on with the legacy of suffering and hardship. It is these marginal people and their story of survival that is the primary focus of this book.

In relating their story we get to reconstruct the "cause and effect" of the disaster from the people's perspective. In the words of Hazra Bi, one of the women who survived the disaster, "that night" is indelibly etched in her mind. "How can I ever forget?" she asks forcefully, setting in motion a narrative whose strands unravel an amazing saga of relentless suffering and battle for justice. Bi admits that she is more than willing to talk about her experience to anyone who asks her questions, for it is the only way she can make sense of what happened to her on that fateful night. Oral history offers an important tool for recording what women like Hazra Bi have to say. She represents people who use their "memories" in a deliberate and conscious effort to make sense of the mammoth process of "containing" and "controlling" that followed the disaster. The fact that twenty-five years later the process of "containing" still continues, tells us a great deal about the relevance of Hazra Bi's testimonials.

What sort of research methodology do I use to uncover an event that has been grossly misrepresented by the media and the ruling middle class? It is surprising that even today when I listen to Bi I am struck by how much is really unknown about the incident. In real terms we are still talking about a runaway reaction of deadly chemicals of unknown components and potency, killing an unknown number of people and causing injury and disability of an unknown kind to an entire community of people living in thirty-six wards identified as severely, moderately, and mildly affected areas, with long-term repercussions for nobody knows what length of time. And this despite the fact that soon after the disaster, an entire bureaucratic mechanism was put in place to deal with the situation, and reams of statistics were produced by government-controlled surveys and studies. Clearly, the task of uncovering "true facts" to pierce the veil of secrecy that gave impunity to those responsible for the disaster is daunting. Importantly, writing on Bhopal can never be a purely academic exercise without drawing attention to its political relevance. In this book I take up the bigger challenge of highlighting ways in which the Bhopal disaster has been "constructed" in the popular imagination by a process that simultaneously commemorates and erases the tragedy. In this way, I am able to show how official methods of coping with the disaster went on to become the basis for a cruel and ruthless denial of justice. I draw on resources provided by oral history methodology, to recreate the interface between what is "reported" officially and the "lived experience" of trauma and suffering as recorded through neglected voices of people.

A great deal of what has been written about the Bhopal gas tragedy veers between dry, inaccessible government-sponsored documents and scientific studies, to human interest stories carried in magazines and popular journals catering to middle-class tastes and imaginative appeal. Consequently, much of the writing falls into the trap of serving different kinds of vested interest. As mentioned earlier, *Surviving Bhopal* treads a middle ground. It is an academic exercise but hopes to have a wider appeal among campaigners and activists working at the grassroots level for the victims and survivors of the event. Moreover, it reflects my own intellectual and emotional engagement with Bhopal. My involvement began from 2002, after my work of nonfiction for children on the Bhopal gas tragedy was published.[3] I was addressing children born after the event, so a large part of my effort was to reconstruct things in a manner that was relevant to youth and the future generation. As a teacher of English literature I had little experience of fieldwork. I had never visited a slum in my life. I was treading on the toes of historians, sociologists, and social scientists. My research had to be interdisciplinary; my subject provided me requisite training in that area. I carried many a baggage with me but in the long run they became my assets. I was able to meet people without ruffling their feathers or seeming like a threat. I discovered that reading and interpreting works of art are seen as apolitical activity that is esoteric and escapist in nature. In any exchange of ideas, even on polemical issues, it was interesting to see how roles got reversed, and I had people quoting Shakespeare to make their point! Today I can say with some degree of confidence that my work uses parameters that are far from stereotypical. My fieldwork took me to bastis inside the homes of the community of Bhopali survivors. I shared their meals, joined their festivities, listened to their victory songs and tales of grief and suffering; I put forward my questions, recorded their answers on tape and in scribbled notes; all this data has gone into writing this book.

The research was spread over years and involved piece-meal gathering of information, as and when I got interested in particular aspects of the Bhopal tragedy. The Fellowship at Nehru Memorial Museum and Library, Teen Murti House, New Delhi offered me the ideal space to put it all together. Riffling through the material I had gathered, I discovered a few areas of interest that emerged like a leitmotif on which I could peg my central argument. It was surprising that very little had been written about the women survivors of Bhopal. And this, despite the fact that the fight for justice in Bhopal is one of the oldest movements in the world, and women have been in the forefront of the struggle. What I have tried to do is fill up this lacunae by studying women's activism in Bhopal, regarding the development model of economic restructuring in the context of globalization. I have tried to explore the different facets of a chemical disaster, involving a giant multinational and its Indian subsidiary, and raised questions on why the economic and medical rehabilitation that followed the disaster failed to mete out justice for the victims of development. I have also shown how women's activism has championed an alternate vision for justice that reinforces the political rights of people to choose a life of dignity.

From August 2007 to September 2008 I was involved with a research project undertaken by Queen Margaret University (QMU), Edinburgh on the Ethnology of Bhopal Campaigners for Justice. It formed The Bhopal Survivor's Movement Study Group, which comprised of Eurig Scandrett (Principal Investigator), Suroopa Mukherjee (Consultant), Dharmesh Shah (Research Assistant), and Tarunima Sen (Research Assistant). Luckily for me, any difficulties I might have faced, given my lack of formal training in taking interviews, were easily overcome. The project conducted interviews with forty individuals who belonged to different groups actively participating in the resistance movement in Bhopal. The interviews were recorded on digital video and audiotape, and it followed the format and norms laid down by oral history project. I am enormously fortunate in being able to use extensive material from the project. I have scrupulously acknowledged the sources that are primarily of three kinds: testimonials drawn from archival sources soon after the disaster, interviews I have personally conducted with details of when they were done, and interviews drawn from the project—these are indicated by the tape number. Wherever necessary the anonymity clause has been followed, and the identity of the interviewee has been disclosed only with permission. Individual voices merge with the collective, but in most cases the point of view comes unmediated. At the same time, the attempt has been to present the conflict-ridden domain where "private" grief and the "public" denial of justice and systemic failure converge in multiple ways. At different points in time I met bureaucrats, doctors, lawyers, politicians, activists, and their group leaders. I have tried to bring together conflicting points of view in strategic relation to each other, in a way that probes oral history methodology and argues for its radicalization. This is specially so when one is looking at the Bhopal gas tragedy from the perspective of a people's movement in the modern context of corporate crime.

The Use of Oral History

I have to admit that what attracted me to oral history was its close association with literature and the fact that its practitioners include historians, sociologists, anthropologists, and literary scholars who have done pioneering work.[4] Some of the names that come to mind are Milman Parry, a Homeric scholar and founder of the discipline of oral tradition, and Albert Bates Lord, Professor of Slavic and Comparative Literature, who studied the epics from Europe and Asia. Both worked on theories of orality/literacy (Parry, 1971) and oral performance/composition (Lord, 1960). The *oral* component in oral history makes it an ancient tool for exploring myths, songs, folklore, and stories that have passed down through word of mouth, from one age to another, across different cultures and geographical locations. At the same time, it serves as a modern device that specifically records the eyewitness accounts of an event of historical importance. Its popularity as such an instrument became a post-sixties phenomenon, bringing to light the experiences of working classes, women, and black history.[5] It is clearly meant as an aid for recording, transcribing, and preserving knowledge that is somehow threatened by external circumstances. Many international oral history organizations have been formed that conduct workshops, conferences and publish newsletters and journals that discuss oral history theory and practices.[6] A major shift was seen in the sixties and seventies; the focus turned from recording prominent voices to recording memories of people from the margins, thus drawing on history from below.[7] Notable scholars in this field are Raphael Samuel, Christopher Hill, E. P. Thomson, and Eric Hobsbawm.[8] More recently the development of video tape recording has brought in the dimensions of gesture along with verbal forms of communication (Kendon, 2004, McNeill, 2005). A lot of work has been done on the use of "memory" as tool and the dynamics of individual and collective memory of the community.[9]

This book uses oral history to study the experiences of the specific social group of women victims/survivors of this industrial disaster who were twice victimized by their positions of marginality in a traditional society undergoing social/economic/political upheaval that accompanied the spread of corporate power in a globalized world. The idea is to draw attention to the testimonials of people who are underrepresented in the mainstream culture. Oral history projects take up the voices of marginalized groups by highlighting the value of experiential knowledge. No doubt, oral testimonials cannot replace traditional historical materials such as official documents, newspaper clippings, and archival materials that include letters, public notices, and other printed matters such as books, journals, pamphlets, and monographs. History unravels the past, keeping in mind trends that are specific to a given historical period, and the individual experiences that give shape to such trends. Cultural anthropologists try to understand the interrelation between culture and the individual and how individuals think of themselves in relation to larger forces operative in society. Folklorists also study culture as expressed in everyday life, and they use the interview method to retrieve the folklore of that particular culture.[10] I draw upon oral history methodology taken from these numerous strands in oral history traditions, but more particularly I look at the dynamics of academic research and finding that are freely circulated in the public domain. In the process, scholarship breaks free from any kind of hegemonic control and becomes the property of those who strive at the grassroots level to bring knowledge within people's grasp. Only then can the indigenous, oral tradition become the means for deconstructing the corporate and bureaucratic "veil," in order to show how they act as tools of oppression.

As mentioned earlier women have led the movement. I study gender politics in the movement by drawing attention to some of the demands made by the Bhopal survivors. The issues of livelihood and healthcare are closely linked, given the fact that most survivors suffer from severe disabilities, which has taken away their capacity to earn a proper living. Here are some of the demands: right to good health, right to a clean toxic-free environment, right to information, and the right to a life of dignity. It is interesting to know how issues of poverty, lack of medical care, and the presence of a polluting factory site get intertwined with worldwide concerns regarding human rights, environmental politics, and corporate liability. I use women's testimonials to talk about their "experience" of living lives of destitution, and the way in which this affects family life, especially that of elderly members, dependents, and children. At the same time, the very process of coping with their ravaged, ailing bodies enables them to understand the nature of the systemic failure that has continued to plague the aftermath of the disaster. The body becomes the site of contestation, and survivors are able to testify through their own experience of the ruthless manipulation that underlies the clash between institutions, official discourses, and their social/political ramifications.

It is in the process of knowing the body that an alternative model for rehabilitation is created, which works on the simple paradigm that economic and medical rehabilitation has to go hand in hand. More importantly, proper treatment protocol has to be accompanied by research, which looks into long-term health issues. Right from the start, both the company and the government were reluctant to admit to the long-term effects of the gas on the body. Clearly, the reasons are sinister and carry serious implications. They indicate that official medical discourse has continued to deny the truth that the gas had affected more organs than just lungs and eyes. The reality is grimmer still. The most devastating effect of toxic poisoning has been on women's reproductive health, resulting in the possibility of a second generation born with congenital defects. Twenty-four years later, mothers affected by chemical poisoning are giving birth to such children, and it is the untold stories of this invisible "wounded generation" that needs to be brought out in the open.

Women are conspicuously missing from official documents—legal, medical, bureaucratic, and those used in compensation courts. Such documents provide historical evidence of a ruthless process of denial and erasure. In sharp contrast, oral testimonials become means for probing memories of people, otherwise written off from formal methods of recording events. Tools of oral history in this context have been used to retrieve lost voices, to show how women have participated in the political process of redefining identities, in terms of collective strength, and the discovery of self. By juxtaposing texts and testimonials I reveal how women's consciousness has "scripted" the story of activism in Bhopal. Therefore, it is not at all surprising that despite the official negation, women have forged their "visibility" in almost every aspect of the social movement in Bhopal.

Writing the Historical Wound

In this connection it would be interesting to draw attention to the concept of a "historical wound," which requires evidence of experience before it is brought openly into public life (Attwood, Chakrabarty, and Lomnitz, 2008). Attwood talks about the "age of testimony" in relation to the "stolen generation narratives," which has a resonance in our understanding of those forgotten histories where authenticity is not dependent on what the written word guarantees as true knowledge (the stolen generation narratives claimed that in the twentieth century, in an open act of genocide, a high percentage of aboriginal children were removed from their families to prevent the race from multiplying).[11] Attwood gives importance to narratives that are projected onto a "range of institutions" that are "not historiographical in nature but memorial, literary, filmic, therapeutic and quasilegal" (78). He talks of a conscious effort to democratize historical methods by breaking out of the positivist or empiricist mould. Oral history is brought in to give people agency by allowing them to participate in the recovery and reconstruction of their experience. This is especially useful in recreating a traumatic experience, by using empathy and compassion to evoke subjective states of mind and heart. He therefore insists on historical proximity rather than historical distancing.

Oral history can be both formal and informal, a set of fixed parameters to get preconceived responses or informal conversations with people who can provide a firsthand account of events. It works on the premise that a lot of essential information can be got by simply talking to people. At the same time, it involves a systematic and disciplined effort to record and preserve the data for future research. The idea is to supplement the written record by bringing in a vast repertoire of narratives from different subject positions and historical sequencing of events, so as to create a more nuanced understanding of how they unfold in a multidimensional way. No doubt, with oral history we are entering an ambivalent domain, which raises queries that are both conceptual and functional.[12] What is the link between the interviewer and the narrator? Is it a dialogue or question/answer session? Is there a degree of preparedness, selection, and self-conscious editing and blocking out of problematic aspects? And how do norms of confidentiality really work? Oral history involves interpretation, making connections, and seeking clarifications. Therefore, it is of utmost importance that the cross-section of people selected for the interview is truly representative. Finally, how difficult or probing should the questions be? And who controls the story—the interviewer or the narrator?

Surviving Bhopal confronts most of these issues; at the same time, it shows how oral history problematizes the whole question of representative voices and historical proximity and distancing. Simply bringing in the voices of oppressed people is not enough to present social reality.[13] This can happen only by shifting attention away from merely personal experience, which is narrated as a good story. Often the intention is to play on the emotionally resonant quality of personal experience, in order to draw the attention of the listener and evoke interest and sympathy. I dare say these are qualities that are associated with literature. I use the first-person narrative very cautiously and only after I have carefully created the larger context. In doing so I draw upon literature's multidisciplinary range and the way it can use history, sociology, and psychology in its study of people and society. Whenever I bring in a single speaker who does most of the talking, I also make sure that the nameless voices appear in the body of the text to suggest the collective struggle that forms the backbone of the resistance movement. The book explores the open confrontation between the survivors and the systems of oppression. I show how survivors were left out of the decision-making process, thus deprived of the freedom to exercise personal choice, and their individual self-expression literally gagged. I draw attention to the unprecedented levels of violence and suffering that are unleashed by the process of marginalizing and erasure. Oral history becomes the vital mode of understanding the nature of this violence and the way in which it affects the day-to-day lives of ordinary people. Testimonials take us deep into the psyche of people who stand at the other end of the spectrum, far removed from such decision-making bodies as government offices and the boardroom of corporate bosses. Instead, we get an inside view of those public spaces, like work-sheds for economic rehabilitation, gas relief hospitals, and compensation claims court, where an ordinary survivor suffers endless humiliation and despair. By listening to people who are at the receiving end of these rehabilitation schemes, we get a clear insight into how systems that are meant to deal with a crisis situation actually work. In recording the impact of a manmade disaster on people who live to recount their personal experience, oral history creates the perfect vantage point between proximity and distance.

A major thrust of my argument is to show how forces of globalization and corporatization, with their models of development, rendered communities as expendable by distancing them from the forward march of progress. By bringing in oral history I am able to analyze how survivors perceived the larger forces of change, and the ways in which it impinged on the lives of people. I believe that it is important to understand the development model from the perspective of those who do not stand to gain by it. It shifts attention from economic to social and moral issues, and it raises ethical questions on the inequitable distribution of resources and wealth. It shows how a merely techno-driven rehabilitation scheme that fails to assuage the demand for justice can set a bad precedent in a world that is willing to pay any price for profit. Bhopal reveals the ugly underbelly of globalization. It is in this context that we see how resistance to global forces had come into shape in Bhopal. Each chapter deepens our understanding of the political process by which survivors gained insight into how globalization operates in the common man's daily struggle for existence. Women speak out, in an eloquent testimony to the spirit of resistance. By rewriting the history of people pitched against monolithic institutions, oral history is able to show how oppression works within systems, and how resistance takes shape in people's consciousness.

A New Definition of Corporate Crime

Over the last few decades there has been considerable interest in corporate behavior and the nature of violations of corporate laws (Clinard and Yeager 1980, Fisse and Braithwaite 1993, Pearce and Snider 1995). The term "corporate crime" is widely used, since Clinard and Yeager (1980) undertook the first comprehensive study in their pioneering book *Corporate Crime*. A new edition of the book (2006) has been brought out recently. In the revised Introduction, Clinard and Yeager makes a distinction between occupational and organizational crime. The former refers to violations that happen in the course of activity in a legitimate occupation, while the latter to illegal methods adopted by large corporations for profit motives. The authors rightly point out that even while the impact of organizational crime is far wider, it attracts much less interest and publicity than occupational crime. It is reported only in business sections of the newspapers. No doubt, powerful corporations influence legislations in a way that enables them to evade the stigma attached to corporate crime. Corporate greed gets diffused within the larger context of declining ethical principles in society on the whole. When the book was first published in 1980, the Bhopal disaster had not happened. Post-Bhopal a new definition of corporate crime is in place. We are looking at the structural complexity of the corporation, its illegal behavior that cannot disentangle itself from economic factors, the nature of delegated authorities, and the ultimate responsibility of the chief executive officer and top management, and most importantly the part played by corporate culture and its practice. As Clinard and Yeager point out, practices that were formerly seen as unethical are now being regarded as crimes (2006, xxxvii).

In the first three chapters, I work on the same premise of a new definition of corporate crimeand trace the linear movement from the day of the disaster to the current situation. I thus provide the necessary background to the industrial disaster and its long-term repercussions in the corporate scene. Chapters one and three are closely linked, and deal with the dynamics of changing times and how in the last twenty-five years Union Carbide Corporation (UCC), UCIL, and Dow Chemicals have come to be associated with corporate crime. In the process, they revisit the history of the offending companies in the context of Bhopal gas tragedy. Chapter one takes us inside the factory to tell us what exactly happened on the night of December 3, 1984 and what factors went into creating conditions for the disaster. Chapter two links the public and the subjective domain. It recreates the perspective of those who survived to tell their experience. At the same time, what comes across as a shocking indictment of corporate crime are levels of ignorance and unknown factors. Oral testimonials are used to "relive" the night of the disaster; at the same time, it becomes the analytical tool for unraveling the nature of the corporate veil. In chapter three the role of multinationals is examined in the context of economic liberalization and globalization. General discussions on the nature of corporate crime get firmly anchored in a case study that vividly recreates the sequence of events, both subjectively (as recounted by those who lived through that night) and objectively (in official forums such as courtrooms, relief and rehabilitation centers, and government offices).

The State versus People

Chapter four begins with oral testimonials that touch on the economic hardships faced by families whose bread-earners died or were grievously injured in the disaster. The focus is on women who were catapulted to positions of being the main or sole earner in the family, and the sort of trials and tribulations they had to face. I take up larger issues of livelihood and the kinds of social displacement that followed in the wake of the industrial disaster. I also bring in gender politics to show how stereotypes were evoked to define a woman's role as homemaker, nurturer, and one who bears the burden of the family. In chapters four and five, my attention shifts from the company to the government and the rehabilitation schemes that were put in place. The Ministry of Bhopal Gas Relief and Rehabilitation was set up in MP directly under the Ministry of Chemicals and Fertilizers (MOCF) at the central government, with a special Bhopal cell headed by a director at the joint secretary level, who reported to the minister of chemicals. It was a closed-door structure that ended up cloning the corporate veil.

I take up larger issues of why systems that were meant to benefit survivors worked against their interest. Fundamentally, the economic rehabilitation programmes were not gender sensitive. The schemes that were planned focused only on short-term relief measures to tackle the crisis situation. Sadly enough, the fire-fighting approach did not change with the passage of time. A gender-sensitive approach would have looked at the long-term repercussions of the disaster, not only in terms of the effect of the gas on the bodies, but also in terms of the social impact it had the lives of ordinary people. It would have taken the second generation into consideration and brought to attention the disruption in families in which children needed constant medical care or parents had to take care of newborns with congenital defects. The need of the hour was to provide health care and livelihood for people who had permanently lost their ability to lead normal healthy lives. Right from the start, the magnitude of the disaster and its political dimensions led to a widening gap between planning and implementation. Some of the other factors that worked against proper restitution were lack of political will, widespread corruption, indifference, and the unsympathetic attitude to real problems at the ground level. These schemes failed because they did not take people into account nor did any of them possess a process of verifying whether survivors really benefited from them or not. As time went by, Bhopal became a problem without any solution in sight. The government reacted by withdrawing schemes, clamping down on information sent out, indulging in false propaganda, and what is worse still, by making policy decisions based on incorrect statistics. When schemes failed to mitigate the suffering of people, the blame was shifted to the survivors rather than the systems.

Oral history registers the voice of people as they critique the rehabilitation schemes and tell us what is really wrong with these schemes and why they failed. What is even more interesting, as they probe the reasons for failure, is that they are able to envisage an alternative vision for rehabilitation. The testimonials combine despair and hope in the way critique and solution seeking become simultaneous tasks. Importantly, there is talk about coping with hardships and the need to break free from entrenched values and to discover self-worth. The rehabilitation schemes were meant to peddle middle-class notions of economic betterment that propagates ideas of improving life style, of changing aspirations with increase in material possessions, and of merging with the mainstream. Therefore, development is accompanied by changes in the urban landscape, with improved roads, plans for city expansion and beautification, and better amenities within the reach of the middle class. No doubt, the survivors felt left out of such development schemes. But at a more insidious level, the Bhopal survivors became living embodiments of everything that had gone wrong with the development model. They carried the body burden of chemicals, and therefore, it was no longer possible to see their problem in isolation from developmental issues. Viewed as a burden and a threat to development, the survivor became an object of suspicion and resentment.

Chapter five specifically links up economic rehabilitation with the first stirrings of activism. Using both archival material and live interviews, I trace the beginnings of movements with women coming together to form action groups and unions. Oral history becomes an important mode of analyzing how women negotiated private and public spaces, and the kind of hardships they had to face when they broke the barriers of home and community to take to the streets. It is important to understand how these women confronted official documents as most of them were illiterate; they—"read" between lines and "interpreted" them—with the aid of inherited wisdom and common sense. Protest actions were meticulously planned by considering individual and collective opinions and especially creating space for dissent. Few of the women became seasoned campaigners, and we listen to their experience of spearheading creative and innovative actions against the government and the company. In providing a gendered reading of economic rehabilitation, the Bhopal movement recounts the story of emancipation from entrenched values and rigid traditions. I analyze the ideological moorings of such movements by showing how the workplace provided the space for empowerment. Emancipation and empowerment became twin terms that enabled women to carve out their own social identities.

The Right to Health and Welfare

Chapter six looks at the nature of the medical catastrophe that followed the disaster and how the poor were at the receiving end of the total failure of medical rehabilitation. Once again it was a failure of vision, combined with an overburdened and outdated system that was hardly prepared to take on the additional burden of mass-scale mortality and morbidity. The unknown factors were overwhelming, and whatever nascent research was hurriedly put in place to tide over the crisis situation, remained disconnected from treatment, which was the need of the hour. As a result, people never benefited from the services offered in government hospitals for gas survivors. Testimonials vouch for the unending trials faced by families reeling under the impact of the gas on the body. An interesting research method I was able to adopt involved analyzing health surveys done by voluntary groups, to see how they differed from government reports.[14] The surveys adopted people-friendly techniques, keeping in mind the crisis situation. The interview method helped to engage people from the bastis, and whenever questions did not elicit honest answers, trial runs were conducted and questions were reframed. Repeated visits were made so that compliance level was at its maximum. The surveys brought in sections of people who had been left out from the official lists of claimants, simply because their names were not included in ration cards. The fatal flaw in the medical rehabilitation scheme was linking health care to compensation money. The women were very forthcoming in participating in the surveys and provided vital information on what was missing in official surveys. Many of them complained that children born immediately after the disaster were left out of compensation claims, despite the fact that an October 3, 1991 judgment of the Supreme Court did make provisions for children born later, manifesting congenital gas-related afflictions. An arbitrary decision was made on the part of government officials in charge of claims registration to disallow children under the age of eighteen to register. Testimonials show how families had to take on the onus of the financial burden, especially when they borrowed money to pay medical bills. It is only by linking health care to economic concerns that we can understand the deep-rooted sociopsychological effect of the disaster. There has been a lot of talk about false claims, but what about denial of real claims? Women giving vent to the sense of denial and exclusion give us the true picture of the suffering.

Chapters five and six are closely linked to chapter seven, where we further explore the link between activism and self-development. The Bhopal movement is directed against exploitative and unequal social relations. Our concern is less with the conflict between men and women and more to do with the possibility of collaborative space. The fight is against monolithic power, which has created "victims" and "survivors" of an industrial disaster, both gender-neutral terms. Victim represents subjugation, while survivor represents emancipation/empowerment. The book traces the shift in perspective. It shows how group organizations had to go through a lot of experience to acquire a gendered approach to problems by engaging with lives of people and entering their psyche. I trace the relation between women and their organizations, in order to understand the ways in which they confront their selves, and how this understanding becomes an instrument of personal learning.

Once again the testimonials gathered reflect how women learn to be articulate, speak out their minds, address a crowd, share their experiences, enter into a dialogue, and face a camera. Their intuitive knowledge of their selves combines with an understanding of serious social issues and with a layman's perception of a technologically advanced world in which concepts of human rights and justice figure importantly. But their real strength lies in an intrinsic ability to share experiences, which adds to the value of oral history. Women, we discover, possess the quality of empathy, which is the cornerstone of their vision for change. In the process they learn to observe, reflect, analyze, and emote. They explore basic emotions such as grief, despair, anger, and faith. As the personal journey merges with the collective movement, emancipation goes beyond the self to embrace larger forces in society. It is at the point where all the different narrative strains criss-cross that we can unravel the making of grassroots organizations keeping in mind the gender perspective.

Notions of Justice

The book deals with larger issues of the betrayal of people by the state. According to the Constitution of India in the Preamble and Part IV, Directive Principle of the State Policy, provides inter alia that the Union of India shall strive to provide justice for all its citizens. As I will show, the infamous settlement of 1989 set the stage for a prolonged betrayal. The Bhopal disaster brings out the weakness in the legal system and the major lacunae in rules and regulations that monitor hazardous activities. Worse still, it shows how double standards operate in the unequal terms and conditions for transfer of technology between a powerful multinational and its subsidiary company. The disaster also raises vital questions in the areas of law, ethics, technology, and ecology. Does the cost-benefit analysis of development include environmental, social, and human costs? Is there a concept of intergenerational equity, which is operative in any sort of high-risk industrial activity? What kind of profit analysis can put aside such vital considerations in the name of progress?

Finally, I analyze why justice for Bhopal is such an elusive concept. My research has amply revealed that there are no simple answers. Post-Bhopal we are witness to many changes. For instance, there has been much talk about a new liability regime for hazardous industrial disasters. A whole new concept of judicial activism has come up. The seventh five-year plan (1985–1990) had brought in notions of sustainable development in harmony with the environment. It is ironical that despite all these changes, two decades down the line, justice is still awaited in Bhopal. It is this larger problem of disconnect between notions of sustainable development and the idea of justice that I take up for discussion in the book. It is important to keep in mind that when we are relating development to environment, we are linking environmental problems with conditions of poverty and underdevelopment. Over the years Bhopal has got absorbed into the global debate on environmental issues, but there is a danger that this kind of mainstreaming will showcase Bhopal as a problem of poverty and underdevelopment, rather than that of injustice and violation of human rights. Perhaps, this explains why the idea of rehabilitation and restitution continues to be defined within the paradigm of development as a poverty alleviation programme, with little space for justice being done.

A worldview that showcases such a model of development is hazardous. It works on the insidious logic that disasters are inevitable and will continue to happen. Legislations become the proverbial paper tiger, and it is no longer the question of proper implementation of laws. Wanton corporate conduct is accepted as an inevitable menace. On the one hand, demand is created for hazardous technology through aggressive marketing policy that seeks to increase corporate profit. On the other hand, the poor are exposed to the hazards and are made to pay the price in an inequitable world. The emphasis is on lessons of Bhopal, but interestingly enough all lessons are directed toward averting another disaster. There is a pressing need to spread awareness about the potential risks of hazardous industrial activities. But the underlying logic is that disasters can at best be prevented in a modern, technological society. Why the disaster happened is never really viewed as a deliberate, criminal act of negligence, and therefore a culpable offence. So the question of getting justice becomes redundant.

Surviving Bhopal attempts to reverse the logic by showing that justice can never be done till we get to the roots of an unjust system. Also, without justice all effort toward rehabilitation and remediation gets nullified. That this lesson comes directly from the affected community makes Bhopal a live issue. Oral history has brought women to center stage. In the conclusive part of the book we see how the nature of the demands that women themselves garnered from their experience became the rallying point of collective mobilization at the local level. Increasing empowerment created an ensemble of identities for women that ranged from the homemaker, bread earner, victim, and survivor, to worker, unionist, and activist. Perhaps, the most significant aspect of the Bhopal movement is the way in which local demands for clean water supply, clean up of the contaminated site, and the need for medical care and jobs get incorporated into wider issues of human rights and corporate liability in the context of globalization. It is the local/global nexus that places Bhopal on the international map.

Bhopal has generated a global debate on the need to rationalize the development model by placing people before nature. Regenerative economy is what environmentalists have in mind when they talk about sustainable development, but such a model alone will not do for Bhopal. "Prevention of continuing Bhopal" is the slogan that comes closest to defining the vision of activism in Bhopal. Prevention redefines the conflict between economy and ecology, and "continuing Bhopal" is a reminder that the problem still persists.

Finally, I would like to draw attention to another aspect of the oral tradition that is not really central to the book, though it finds expression in almost all the chapters. The dynamics between the written text and the oral testimonials can best be negotiated by visual representations. Any Web site on Bhopal throws up myriad images that are eye-catching and symbolic. The images range from the sick, aged, destitute, and the mourners to the young, angry, volatile, and the protestors. I have merely evoked these images through the underlying narrative that runs through the book, working on its thematic relevance to the issues that have been explored. What they capture is protest and celebration in the face of enormous suffering. At the same time, there is something stereotypical in the way the images evoke the middle-class approach to the disaster. We have all seen motley crowds of the poor and the disadvantaged protesting on the streets, and we instantly recognize them as commonplace and yet distanced from our own concerns. We are troubled because they are a reminder of forces that stand in the way of middle-class compliance with status quo. We feel sorry, and almost simultaneously we recoil and turn away, and move on with our lives. *Surviving Bhopal* tries to deconstruct the multiple ways of viewing the tragedy through the lens of popular culture, media representation, and the economic, sociopolitical, and scientific approach. In this way, it tries to demolish the politically expedient formula of remembering and forgetting, by problematizing the issues and thereby compelling us to engage with them. This is the only lesson of Bhopal that can and should be learnt.

CHAPTER 1

The Killer Factory: A Disaster Waiting to Happen

A Hand in Things to Come: Union Carbide.
—Union Carbide run advertisement in *Fortune Magazine* (April 1962).

The Company, beginning its operations in India at the dawn of this century, has ever since shared the country's dreams and aspirations and contributed to the nation's growth.
—*A Time for Nostalgia,* Hexagon, The Commemorative Issue: Golden Jubilee (June 1984).

In 1975, I was in the middle of studying for my diploma in pharmacy when there appeared in the newspapers an advertisement of job vacancies in the Union Carbide factory in Bhopal. Family and friends in my small hometown—150 km from Bhopal—said that I should try for a job in the Carbide factory, since it was quite a good opportunity... For the first six months when we took part in classroom training we considered ourselves pretty important people. The bubble burst when we were sent for training on the job.
—T. R. Chouhan, worker in MIC unit, UCIL and author of *Bhopal: The Inside Story.* 2nd ed. (2004).

For a long time we thought the factory made medicines to kill rats. In J. P. Nagar we hardly knew anyone who had a job in the factory. Such a person would be an object of envy for we had heard the company paid higher wages than government jobs.
—Hazra Bi, Gas Survivor.

In 1984, the year of the Bhopal industrial disaster, Union Carbide Corporation (UCC) was the seventh largest chemical company in the world. Based in Danbury,

Connecticut, USA, UCC owned and operated through its divisions, subsidiaries, and affiliates 500 manufacturing facilities across 137 countries, with a workforce of 120,000 employees and earning a profit of $10 billion.[1] The inception of its industrial empire dates back to the late nineteenth century, when it launched the company through acquisition and incorporation of a number of smaller companies that produced carbon and batteries, arc lamps for acetylene street lighting, and headlamps for cars. It was during World War II that UCC began manufacturing synthetic organic chemicals for supplying equipments to the army. Soon it acquired a dominant position in petrochemicals, hydroelectric power, and mining of steel alloys and uranium as part of nuclear weapon projects. It first entered India in 1905 as the National Carbon Company (India) Ltd and subsequently became Union Carbide India Ltd (UCIL). After 1947, the year of India's independence, UCIL started diversifying from the manufacture of battery cells in its modern plant in Calcutta to the distribution of a wide variety of chemicals, plastics, and allied products. It opened facilities in other metropolitan cities. In 1968, UCIL shifted its agricultural products division from Mumbai to Bhopal, the state capital of Madhya Pradesh (MP). The saga of the Bhopal industrial disaster begins from this point with UCC riding high on its success story. At the same time, another story—as yet unsung and unwritten—was already coming into shape.

By 1976 UCIL had developed indigenous process technology for the manufacture of carbaryl pesticides, and a 2 crores R&D facility for agricultural chemicals was inaugurated in Bhopal. The company diversified into producing pesticides for the agricultural market. New pesticides, under the brand name of Sevin and Temik, were toted as magic potion for farmers. Cost effective and less wasteful, these pesticides exterminated not only pests that infested crops, but their eggs and larvae as well. The Sevin formulation unit was set up in Bhopal, and as a part of its expansion plans, the methyl isocyanate (MIC) production unit was added to the Bhopal facility in 1979. Till then MIC, which when combined with alpha-naphthol produced the pesticide Sevin, was being imported. With the set up of the MIC unit, UCIL was licensed to manufacture 5,250 tons of MIC-based pesticides per year. But right from the beginning it was a business venture that never quite took off. By 1984, despite UCC's global success story, the Indian subsidiary was running at a loss with production barely touching 1,657 tons. UCIL that was meant to be a state-of-the-art factory using highly sophisticated, complex technology was in a condition of utter neglect and had been rendered a loss-making organization. Success and failure was a mirage that hid the grim reality of a disjunction between the global enterprise and the local realities.[2] When UCIL was celebrating its golden jubilee in the year 1984, UCC had already begun a massive process of dismantling the loss-making Indian plant in Bhopal. By year-end the world witnessed the cruel fallout of the process. All it took was a single night to convert old Bhopal into a killing field.

Bhopal gas tragedy has been described as a modern, technological disaster (Bogard 1989, Shrivastava 1992). To put it even more succinctly, the disaster was largely a result of the failure of interdependent systems of technology, information, and law (Cassels, 1993, 11). It is at the point of interface of all three systems that the history of the "making" and "dismantling" of the company gets written out. By profiling the company history the corporate structure is unraveled and shows how it operated within the social and regulatory regime of industrial production. It is important to keep in mind the general political climate that fostered industrial activities in an economically backward state like Madhya Pradesh. In the context of globalization, this move to expand business was part of a worldwide phenomenon to identify hotspots in third world countries as fertile zones for creating chemical hubs. It was a process of mutual give and take, and developing countries increasingly opened their markets to foreign investments with the assurance that the risks were borne by the marginal, expendable section of the society. Bhopal disaster happened because something went terribly wrong in the cost-benefit calculations, on the part of both the corporation and the government. What really went wrong is the focus of this chapter.

In the *Union Carbide Report* (March 1985) on the accident, Warren Anderson the then chief executive officer of UCC, went on record to say, "Non-compliance with safety procedures is a local issue. UCC can't be there, day in and day out. You have to rely on the people you have in place. My board does not know what valve is on or off in Texas City. Safety is the responsibility of the people who operate the plant. You can't run a billion dollar corporation all out of Danbury" (Jones, 1988, 37). The tone is flippant but the position taken is official. Safety, responsibility, the uneasy relation between parent body/subsidiary, and who takes liability for a billion dollar enterprise are the key factors that define a technological disaster. Tara Jones in his book *Corporate Killings: Bhopals Will Happen* (1988) raised the larger question of whether the event on that fateful night was an accident or a corporate genocide. By juxtaposing different points-of-view, we can isolate the various strands of opinion making that went into defining the nature of the disaster. According to Jones, UCC saw Bhopal gas tragedy as an "incident"; the mass media saw it as "world's worst industrial disaster"; observers saw it as "murder"; and the survivors saw it as "tragedy." We can take the analogy a step further to show how different stakeholders came forward with their own agenda, thus creating the dynamic field that became the hotbed for clash of opinions. This chapter explores the power play between politics, economics, and science to show that the "cause" of the disaster and its tragic aftermath can best be explained as a total systemic failure.

Development Models, Perception of Hazards, and Risk Calculations

In a commemorative brochure brought out on the occasion of the golden jubilee, UCIL highlighted the company's role in India's national development. Over the years the company's best-known product, the Eveready battery, had become a household name; so had the popular campaign of the "Eveready Man" as a friend of the people. But early in 1964 *Business Week* was already reporting dismal conditions in the plant at Calcutta with "the assembly operation bursting at the seam" (Weir 1986, 12). However, such rumblings went unnoticed. Instead, the setting up of a brand new chemical factory in Bhopal, on a 5-acre plot of government land given on an annual rent of $40 an acre, was seen as a clarion call by the Indian government to a corporate giant for participating in the task of nation building. As a fledgling city and state capital with excellent road/rail links to major ports in India, Bhopal seemed a good choice. The factory site that was identified in the Bhopal Master Plan as an industrial area was barely 3 km from the railway station. In 1975 the Ministry of Industry and Civil Supplies gave the approval to UCIL for manufacturing pesticides. The end product was registered with the Insecticide Board and the manufacturing process was registered with the Ministry of Chemicals. With a fully functional MIC unit, UCIL grew into a manufacturing facility sprawling over seventy acres of land. India had entered into the big league with toxic capital, riding high on its promise to usher in the Green Revolution, to increase food production, and to combat hunger and poverty through the introduction of chemical fertilizers to mechanize agricultural production (Sarangi in *India Disaster Report* 2000, 337). The setting up of this factory was part of an integrated vision of progress and development, and therefore it was easy to miss out on the "hazards" that were slowly and insidiously creating the perfect scenario for a disaster waiting to happen.

The methods for assessing and managing risks cannot be placed within a single analytical framework. Right from the start, the company's decision to manufacture pesticides proved to be an unprofitable venture. By 1984 the Bhopal plant was $4 million into red (Weir 1986, 15). The estimates of social benefits were wide off the mark. The company was having doubts about the technology chosen and its appropriateness in relation to local needs. But at the same time, it used all its influence to create a niche for itself in a class-structured society like India. This gave rise to mutual dependency, and an ideological consensus among the power elite to endorse given models of development. The rampant use of pesticides in the Third World had always posed a major hazard. The buoyancy of the market often overlooked the grim side of the picture. In a chain reaction, the excessive use of chemical fertilizers had resulted in the "pesticide treadmill" that in turn increased the price of food with profit concentrating in the hands of manufacturers.³ Large companies such as UCC manufactured hazardous products in small, but highly concentrated division of the industry that worked through networks and subsidiaries across the globe. Given its wealth and size, UCC enjoyed tremendous bargaining power in the host country. It continued as a major player in an intensely competitive market. The emphasis was on technocratic and rational approaches to development issues. In his book *Ecological Nightmares and the Management Dilemma: The Case of Bhopal*, Ashis Gupta gives a comprehensive analysis of how UCC was provided with an ideally protected market for its agrochemical products in India.⁴ All this continued to happen despite the fact that the Green Revolution could not accelerate the overall rate of growth in agriculture, and technology failed to reduce poverty. What created this implicit faith in technology remains a moot question, resulting in an illusion of security that was matched by a general lack of understanding of hazards at every level.

People of Bhopal never showed hostility toward the plant. The government and the industry continued to cooperate with each other. On the one hand, allowing a foreign company to operate in a host country meant a symbiotic relation between new kinds of capital, technology, and skills and the domestic economy that took roots in the community itself. On the other hand, the state did have the power to withdraw the company's license or to increase its obligations. On paper a transnational corporation was never meant to feel secure in a host country. But the ground reality was starkly different. Instead of taking cognizance of the dangers posed by hazardous chemicals, Government of India (GOI) took care to invite UCIL to expand business. In 1979 when the MIC unit became fully operational, drought conditions were prevailing in India that drove farmers to take loans and to buy cheaper pesticides from small-scale producers rather than foreign companies. The market was rapidly shrinking, so UCIL had to come up with strategies to override the situation. It started using strong-arm tactics and behind-the-scene negotiations. It also used aggressive propaganda and systems to reward agencies that promoted pro-Carbide policies, thus ensuring its unregulated growth and expansion. The perception of hazards mostly remained as a possibility. So paradoxically it was the poor who believed that the hazards in the Bhopal plant were well under control or was part of a larger benefit. The safer the people felt the more real the danger became by simply vanishing from public view. The task of defining hazards was in the hands of the technocrats—corporate executives, scientists, government officials, and safety planners. They propagated a theory of calculated risks that diverted attention from the actual production of lethal chemicals. The company brochures continued to draw an optimistic picture for the plant's future despite the cutbacks. It was a double bind. The brochures were meant only for the technocrats and not for the local residents. So, specialized knowledge of the company circulated in closed-door forums. The conscious attempt was to keep scientific knowledge apart from issues that were viewed as polemical. At the same time, promotional literature was widely disseminated for the sole purpose of advertising the plant as safe. This kind of falsification of information lulled everyone into a false feeling of safety.

Wall Street Journal was grossly wrong in claiming that "regulations driven by nationalism" was at the "core of any in-depth explanation of Bhopal tragedy" (January 21, 1985, cited in Jones, 1988, 37). It is important to understand that regulations are usually in a state of "disjunction" from national considerations when one is looking at a technological disaster. The fact of the matter remained that GOI allowed major ownership (59.1 percent) to UCC, despite limitations on foreign investment, because of the technological sophistication of the operations at the Bhopal facility. So UCC was expected to choose the production processes, supply the plant design, designate operational procedures, and conduct safety audits. The fact that the company failed to fulfill its commitment and the government betrayed its people by refusing to hold the company accountable goes to show that something was seriously wrong in the way the technology driven system operated.

In a press conference in March 1985, Warren Anderson went on to make tall claims that if he "knew personally of any location in the corporate world of Union Carbide that had an unsafe operation, it would have been shut down."[5] Actually the company had evolved a system of pruning down any operations that was seen as loss making. This was done on grounds of "streamlining" the system and making it more efficient and profitable. But broader issues of production of hazardous chemicals were not allowed to come to the foreground. What was wrong with the plant was never a question of its safety. The idea was to separate profitability from detection of hazards and to prevent the issues from becoming a political agenda. The best way to do so was to seek technocratic solution to social problems. William Bogard in his book *The Bhopal Tragedy: Language, Logic and Politics in the Production of a Hazard* (1989) shows how industrialization in the eighties had changed the face of urban India. The demographic profile of a basti like J. P. Nagar clearly shows how the process was underway. Villagers were coming to state capitals in search of jobs. With no housing and very little work, most of them were forced to live illegally on vacant land. Electoral politics prevented the local government from relocating them. The Madhya Pradesh Town and Country Planning Board had classified the Carbide plant as belonging to the general industry category rather than a hazardous unit. So instead of relocating the plant it was allowed to stay. It was hardly surprising that maximum number of deaths and injuries were reported in J. P. Nagar, given its proximity to the factory. Yet the discursive logic that was commonly used to detect hazards saw much greater danger in the plant closing down on grounds of unprofitability. All that the company had to do to overcome risk factors was to ensure profitability.

GOI, in turn, had to make sure that there were no roadblocks in its drive toward greater modernization. Regulatory resources in a developing country were limited, and as pointed out the bargaining power of industry was enormous. Environmental objectives were largely the result of negotiations between government and industry, so, much depended on the political will. Also government regulatory agencies, understaffed and not properly funded, depended heavily on the industry for information. The industry in turn viewed environmental offences as part of the cost of doing business (Cassels 1993, 30). So both the costs and the risks were absorbed by the system itself. The people who populated the slums—the daily laborers, construction workers, sweepers, cleaners, and those doing service jobs in households, shops, and roadside kiosks—faced the real danger. In the case of Bhopal, the middle class from whom the pressure for environmental and industrial safety normally emanates was missing. Therefore the environmental and safety issues never figured prominently in the government agenda. The company, on the other hand, went about its business of diverting attention from issues of health and safety. It began centralizing its decision-making and public relations activities. It adopted the twin process of acquiring more companies, and at the same time divesting itself of those affiliated companies that had low-growth potential and limited profitability (Dembo, Morehouse, and Wykle 1990, 15). By the eighties, Carbide was acquiring the reputation of being "an unwieldy giant run amok" (17). Dembo argues that a series of accidents in the Carbide plant in Puerto Rico in 1976 and a tank explosion in Syracuse, New York, in 1977 were compelling the company to clean up its tarnished image. It did so by centralizing its public relations activities and strengthening government lobbying, and controlling media. But more importantly it began identifying core business segments for expansion while initiating cutbacks in sensitive areas of workforce and safety. This happened simultaneously with drastic reorganization of its management. In effect, the setting up of new business/development programmes went hand in hand with huge disinvestments. The idea was to make the giant leaner and more efficient. There is little doubt that the setting up of the agricultural products division in Bhopal was part of the company plan to both expand and disinvest.

Slow Bhopals and Routine Accidents

UCC went out of its way to propagate the theory that the Bhopal disaster was an isolated event caused by a corporation that otherwise had a clean environmental and safety record. It is debatable whether we have evolved an effective mechanism for gauging the social performance of a corporation.[6] Normally a multinational company has societal accountability regarding the health and safety of the workers and the protection of the environment. But this obligation is only nominal, and corporations do not regard themselves as accountable to the local communities in the places where they have their facilities. In contrast, the economic performance of a company can be easily tracked, for the benefits are more readily identifiable in terms of creation of jobs, increase in production, sales, and capital. But there are few tools for tracking social performance. Far from having an impeccable safety record, UCIL was notorious for its willful disregard of both the workers and the community. This section looks at routine accidents or the "slow Bhopals" that were happening daily.

Right from the start, minor accidents inside the plant were happening regularly, causing death and injury to a handful of people, mainly workers. At the same time, slow poisoning of both workers and residents was being caused by the release of low levels of toxic chemicals into the air and water. Yet small-scale accidents were treated by the company as normal and part of the routine. Jones argues that "toxic capital's profits exist on a balance sheet of death" (1988, 12). It brings death, which can be swift or slow, and both are an integral and unavoidable part of toxic development. There is no doubt that attention has to be focused on "slow Bhopals" for it highlights the universal nature of the threat. But there is always the danger of minimizing the role of UCC in the disaster by showing how toxic poisoning is an inevitable part of the system. It is important to remember that Bhopal continues to bring slow and living deaths of a kind that redefines the nature of toxic development. Only then can we understand the full scope of corporate liability in terms of both economic and social performance.

The rest of the chapter looks at the pre- and postdisaster scenario to understand why Bhopal was more than a simple aberration in a flawless system. Moreover, Bhopal became a public relations crisis. From the corporate point of view, it was important to rebuild public confidence by insisting that the incident was rare and would not be repeated. A lot of effort was made to limit the event to India, and to show that it was largely a question of lower standards of operation, labor, and regulation in the host country. From the government point of view, it was important to minimize its own complicity and to curtail financial costs to the state by scaling down the magnitude of the disaster. The only thing that was ignored was the social costs of toxic production that were borne by the workers and the people. The people's perspective was conspicuously missing for it was systematically excluded from the process.

Inside the Factory

An outcome of the development of technology and its applications is the fragmentation of traditional tasks and increased specialization and routinization. T. R. Chouhan, who had joined UCIL in 1975 as plant operator and was working in the MIC unit at the time of the disaster, provides an insider's view of the appalling working conditions inside the plant. His book is aptly titled *Bhopal: The Inside Story*. His individual experience has been used as a case study to analyze the worker's vulnerability and complicity in a system of gross negligence. The workers were given a mandatory training that lasted for not more than six months; during training the plant was described in detail with the help of a model. Workers were also apprised of the hazardous nature of the chemicals produced, stored, and used in the factory. Showing a perfect model created a sense of awe for the advanced nature of technology and lulled the questioning mind. However, things turned out to be different when the plant started operating. The workers learnt of the dangerous effects of chemicals from on-the-job minor accidents, such as acid burns and allergic reactions to chemicals. The picture was grim, and the gap between the projected public image and the reality was ever widening. Did this alert the workers to the dangers of working with toxic chemicals? The answer is no, for the entire system worked on the basis of hierarchy, division of labor, and nurturing feelings of segregation. The hierarchy got reflected in the way the information was kept out of the reach of those who worked at the level of the shop floor and handled hazardous material. In other words, the most vulnerable segment remained the most ignorant. This created a culture of apathy and self-interest.

The workers were never trained to develop a sense of obligation toward a larger community. The idea was to keep the workers restricted to their workplace. By workplace it meant the unit or segment in which the individual was posted, so a person working in the x-naphthol unit was not meant to know or intervene in the MIC unit. Nobody was allowed to build up loyalty toward the "whole" factory or workforce or the people residing in the neighborhood. The workers were paid at an hourly rate, denying job security and control over the workplace. When things went wrong and this happened regularly—with supply lines getting choked, equipments turning out to be of inadequate capacity, and control instruments failing to operate—the workers were too distant from the technology they were working with to really care about the safety issues.

Chouhan shows how modifications from original designs were made from automatic and continuous to manual and batch processes (2004, 16). The most rampant malpractice happened in the x-naphthol unit, where contract workers were employed to manually crush naphthol with hammers. A lot of the dust would escape and create unbearable conditions in the work sheds; at such times the plant was closed down for a few days and then reopened. In this particular unit, the factory doctor did a six-monthly medical checkup, but the reports were rarely given to the workers. The workers with pronounced health problems were simply shifted to the utility division. Manual work, contract labor, and ignorance were clearly a fatal combination in an otherwise mechanized system. But was it simply a question of inefficiency and corruption or was it management decisions based on an ideology that put profit before people? Systems were meant to be cost effective, while the jargon used was modifications done to suit the Indian job market.

Chouhan describes a big fire that broke out in 1978 destroying x-naphthol worth Rs 6 crores (2004, 17–18). In December 1981, a worker was fatally exposed to phosgene. In January 1982, a valve in the phosgene line in the MIC plant broke off and a thick cloud of phosgene leaked out. Twenty-four workers had to be hospitalized and the rest ran in panic to the fields behind the factory. The death of the worker and the incident of chemical leak were reported in the newspapers and did create alarm among the workers and their union leaders. Letters were shot off to the managers, State Ministry of Labor, and the chief minister, but nothing came of it. Neither the management nor the government officials came out with any report on the incidents. The sensation soon died down. The Sevin plant was closed down the same year but on grounds of nonprofitability. Larger issues of safety were never taken up. Clearly hazards in a workplace or accidents—frequent or infrequent—cannot gain the attention of the larger community. The workers too felt insulated from stray accidents. The apprehension was that the plant would close down. This prevented agitations from going out of hand, and the management responded with punitive measures and a few cosmetic changes. Thus, workers were provided with safety gloves and masks, and by 1983, a five working-day week was introduced. It meant that for two days the plant was less supervised; not surprisingly the night of December 2, was a Sunday. So long as the workers linked hazards to the workplace and did not have a sense of carrying the threat home, the danger seemed out of sight. When the plant started running at a loss, a voluntary retirement scheme was introduced, and many workers who were dissatisfied with the working conditions left the job. Clearly the issue of safety was redundant inside the factory.

Voices in the Wilderness

It was not that voices were not raised in protest but they went unheeded. This section draws attention to some of the issues that were raised by individuals from different sectors, and the way in which these issues were simply glossed over. Clearly it is not enough to say that these issues were misguided intentions and every system has scope for errors. Ultimately, the errors were there for everyone to see, but people in power—officials, professionals, and the average middle-class citizen—chose to look the other way. Worse still they chose to mislead and spread disinformation. There was a calculated way in which risks were disguised and false knowledge was disseminated with the assurance that "you are safe" while "others might be at high risk." This assurance was readily available and often endorsed by people in the power. Bogard sums up the situation forcefully when he writes, "A technocratic class that predictably elects profitable, low cost, high-tech answers for human misery was responsible. Theirs is responsibility grounded on intentional ignorance, deliberate omission and misguided optimism" (1989, x). Everybody knew that it was a disaster waiting to happen and almost everybody let it remain at that.

It is equally important to understand how systems get modified and create space to accommodate this kind of deliberate peddling of false notions of safety and benefit. The government began cloning the corporation, and both survived parasitically by creating a closed-door system. In September 1982 Rajkumar Keswani, a local journalist shot off his first article in *Jansatta*, a Hindi daily with wide readership. He carried out his one-man crusade till as late as June 1984 when he warned that the Bhopal population would be wiped out by a disaster that would defy imagination. Keswani was the lone David against the twin Goliaths, a multinational and the state government. His rhetoric "Wake up people of Bhopal, sitting on the edge of a volcano! No sorrow will save you from this foreign death!" (*Rapat Weekly*, Issue 2, October 1, 1982) could be ignored, but the issues he was raising could not be ignored. He drew attention to the minor accidents that were happening regularly and were being covered up. He said UCIL paid for the government's silence. A week after the disaster Keswani lamented his failure by divulging a volley of incriminating evidence against the company and the government. The following are some of the incriminating facts that he provided: the former inspector general of MP Police was employed by Carbide as security advisor; the Carbide guesthouse was at the disposal of the ruling party, with a separate suite for the chief minister; the company provided jobs to sons and relatives of politicians and civil servants (*Free Press Journal*, December 16, 1984). In the *International Conference on Bhopal Gas Tragedy and Its Effects on Process Safety* held at Indian Institute of Technology (IIT) Kanpur on December 1–3, 2004, Keswani presented a paper where he stated eloquently that his lack of a technical background made his warnings a mere "premonition." "But little knowledge is not always dangerous," he went on to clarify, "Dangerous is the attitude of those in positions of power... I regret I am proved right. I regret the people in power could not get me right. I regret I failed in my campaign."[7]

On March 4, 1983, a local lawyer Shahnawaz Khan sent a notice to the UCIL management as a "responsible citizen of Bhopal." He pointed to the "specter of death that loomed" over the local residents, thus drawing attention to hazards that went beyond the workplace. J. Mukund, the then works manager of UCIL responded on April 29, 1983 with typical shortsightedness, "Our pesticide complex at Bhopal like any other complex in the world is equipped with sophisticated devises for handling various types of chemicals in our manufacturing operations and all precautions are taken for the safety of persons working in the factory. Your allegation that the persons living in the various colonies near the industrial area remain under constant threat and danger is absolutely baseless."[8] Typically the worker and the local resident are seen as two separate entities that had to be tackled by using different management strategies. It was not that sporadic actions were not taken. Following the phosgene leak, an enquiry was ordered in January 1982 with a local science college chemistry professor heading the committee. The committee took two years to bring out the report that waited for months in the lower offices of the under secretary before it was handed over to the higher authorities. However, no action was taken on the basis of report. When the chief minister asked for the report after the accident, it took a week before he got it (Grazia 1985, 58). Letters exchanged between Mukund and authorities in Danbury make it very clear that danger was classified under two headings, major and less serious. Routine accidents did not qualify as major hazards. The emphasis was on the possibilities of exposure of maintenance and operating personnel, so that primary concern was with procedural and personnel safety-related issues (Cited in *Union Carbide Corporation Research Compendium prepared for Communities Concerned about Corporations,* 1994).

Representatives from another sector tried to put up a fight in the factory. The Carbide workers unions were organized shortly after the MIC plant was commissioned in 1979, and the Union Carbide Karamchari Sangh (UCKS) was formed. A majority of Hindu workers joined the UCKS. Another union, Union Carbide Workers' Union (UCWU) was started under the leadership of an activist affiliated to the ruling party (Vivek 1990, 19). This union was more or less sponsored by the management. Issues of safety and health were taken up only after the death of the worker from phosgene leak. Both unions sent joint memorandums to state and central government demanding that the Bhopal plant be categorized as heavy chemical industries and subject to more stringent safety laws. The letters were not even acknowledged. The workers organized a poster campaign to alert the community to the dangers inside the factory but the response was one of suspicion. The residents feared that too much protest would go against their interest, and they would get displaced. The *Bhopal Reader* quotes from a letter that was written as rejoinder on the part of the management to UCWU's plea that corrective measures were needed urgently. "We wish to impress upon you that the management is aware of its responsibilities to provide protection to its employees and has therefore imparted technical skills of a very high order through intensive in-house training programmes" (2004, 13). This fact was not only far removed from the truth, but at a more pernicious level claims for safety were being made falsely without proper assessment of the situation. Despite all the talk about technical skill, there was no attempt to probe the affects and reach of the chemicals. At the same time, the *Bhopal Reader* tells us that Carbide's own internal documents, which were classified and clouded in secrecy, spoke about the use of "unproven technology." "Naphthol processes have not been tried commercially and even the MIC to Sevin process has had a limited trial run. It can be expected that there will be interruptions in operations and delays in reaching capacity or product quality" (2004, 20). Scientific discourse was manipulating the truth by walking the fine balance between expert knowledge and political persuasion. The language of profit, commercial use, and viability was being used to divert attention from the real hazards.

The Question of "Who" Paid the Price

When a hazard goes undetected, it increases the vulnerability of a section of society most likely to get affected by an accident. At the same time, it undermines the ability to plan out collective action for dealing with the crisis in the eventuality of such an accident. This is precisely what happened in Bhopal. But what was the nature of the vulnerability? It was at the level of hazards faced everyday by the most vulnerable section of society—the poor and the disadvantaged. The slow Bhopals fed into the world's worst industrial disaster. It was easy to miss out on the consequences of minor accidents that happened sporadically and whose long-term effects were uncertain. Therefore, "events" projected into an uncertain future could not capture the "potential" character of hazards. But it is important to remember that the hazards went undetected primarily for the community living near the factory, because they did not possess the means for detection. In a sense the most important lesson of Bhopal was that detection of hazards is not merely a scientific process, involving dissemination of specialized knowledge or the question of who controls information. Detection is conditioned by cultural and political values. Therefore, whatever little information was available was circulating in a restrictive manner that failed to reach the people, to whom it would have mattered most. They were truly deprived for they did not have the material resources to escape the hazards or to make contingency plans or cope with the consequences. The factors that made the poor vulnerable were class specific: poverty, illiteracy, poor sanitation, crowded and ill-constructed dwellings, and total dependence on the state to reduce their vulnerability. Almost no one was employed in the factory. So the dangers they faced were separate from workplace hazards and therefore not even recognized. No evacuation plans were in place for them. They were never informed about the true nature of the hazards. They were not even equipped to get proper compensation for any loss. After all, warnings have to be heard and also understood. Faced with so many disadvantages, the Bhopal victims had little choice. They were neither complicit nor part of the system that destroyed them, by excluding them and leaving them unarmed.

In the case of Bhopal, technocratic discourse—whether scientific or political—carried high stakes. It was after all a matter of grave consequence that profoundly affected the safety and well being of a large number of people. It was also a question of gaining legitimacy for industrial activity. What the technocrat managed to do was to define acceptable levels of hazardousness and vulnerability.

Cost-benefit analysis offered a range of technical options with benefits proportionate to the costs. What remained hidden from view was the inability of such an analysis to quantify the cost-benefit value of human life. Social costs of industrial progress have never really been calculated for the poor. Dr. Varadarajan, Director General, Council of Scientific and Industrial Research (CSIR), spoke on behalf of the technocratic class of administrators, when he said at a press conference on December 15, 1985 that "the whole issue has to be seen in the context of the cost-benefit ratio. No technological operation is entirely without risks."[9] Following the disaster, both the government and the corporation found themselves answerable to the public. That they managed to come out fairly unscathed speaks volumes for the power play that accompanied such a discourse. But Bhopal was to outlive itself as a crisis. In the years to come the compensation that it demanded was beyond any calculations made by the government or the company. It was precisely the staying power of the people's movement, bolstered by the mammoth unpredictability of events that helped nail the lies that were actively propagated in different official forums.

Containing the Crisis

Postdisaster the immediate task before the multinational was to contain the crisis and to protect the company's continued existence. This involved getting the best legal advice and forming a crisis management team that consisted of experts in the field of law, finance, and public affairs. At the same time, media attention was being dispersed from hard scientific facts to people's sufferings and its "tragic dimensions." The public uproar and the floodgates of emotions that followed became selling points that inadvertently helped to divert attention from the truth of "why" the disaster happened. There was always the danger that once the "why" became public knowledge, the question of holding the corporation guilty would follow. But industrial disasters are never known to punish the individual entities, and by definition multinationals are well protected by the "corporate veil." The corporation was able to use its well-oiled PR machinery to tackle the tide of public outrage.

The more pressing danger was that the individual suits filed against UCC in the United States could lead to a financial crisis. Uncomfortable questions—"Can such a disaster recur elsewhere? How adequate are emergency systems to deal with mass disasters?"—were bound to rear their head and seek clarification. The initial knee-jerk reaction of the company was to claim that the Bhopal plant was no different from the West Virginia plant on grounds that the design and safety standards were identical; the accident was, therefore, a result of human error or an act of sabotage. The latter claim was made at a conference on *Chemical Industry after Bhopal* held in London in November 1985 as part of a scientific paper, but its absurdity was meant to strengthen the propaganda that no individual entity can be blamed for an industrial disaster. The sabotage theory was soon abandoned. Instead, a well thought out, calculated move was made to disassociate the parent body from the process of implementing safety standards by putting the onus on the Indian subsidiary. The company was not only trying to save its skin, but it was also propagating the cause of toxic capital by limiting liability. Developed versus developing countries was only the shadow battle. UCC was trying to appease the class of people in the host country who were feeling threatened or enjoyed immunity from the crisis. Later it was these people who presided over litigations, medical surveys, and became heads of committees. They controlled information and its circulation.

The focus in this section shifts to the courtroom where a mammoth battle between contending discourses was preparing to unfold. Here the corporation had an upper hand because its efficiency could hardly be matched by the tardiness that is inherent in all other systems, legal or bureaucratic. Potentially Bhopal litigation could have redefined industrial disasters by getting full justice to the victims and creating new codes of conduct to govern transnational business operations. But right from the beginning, UCC wanted a settlement that would help the company to bury Bhopal forever and retrieve its tarnished corporate image. Meanwhile, the only other thing that was happening at a steady, relentless pace was the rising number of people who were dying, falling grievously ill, or suffering the acute aftereffects of social dislocation. Pitched into such a volatile arena, UCC did what it knew best—continue with the process of disinvestments that was already underway. If anyone benefited from the Bhopal disaster it was the company; it could close down a plant that was already devalued and discredited. The real lessons of Bhopal was learnt by the company that accelerated the process of downsizing by shedding old capacity, focusing on profitable specialty chemicals, and shifting to new technologies that would cut costs and raise efficiency (Fortun 2001, 118). It is not at all surprising that the 1990 company *Annual Report* could boast—"In the past five years at Union Carbide we have fashioned a new company." The nightmarish Indian chapter was laid to rest with a settlement in 1989 that was hailed by the industry as a major victory. In a sense the settlement was an intrinsic part of the way in which the company redefined itself as a monolithic entity by a careful process of "structuring" and "dismantling." In the rest of the chapter we take a look at the legal jargon used by the company to undergo such a process of redefinition, and how this resulted in the most ruthless violation of the principles of justice and fair play. As a result, "why" the disaster happened in the first place was buried under a paper cloud, which proved to be as noxious as MIC.

The Monolithic Entity

On May 12, 1986, Judge Keenan issued an order that declared the US courts as an inconvenient forum for fighting the Bhopal litigation, thus throwing the case back into the Indian courts.[10] The message was loud and clear; India had to take responsibility for her own people. Before that on March 29, 1985, the Indian Parliament had passed the Bhopal Gas Leak Disaster (Processing of Claims Act) that gave the government the sole right to represent thousands of victims, who were too poor and illiterate to take action against a powerful multinational corporation. In other words the two monolithic entities were to come face-to-face in a forum that was meant to give a fair hearing to both and adjudicate in favor of the bereaved party. A smokescreen was created to keep the victims out of the political process of exercising choice. At the same time, an entire techno-legal discourse became operative in a way that kept real issues out of sight.

The grounds for dismissal were quaintly myopic and self-serving (Baxi 1986, 35–69). Although India was hailed as a "dynamic democracy" with the greatest number of "technical experts in any country of the world," it was castigated for wanting to take advantage of liberal US federal laws in cases of strict liability for tort. Keenan felt it would set a bad precedent by making American courts extremely attractive to foreign plaintiffs. He feared it would put heavy financial burden on the tax paying American public, whose connection with the case was tenuous. Weighing India's "private interest" against worldwide "public interest" Keenan thought the scale tipped heavily in favor of India, so that private interest stood to gain. It was not that Keenan was not aware of the public interest that would get served. This is what his order clearly stated: "When US corporations assume responsibility for accidents happening on foreign soil it will create a precedent, which would bind all American multinationals hence forward; it will promote international cooperation; it will avoid assertion of double standards and the prevention of economic blackmail of hazardous industries which extract concessions on health and environmental standards at the price of continuing operations" (Baxi 1986, 62). Keenan went on to reiterate that public interest was not sufficient to justify the enormous commitment required by the US courts, in terms of both time and resources. Clearly something more insidious was happening here. It was not so much American corporation versus Indian government. The real conflict was between corporation and people. It was also between the marginal people and the rich and powerful.

The convenience of the forum was tied up with the nature of evidences required by the court. Keenan was quick to point out that all the evidences relating to liability and relevant to damages were located in and around Bhopal, in India. But clearly this issue was only eyewash. The real issue was the relationship between the parent body and its subsidiary. Taking recourse to legal reasoning and persuasion, the corporation was reconstructed step-by-step by breaking it down into single units within a monolithic structure. This was done in the entire course of the legal battle that was fought out in India till the time of the settlement in 1989 (Baxi and Dhanda 1990, 33–107). Thus the plant was described as part of UCIL's Agricultural Products Division, which had limited contact with its Bombay headquarters. The Bhopal facility had seven operating units, each headed by a manager of Indian origin and employed by UCIL. The managers reported directly to the works manager or one of the three assistant works manager. The three units, which were potentially involved in the MIC leak, employed sixty-three people, all Indian nationals. The maintenance units were subdivided into Instrumentation and Mechanical Maintenance. Other functional units were Quality Control, Purchasing, and Stores. It was the Safety/Medical unit that was responsible for safety performance, monitoring safety statistics and planning and implementing safety drills. The idea was to show how a complex process was made functional by carefully distributing responsibility. Each unit in a monolithic structure carried its own method of surveillance. Therefore all evidence brought before the court were daily, weekly, and monthly records of plant operations. In the ultimate analysis, not only was information gathering rendered an impossible task, pinning liability was made out to be time-consuming and fraught with uncertainties. Even where data was available to prove complicity, it was manipulated to score a legal point. For instance, GOI's plea that three of the safety audits were conducted by UCC and not UCIL was overruled by simply arguing that three events were a small fraction of the thousands of safety drills conducted daily at the Bhopal facility. The fact that these three audits were conducted in 1979, 1980, and 1982 and its frequency showed that safety had become a cause of worry and was overlooked. Clearly the focus was on the power relation between the parent body and the subsidiary, without highlighting the attendant responsibility.

Keenan had anticipated the direction of the legal battle. While declaring the forum as inconvenient, he made it clear that he was not convinced that India's private interest was a matter of overriding concern. "India no doubt valued its need for a pesticide plant against the inherent risk in such development" (Baxi 1986, 65). Risks and benefits were highlighted as two sides of the same coin and intrinsic to the development model. In other words, India should have known better when it signed the Design Transfer and Technical Service Agreements way back in 1973. Also India was described as a country with vastly different standards of living, wealth, levels of health care and services, values, morals, and beliefs. Therefore, it was India's interest and not that of the multinational to create standards of care and enforce them. By shifting the litigation to Indian courts, Keenan was offering the Indian people the chance to learn their lesson from an event that was of national interest. Though Keenan claimed that he did not want "to revive a history of subservience and subjugation from which India had emerged" (Baxi 1986, 69), he could barely hide his contempt for a country that could not take care of its own people. Worse still, he was able to reduce the world's worst disaster to an event that catered to local rather than international interest.

Lethal Litigation

From September 5, 1986, when the first suit for damages was filed in the Court of the District Judge in Bhopal, to February 14, 1989, when the Supreme Court announced a settlement, the Bhopal legal case was bureaucratized and politicized in a way that can best be described as the second catastrophe. "MIC entered the soul of Indian jurisprudence" (Baxi and Dhanda 1990, 2). The settlement failed on almost every count. It could not determine the cause of the disaster. It could not fix the liability. It could not award damages and compensation commensurate with the suffering. Relief and rehabilitation, which should have been a matter of high priority, irrespective of the outcome of the litigation, were used as ploy to deny justice. It was as though Bhopal had ceased to be India's interest. In its attempt to gather evidences, GOI had to identify patterns of injuries that were then classified under broad categories of severe, mild, and no injuries. The victim's suffering had to become a quantifiable unit of injury that could be compensated in monetary terms. As a result, the victim became a disembodied object without a name, face, gender, or sense of self-worth. The media lost interest in the spectacle of suffering. The middle class people were able to go back to their routine life. There were however innovative components in the suit for damages that was filed in the District Court on September 5, 1986. In a bid to make the damages all encompassing, it stated in no uncertain terms that the Union of India was claiming damages for "*all* persons for any and all claims in respect of death, personal injuries to individuals, loss of property... *business loss, damage to environment* and other losses, *present and future* arising from the disaster" (Baxi and Dhanda 1990, italics mine, 4). Here was a comprehensive statement about the loss of livelihood, damage caused by contamination of air, soil, and water, and the need to take care of the future generation of victims. It went on to define the monolithic multinational as a complex corporate structure with a network of subsidiaries and divisions. As a single entity, it operated through a neatly designated network of interlocking systems with global distribution and marketing, financial, and other controls. The inherent duty of the corporation was to exercise reasonable and effective means to promote safety, and this was an absolute and nondelegable duty. The disaster should have been foreseen and prevented. Therefore UCC was termed as absolutely liable.

UCC responded by entering into a denial mode that virtually negated its own existence. The allegations were dismissed as rhetorical because they were not even directed toward the defendant. The vanishing act had begun! Ownership of UCIL was denied on the grounds that it functioned as a distinct corporate body. UCIL had a managing director appointed by the board of directors of UCIL. Its identity as a corporate body was approved by the shareholders of UCIL and duly sanctioned by the central government. UCIL had many shareholders that included Indian public financial institutions. Similar to other shareholders, the only assets of UCC were shares, and it did not have any propriety or ownership interests in the assets of UCIL. At any given time, UCC was only a "contractual provider" of certain technology and knowledge. The detailed designing, fabrication, and installation of the capital plant, machinery, and equipment of the plant were done by UCIL. The denial reached a crescendo with the defendant submitting that there was "no concept known to law as Multinational Corporation or as monolithic multinational." UCC had "no operations in India, did not operate in India or all relevant times were never recognized as having carried out any business in India…The provisions of statutes, regulations and policies of GOI, especially since 1960 had in fact not permitted alleged multinational corporations as alleged monolithic entities" (Baxi and Dhanda 1990, 62). The denial of its corporate being transformed UCC into an obscure American corporation that merely held some "capital stocks in separate incorporated companies in foreign countries."

The denial was carried even further. It denied that there were any future generations of victims as alleged. This was based on its denial that MIC, which in certain conditions was toxic, inflammable, and hazardous, was ultrahazardous. It also denied that most of the claimants were physically and financially incapable of individually litigating their claims. Taking the argument further it denied that the Union of India was entitled to file suits on behalf of unknown and unspecified people. Finally UCC went on record to state that there was no evidence of any alleged consequences or long-term adverse genetic or carcinogenic effects resulting from MIC exposure. These sweeping denials were made despite its own contention that no proper surveys or studies had been done conclusively to arrive at a comprehensive assessment of the situation.

The Final Betrayal

Although UCC denied that it was ever a multinational enterprise, it did everything in its power to reach a court directed settlement. The four years lost in litigation was part of a planned move to convince everyone that legal initiatives would come to naught. The company went out of its way to prove that Indian jurisprudence could not enforce American due process requirements. It saw to it that prolonged waste of judicial time made the settlement seem inevitable and legitimate. However, this did not come as a surprise to the Indian people, given the fact that a transnational corporate entity by its very definition believed in profit and power. It was the Union of India and the Supreme Court that finally betrayed its own people.

The February 14, 1989 order laid out the grounds on which the settlement was reached. After careful consideration of the "mass of data placed before us," "the offers and counteroffers made between parties," "the complex issues of law and fact raised before us," "the enormity of the suffering," "the pressing urgency to provide immediate and substantial relief" the court arrived at the decision to settle for the sum of $470 million. There was shock and outcry from every sector of the society. The survivors of the Bhopal disaster had been let down on almost every count. The Supreme Court knew that the data was incomplete and delay was endemic and innovative methods could have dealt with the situation. The survivor groups had moved the court on public interest to grant interim relief to tide over the situation. In the December 17, 1987 landmark decision, Judge M. S. Deo had asked both parties to pay "reconciliatory substantial interim relief." UCC accused the court of prejudging the case. The Union of India's reaction was vague and directionless; it spoke of the need for a "fair and just settlement" (Baxi and Dhanda 1990, 225). The grounds had already been prepared for the settlement, so whatever careful consideration had gone into it was preplanned. All references to the complexity of the legal system and the enormity of the suffering were only meant to divert attention from the nature of the sell out.

The Supreme Court made a feeble attempt to justify its decisions in an amended order brought out on May 4, 1989 (Baxi and Dhanda 1990, 539–549). The tone of the order was curiously apologetic. It agreed that no decision can be infallible but insisted that things were done in the best public interest. "Considerations of excellence and niceties of legal principles" were overshadowed by "pressing problems of survival." The juxtaposition was blatantly false, for all previous references had been on points of technicality. In real terms, what was being endorsed was a system that could not be changed, even in the face of an extraordinary situation. So the magnitude of suffering and its impact on society were being highlighted and underplayed at the same time. The settlement was described as "fair" and "just" though it was done on behalf of people who had no voice or power to participate in the political process of decision making. All talk about niceties and moral responsibility only concerned those who made policy decisions. The survivors were conspicuously missing from the discourse, though all terms of reference began and ended with them.

The next issue that had to be tackled was the sum of money that was settled as "reasonable." The amount ranged between $426 million offered by UCC and $500 million suggested by the attorney general, so both parties accepted a compromise amount. Once again the third party concerned was missing. The proposed good that was toted to come out of the exercise was immediate monetary benefit for the survivors. It was a false assurance, since exact numbers had not yet been determined and the method for disbursal of money was fraught with uncertainties. The order did go on to talk about modern industrial technology and "its pernicious potentiality." It raised the problem of the "inadequacy of legal protection" against "exploitative and hazardous industrial adventurism." But these were only matters of academic interest. The real concern was the ground level situation that had to be tackled on an emergency basis. Here the question of the enforcement of the order became paramount. "The decisions of the court cannot be altered or determined by agitational pressures, for the manner of corrections has to be recognized by law." A clear warning was sent out to pressure groups, asking them not to take recourse to agitation. Simultaneously people were told to hold on to their faith in the legal system. No doubt, courts were "human and fallible" but corrective measures also needed recourse through law. This indeed was pernicious logic since law had been bypassed to arrive at a settlement.

What never emerged from the settlement was the bitter truth that the "cause" of the disaster was part of the very systemic failure that had made it so difficult for the legal system to give a comprehensive judgment for bringing the culprits to book. Matters of grave concern that could have emerged in the course of the legal battle were simply swept under the carpet. Here is an example. The Union of India's reply filed on January 6, 1987 showed how as early as 1978, when the Bhopal project was midway to completion, a high-level review meeting was held in New York to discuss potential cost overruns and the diminishing size of the pesticide market in India. The decision taken was to proceed according to the original plan as the project had moved too far. By February 1984 a new plan was submitted to sell or lease the Bhopal facility. When no buyers were found, UCC came up with an alternative. At a Danbury meeting in October 1984, a decision was made to dismantle the plant and ship it to Brazil or Indonesia. UCIL was not represented in the meeting. The plan for dismantling and shipping was prepared for submission on November 29, 1984, just three days before the gas leak. This was the final act of disinvestment that became the direct cause of the disaster.

December 3, 1984

What happened on that fateful night? The first rumbling of trouble started after midnight. An operator in the MIC unit discovered that the gauge on the control panel was showing that pressure was building in tank E610 that contained forty tons of liquid MIC. The operator knew that heat and pressure would turn MIC from liquid to gas. He alerted his supervisor and the internal alarm system was sounded inside the factory. But the situation was already out of control. The huge 40 ft by 8 ft tank, which was partially underground with a concrete reinforcement on top, had started vibrating so violently that the reinforcement cracked. With the temperature reaching more than 250 degrees the safety valve had given way, releasing the gas into the seventy feet pipeline leading into the vent gas scrubber. From 12:30 a.m. to 2 a.m. tank 610 emptied its entire deadly contents into the atmosphere.

In a charge sheet filed in 1987, the Central Bureau of investigation (CBI) the apex investigating body in India gives a run through of what went wrong. From the material seized from the factory site, which included company literature and manuals, CBI concluded that MIC is reactive, toxic, volatile, and flammable. It has to be stored and handled in stainless steel containers of the highest quality. MIC cannot be allowed to come into contact with iron or steel, aluminum, zinc, or galvanized copper during the course of storage, transfer, or transmission. MIC has to be stored in tanks under pressure by using nitrogen that does not react with MIC. The temperature of the tanks with MIC has to be maintained below 15 degrees centigrade and preferably at about 0 degrees centigrade. The storage system and the transfer lines have to be free of all contaminants, for even a trace can initiate a runaway reaction resulting in dangerous and rapid timerization. The heat generated can cause reaction of explosive violence. In particular, water reacts exothermically to produce heat and carbon dioxide. Consequently, the pressure in the tank will rise rapidly if MIC is contaminated with water. UCC manuals underline the fact that with bulk system, contamination is more likely than with highly compact sealed drums. Therefore storage of large quantities of MIC in big tanks is fraught with considerable risk.

It is a well-known fact that all the safety systems that were meant to prevent such a disaster failed. On December 2, routine water washing exercise to clear blocked pipes in the Relief Valve Vent Header (RVVH) piping configuration was undertaken, before the night shift came in. When the control room was alerted to water and gas leaking from the MIC structure, nobody seemed to realize an emergency situation. The thirty-ton refrigeration system that was especially designed to maintain temperature of liquid MIC at 0 degrees had been shut down as part of the cost-cutting drive. When temperature started rising in the tank, there was nothing to counteract it. According to rules a spare tank had to be kept empty for emergency transfer of MIC, but tank E 619 also contained MIC. The thirty meter high flare tower or chimney as it was called had a pilot flame that was always kept burning so that it would burn off the toxic gas before it could reach the atmosphere. The pipes connecting the scrubber to the flare tower had become corroded and had been removed for replacement. So the flare tower was disconnected and the pilot flame extinguished. Normally caustic soda was released into the vent gas scrubber to scrub the poison and neutralize the toxic substances before letting it into the atmosphere. But the vent gas scrubber had been put off to a standby position. Finally the water curtains or network of water outlets that were meant to shoot a jet of water to absorb the gas was only set off at 1 a.m.

Clearly safety standards in the factory were not up to the mark. There was considerable human error as well. Till three hours after trouble began workers still did not realize that anything was seriously wrong. They did not have the wherewithal to locate the problem or to contain the chain reaction. Was it merely a case of insufficient training? Or was the problem more endemic to the system in place? The fact of the matter was that safety systems were not designed to cope with extremes or worst-case scenarios (Everest, 1985, 34). For instance, the vent gas scrubber was not designed to handle a massive runaway reaction. The normal feed rate was 190 pounds per hour at 35 degrees centigrade; on that night gas poured at the rate of 40,000 pounds per hour at 200 degrees centigrade. The flare tower could handle only small quantities of MIC. And the water curtain could not reach the height at which the gas was escaping into the atmosphere. Attention was only paid to routine safety, and major disasters were not in consideration. This happened despite the fact that UCC complained about the lack of safety culture in India. Local realities were grim, given widespread and rampant corruption, laxity in regulations, ignorance, illiteracy, and general disregard for the safety of workers. UCC used all these factors to its own advantage, by propagating a culture that placed profit before people, in which high return on investments and diminishing capital in matters of safety went hand in hand. It was a contradiction in real terms. It resulted in double standards. The Bhopal plant was expanded from a formulation unit to a production plant to help India become self-reliant. At the same time, the technology was entirely imported, so UCIL never became an independent entity. In crucial areas such as exchange of technical know-how, a measure of dependency was maintained. Yet the operation of the plant was allowed to become indigenous. Here if nothing else was a perfect recipe for disaster.

The Bhopal disaster was not an accident but the inevitable result of a series of corporate decisions. UCC did everything in its power to shift the blame from the company to the government, but both were culpable. The year 1984 saw a change of guard at the helm of Indian politics. Prime Minister Indira Gandhi was assassinated and her son Rajiv Gandhi came to power. He carried the mandate of the Congress party to liberalize India's economy. In the two decades following the gas disaster, India began its forward march toward greater progress and development in an increasingly global scenario. The story of Bhopal gathered momentum in directions that were determined by the power play of national and global forces of development and the lapses that were specific to the conditions of progress. In chapter three, we take stock of the sociopolitical scenario and the kind of economic changes that was paving way for greater corporatization of society. We see these changes in the specific context of the disaster. Thus, we are able to link the fate of the nation to the destiny of people struggling to survive in a hostile world. But before we can get this larger perspective in place, we need to shift attention to a more neglected aspect of the disaster. Chapter two uses oral testimonials to record the "voices" of people who survived to tell their tale. In the process, we use the grassroots' perspective to get a more vivid picture of what can best be described as a nightmare without an end.

CHAPTER 2

Monstrous Memories: "Reliving" the Night of the Disaster

Aim a blowtorch at my eyes
pour acid down my throat
strip the tissue from my lungs
drown me in my blood
choke my baby to death in front of me
make me watch her struggle as she dies
cripple my children
let pain be their daily and only playmate
spare me nothing
wreck my health so I can no longer feed my family
watch us starve
say it is nothing to do with you
don't ever say sorry/poison our water
cause monsters to be born amongst us
make us curse god
stunt our living children's growth
for twenty years ignore our cries
teach me that my rage is as useless as my tears
you are a wealthy American corporation and I am a gas victim of Bhopal.
—Anonymous (2004).

Every year a ritual of remembrance is enacted on December 3. The time is close to midnight and the venue is J. P. Nagar, just opposite the defunct Union Carbide factory. A group of men, women, and children walk toward the memorial statue created by Ruth Waterman of the fleeing woman and her two children; they hold candles, banners, and posters in their hands. The media is there and so are the police as watchdogs. There is nothing really to usher in the moment except the dogged determination of the crowd that is growing steadily in number, and they are here to mark the site of commemoration and register their grief and protest. The candles are lit, and any attempt to raise slogans is soon muted by the overwhelming nature of the memories that swamp the faces. People come forward and place the candles at the foot of the statue, the lighted flames glowing in the dark. Soon the crowd begins to disperse. The street stands empty. There is nothing to indicate that twenty-five years back, this vacant spot had witnessed a scene so macabre that it defies imagination. In a real sense, the story of Bhopal can never be told.

This chapter takes a close look at the "night of the disaster" as seen through the eyes of those who were caught in the vortex of the tragedy. I use testimonials to highlight the oral and experiential nature of living through the night, and the fact that all those who were caught in its monstrous proportions were part of the action, without any scope for objective viewing. It is interesting to know that questions that are continuously raised about the need to relive the night or its authenticity or whether it can further our understanding of an industrial disaster are not really relevant from the survivor's point of view. When I asked Champa Devi Shukla to describe the night to me, she only said, "We were all in it. There was no time to think or ask what had happened and why. Those questions came much later and we are still trying to find answers. But that night was different. We were only trying to save our lives." It is the starkness of the tales of survival that I seek to capture in the following pages.

Two kinds of testimonials are used, those drawn from archival sources and live interviews.[1] I have used them in a seamless way to recreate the immediate response that followed the disaster with those that look back with hindsight. Some of the voices have become well known and have been used repeatedly in different forums for highlighting issues. Exploring the different kinds of source material helps us raise interesting questions on the nature of oral history and its use. In a sense, any attempt to create a memorabilia for the Bhopal gas tragedy has its own limitations. Right from the beginning, two kinds of testimonial gathering were undertaken, one by survivor groups and the other by the mainstream media. The first kind was meant to feed into activism, keeping a target audience in mind, while the second was largely used to highlight human-interest stories. As mentioned earlier, human interest remains a staple middle-class response, and both types of testimonial gathering have been criticized for catering to populist demands and therefore discounted by oral history. It has been recognized that oral testimonials are "used" by hegemonic discourses to appropriate "voices" of people who are otherwise never heard. Does oral history offer safeguards against the possibility of misrepresentation? Clearly, like any other form of writing there are pitfalls, without any predictable ways of avoiding them. What I would like to show is that in Bhopal, testimonial gathering was being done by grassroots organizations against all odds, often by dedicated individuals who worked in a politically charged atmosphere, in the face of immense pressure from monolithic systems of silencing and effacing. In using oral history I recreate such a context in order to explore radical use of people's perspective to destabilize entrenched middle-class values. We all like disaster narratives. But more often than not we feel sorry but insulated from people we do not identify with or from circumstances that are not our own. In this case, as we listen to the stories an innovative method of imaginative reconstruction comes into play that highlights the continuous process of remembering, forgetting, filtering of truth, emphasis, recalling, and trying to make sense of things that becomes part of the telling. "Telling" and "listening" are the twin process of identity formation that redefines our role in the tragedy. This is as much our story as theirs, and we need to keep this in mind while empathizing with the events of the night.

Throughout the chapter, individual and collective memories are used in a way that places individual stories in the wider context of the socioeconomic and political background. The testimonials are gender specific in that they capture women's voices, though the male voice is brought in to give comparative points of view. The narratives are drawn from different age groups, given their strategic positioning on the night of the disaster and how they survived to tell their tales. Many of these are women I have known personally in the course of my involvement with the movement, therefore I am compelled to create pen portraits that are both intimate and touching in the way they bring out the foibles, eccentricities, charm, and strength of these extraordinary women. I have tried to maintain the inflection of their voices as much as possible, to get across their points of view without really trying to mediate.

Bhopal survivors are more than willing to talk for various reasons. Since they live with the trauma daily, they feel the compulsive need to talk to anyone who is there to listen. Besides, they constantly feel neglected and humiliated by the official processes.[2] Bhopalis have also realized that they need media attention to keep their fight for justice in the limelight. They are used to journalists hounding them for pictures and sound bytes, and they can play to the gallery when the need arises. "Everybody wants to talk about the night," Champa Devi tells me, "but nobody has the patience to listen to what happens afterward. Then suddenly it is no longer a matter that concerns them. But I am not complaining! After all, these stories can move people to tears."

But there is another more serious dimension to this, which is encouraging. Survivors are willing to talk to researchers and fellow activists because they understand the need for serious documentation. Importantly, these testimonials offer a powerful intellectual and political weapon for piercing the secrecy code that protects systems of oppression, whether it is corporate or state power. Listening to Champa Devi, we notice how years of being in the forefront of the resistance movement has sharpened her insight: "First the company tried to minimize the number of those affected, then the government joined them in speaking the same language. You would think the government is for us—the people—but living through that night made it very obvious who is with us and who is against us."

A great deal has been lost as memories get dim, facts and figures get muddled, and much that is said is based on hearsay, rumors, or exaggerations. I take this loss as part of the risks involved in oral history methodology. At the same time, this feeds into an important aspect of the research that is to negotiate the space between experience and the process of constructing reality in spoken words. Nowhere in the book is the sense of "*dancing* bodies," which is basic to the understanding of oral testimonials, brought out as vividly as in this chapter. These testimonials are visual and as we hear and see the ravaged bodies and minds we understand how words get interlaced with bodies, using both as expressive tools of self-expression and as resistance.

I do draw on the finer distinction between personal narratives, stories, and testimonials that act as affidavits and fact-finding devises. In the later chapters, I evoke the specific connotations of testimonials as "submissions" or "dispositions" that would go into a more conscious project of evidence gathering. In this chapter, my task is to unfurl, somewhat like peeling an onion, the various layers of memories of a night telescoped through twenty-five years of living hell. I use testimonials to get across voices that are otherwise neglected or never heard. In the process we get an alternative perspective that gives a fairer, more balanced picture of a complex reality.

"I saw It...an Insidious White Cloud"

December 2–3, 1984. It was a routine winter night, and most accounts of "what happened that night" always begin with *pre-disaster moments* that capture the commonplace, family scenario. All this would have gone unrecorded as an ordinary day in the lives of ordinary people, if the scene had not changed so irrevocably, and in the most extraordinary manner.

Here are some firsthand accounts of such moments drawn from the Bhopal Group of Information and Action (BGIA) newsletters. As described by Bano Bi, "The night the gas leaked I was sewing clothes sitting next to the door. It was around midnight. The children's father had just returned from a poetry concert. He came in and asked me, 'What are you burning that makes me choke?'" Like many others Aziza Sultan was in the prime of her life, married into a joint family with young children to tend: "I was living with my husband's family at that time. My daughter Ruby was three years old and my son Mohsin about eight months old. That night my husband was away from Bhopal on work. Our whole family watched a Hindi film 'Damaad' till 9 p.m., then had dinner together and went to bed at about 10 p.m. My children had gone off to sleep long before the movie ended. The rest of the people in the community also went to bed around the time." These mundane family scenes acquire pathos because the disaster was about to destroy family units forever and tear apart the lives of its members. The testimonials gathered soon after the disaster carry this sense of a recurring nightmare where the home is permanently destroyed.

It is equally important to record the precarious nature of these housings, and the fact that the makeshift construction without proper doors and windows made the household peculiarly vulnerable to a gas leak of this scale. Most families lived in crowded slums with poor sanitation, no ventilation, in congested narrow alleys with absolutely no greenery around. Many of the women I interviewed told me that initially they did not understand the nature of the gas that was creeping through the windows because they were used to cooking on stoves that emitted heavy fumes, and the pungent smell made them wonder if anyone was burning chilies. A majority of the families with many mouths to feed and limited resources lived below the poverty line, so that their lives were perilously fraught with danger. However, the city was totally unprepared for a chemical assault. According to Aziza, "a glow filtered into the room through the slats from the street lights outside. So the room wasn't exactly dark. And in this half light I saw it, an insidious white cloud that had crept in stealthily and all but filled the room."

The testimonials invariably begin with the rerun of the nightmare since this is the starting point from where the survivors "relive" their experience of death and mayhem. The narratives have a peculiarly compulsive and repetitive quality about them, but there is need to capture the nuances of voices, so as to get a sense of how the gas affected the "individual" lives of people. Aziza's story is representative, but the emotive force underlying her experience is fiercely subjective. The methods of classification used in disaster management try to reduce individual trauma to collective suffering. The testimonials take on a different stance by compelling us to listen to the survivors trapped inside the demon of their own personal trauma. Each of them speaks aloud of fears, sense of helplessness and guilt as they watched their loved ones writhe in pain and die. "It should have been me," remains the constant refrain in the survivor's narratives.

Women have memories that are rooted in the interior space of their homes and the way in which the poison clouds made inroads into it and destroyed its privacy. Men have memories of the outdoor and the assault of the gas that destroyed homes and made it impossible to return to its safe refuge. The BGIA newsletters provide some interesting stories. Jeevan Shinde narrates, "I used to be an auto rickshaw driver and around 12:30 a.m. on the night of the disaster I was driving through Bharat Talkies going toward home. I suddenly started feeling really hot. At that time I could not see any signs of the gas or the turmoil afterward. I got home and went to sleep not thinking anymore. At 2:30 a.m.

I suddenly woke up to find that my quilt was on the floor despite it being a winter's night. Smoke had started seeping from under the door. That was when the coughing started." Ramnarayan Jadav had an interesting insight to offer on why everybody was taken by surprise by the happenings of the night.[3] Jadav who was a city corporation bus driver first smelt the gas around 11:30 p.m. He did not leave the area for the next forty-five minutes, because too often people smelt gas in the vicinity of the factory, causing irritation in the eyes and chest. Since matters usually returned to normal, there was nothing to tell that things were different that night. When the realization did dawn on everyone that things were fatally wrong, it was already too late.

The most chilling narratives are from children just seconds before the disaster struck and their normal family routine was shattered forever. Ramesh was twelve years old then and lived in J. P. Nagar, the colony most perilously close to the factory: "My friends and I were relaxing in the evening and we watched a movie on television. I must have gone to sleep around 9 p.m. It was cold and I had covered myself with a rug. Sometime in the middle of the night I heard a lot of noise coming from outside. People were shouting." Sharda Vishwakarma was barely ten years old and all she can remember are bits and pieces of conversation between her family members; she recounts what must have frightened her the most: "My father said, 'let's not run away because we will surely get separated from each other in this crowd and darkness. If we have to die let us die together.'"

Aziza was right when she spoke of the gas cloud as "insidious" for it permeated every nook and corner of their lives, reducing everything to ruins. It is the quality of the unknown that Champa Devi describes to me, "We had no idea what was happening to us. We did not know what sort of gas it was and why it was making us writhe with pain. It was only much later that we knew the gas had come from the factory. Actually nothing of the real situation has been described anywhere, simply because nobody would have known what to write. In that sense a great deal of what happened has not been recorded at all. For instance, we are told that an entire colony of gypsies who lived on the pavement near the railway station was completely wiped out. But nobody recorded their names or who they were. Bhopal is full of untold stories that are lost forever." Perhaps the most telling account of how lives changed overnight comes from Sunil who was thirteen and lived with his parents and seven siblings in J. P. Nagar.[4] He got separated from his family and ran for about 2 km before he climbed into a bus. He found himself in Hosangabad, which is 70 km away from Bhopal. When he returned to Bhopal the next day, he wandered through the streets crying, looking for his family. He saw posters with the faces of unidentified bodies with a numbered scrap of paper pasted on their brows. He learnt from there that his parents and three of his brothers and sisters were dead. He kept on searching for the others and miraculously found his sister and his infant brother. He brought them back home and from that day onward became the sole guardian of the family, taking on the responsibility of looking after his siblings. The story of Sunil is fairly typical for when the gas entered the homes of the population living in the old city it destroyed the very fabric of social life. It changed relationships within the family, and left women and children destitute by killing heads of the family and bread-earners; in some cases support systems were snatched from those who were old and dependent. Families faced the trauma of future generations completely wiped out. The total annihilation and suffering were of a kind that was unprecedented in its scale, and in the trail of devastation that was left behind.

"It Seemed Like the End of the World"

We begin following the trail with vivid accounts of scenes of total havoc immediately after the gas leak. There are some images that are recurring and worth recording, for much of the official recounting of the sequence of events draws on the imaginative terror these scenes evoke, without really pinpointing what had gone wrong.[5] I choose testimonials that challenge such populist readings of the events. What gives the testimonials its particular emotive power is that survivors do not flinch from giving graphic details, despite the fact that the process of remembering has been painful. "Time is a healer" the popular adage assures us, but in the case of Bhopal the passage of time has only sharpened the pain, making memories more volatile.

A common thread runs through the narratives of those who survived that night—their memories of people running. I ask Bano Bi to describe the moment and she lowers her voice to a hoarse whisper and says, "So many years have gone by and yet my hair stands on end whenever I look back and remember those scenes! We left the door of our house open and began to run. We joined the surging crowd. We ran blindly. Everybody was running; those who were weak and gasping for breath fell down. We did not stop to pick them up." Hazra Bi is more analytical: "The fact is that we were running without any sense of direction. If only somebody had told us not to run in the direction of the gas. The children were groaning so much that we just picked them up in our arms and joined the masses of people. Believe me it seemed like the end of the world!" An impromptu discussion session has been organized in Hazra Bi's tiny one-roomed hovel. All the women who are gathered there could not agree with her more. The interview sessions with Bhopali women are always interesting, because I am invited to actively participate in the discussion. The formality of carrying a tape recorder dissolves and my questions give rise to more questions that are addressed to each other. Bano Bi turns to Hazra Bi to ask if she agrees with her: "It was the ones with money and resources who managed to flee in whatever transport they could get; only the poor, the feeble, the old and women and children got left behind." Hazra Bi instantly responds, "Rich or poor, nobody could escape the gas. But something else was seen that night, which nobody talks about. It was the common people who came forward to help each other. People showed a lot of courage. Women would tell you that perfect strangers covered them with blankets and people gave water to drink. But there is the other side of the picture. When you are running to save your life you become selfish. A lot of people got left behind and many were caught in the stampede and trampled to death. But why complain, even god was unfair! New Bhopal escaped the gas because the two lakes absorbed the poison. Those with education can give explanations for all this. All I know is that the gas did not spare anyone, and for those of us who came in the path of the poison cloud, there was nowhere to go."

Sunil, who was my companion and guide through the interview sessions I conducted with the orphans of Bhopal, as part of an individual project I had undertaken in 2003, summed up his experience with a characteristic touch of irony: "To tell you the truth, since that night I have not stopped running."[6] As I listen to Sunil I realize that the running was metaphorical, for the directions in which people ran were meant to provide the possibility of amelioration. But neither the company nor the government had any of its safety systems in place, so there was nothing to offer people for coping with the disaster or escaping its consequences.[7] As people ran for safety they ran into the poison cloud, and none of the directions they took, whether it was the hospitals, the barricaded gates of the factory, the beautifully laid out parks in the new city, the morgues or the cremation grounds, seemed the right direction. So people did what seemed the best alternative, abandon their homes and rush out in search of help—whatever came their way was a result of the human bid for survival—and when everything else failed they returned home empty handed, bearing the burden of their loss.

On the morning of December 3, the city woke up to sights so horrific in its dimensions that testimonials fail to capture its imaginative range. It is this dialectical tension between what cannot be described in words and what has been verbally constructed that gives oral history on Bhopal a peculiarly destabilizing and subversive quality. The purely descriptive often gives way to the symbolic. It is not at all surprising that a lot of creative modes of protest have arisen from the Bhopal movement, and the artistic method of story telling, spoofs, caricatures, and also poetry have been used to point to the limits inherent in a purely technical discourse. One such bizarre image of people's attempt to escape is provided by Alfred De Grazia in his book *A Cloud over Bhopal: Causes, Consequences and Constructive Solutions* (1985). Grazia tells us that people covered great distances while running, though most of them were escaping on foot; many found themselves in the outskirts of the city. When the director of Medical Services came out to enquire, he was met by a rush of people who surrounded his car. Many of them tried to board the roof and the bonnet, and scores of them were found dead on top (1985, 13). It is these images of death that I take up next. The Bhopal saga is riddled by the contradiction between the instinct for survival that is ruthless and amoral and the instinct to protect, help, and save loved ones and strangers. It is in this context that we understand what Rashida Bi meant when she said in one of her television interviews: "The lucky ones died that night."

"It Was a Stampede of the Living and the Dead"

Bhopal has often been compared to Auschwitz and Hiroshima keeping in mind that it was a man-made industrial disaster.[8] A massive explosion of a vast quantity of lethal gas transformed the city into a gas chamber. The effect of the explosion was different from smaller, workplace accidents that were happening with disturbing regularity. Its impact was also different from slow, chronic poisoning, which usually accompanies industrial pollution. David Weir coined the phrase "Bhopal Syndrome" to show that Bhopal remains a blot on the forward march of civilization, simply because it represented what was "fundamentally wrong in our stewardship of the world" (Weir, 1985, v). As pointed out, Bhopal has been defined as a technological disaster that soon became a crisis with a rising death toll, which was spread over days, months, and years.[9]

Over the years the images of death have proliferated and are constantly juggling between statistics and speculations. Oral history covers the middling ground where the deeply personal experience of death shares space with official methods of classification. Later we look at the politics of the number game and the role it played in the infamous settlement, but here it is enough to remember that the question of how many died on the night is redundant from the survivor's point of view. The images of death evoke the faces of loved ones and the piles of anonymous corpses. Thus we are told that hundreds of people working, waiting, and sleeping on the railway platform died instantly or courtyards of hospitals were lined with bodies or dark rumors were circulated of bodies being dumped in trucks in the nearby forests and the river Narmada (Fortun, 2001, xiv–xv). Such images can both titillate and evoke horror but as we listen to individual narratives, we realize that "who died in the family and under what circumstances," was all that mattered to the many who suffered acute feelings of bereavement and personal loss.

Archival sources (BGIA newsletters) provide the most graphic descriptions with purely visual attributes. Razia Bee narrates, "My three year old daughter Nazma had swollen up so much like she would burst. We took her to Hamidia Hospital. We stayed with her in hospital for fifteen days and then the doctors said she would not survive. We were feeling so helpless because there was no doctor around who knew how my baby could be saved. She died on the fifteenth day." It is the fear and helplessness of witnessing the death of near and dear ones that gets repeated in narrative after narrative. Zubeda Bi said, "My grandson was one year old then. I put him on my chest to protect him as much as possible. But his face swelled to twice its size, his eyes were puffed tight. We were really scared." The descriptions are clinical to the last detail as though emotions had all dried up. After all it was not just one member of the family who was dying. Razia Bee narrates, "My husband Rafique suffered the most in the family. He would need to sit under a fan. His mouth stayed open and he had those violent coughing bouts. Often he would cough blood. After months of his being in the hospital (Hamidia) the doctors said now take him home we can't do anything to help your husband... Finally I took him to Shakir Ali Hospital but the treatment there did little good. Though we were supposed to get free medicines the doctors said that if you want to get better medicines you should buy them from the market. One morning the doctor wrote a prescription and I worried all day about where to get Rs 500 to buy all the medicines. My husband died the same evening at four o'clock." It was not Zubeda Bi's grandson but her son who died a month later, while her daughter-in-law, who was pregnant at the time, gave birth to another grandchild who was born deformed. It is the prolonged nature of the process of dying and the fact that grief had to be distributed among the living, the dying, and the dead that gives these narratives their peculiarly haunting quality.

Sometimes the images of death can acquire a touch of the macabre. Sifting through the material, I found this particular story of Basanta Bai in the BGIA newsletter that is worth recounting. "Right after the gas leak my husband took me to the hospital. By the time I reached there I was completely unconscious. The doctor put a slip of paper on my forehead and I was thrown into the morgue among the dead bodies. My husband and brother were sitting outside. When they went in the doctors stopped them and said, "Your patient isn't here. She's dead." Then they came to the morgue and found me still breathing. So my husband lifted me up and brought me outside to the tent. I was given some injections during the night and after three or four hours I regained consciousness. When I was admitted no forms were filled for any patients. Papers were given neither to me nor to my husband." Bano Bi has an almost similar experience, when she is separated from her husband at the Bharat Talkies Crossing and taken to hospital by strangers. Later her husband's co-worker finds her almost by chance on the hospital floor "among piles of dead bodies."

Here is twelve-year-old Ramesh's experience of being in the midst of the dying: "As we reached the main road we could see a lot of people lying around. We did not know whether they were dead or unconscious. One fellow was sleeping with a rug over him. I crawled under the rug with him and that fellow made place for the rest of us. But after a while we could not breathe and it got very uncomfortable under the rug. So we got up and started walking... I saw a lot of dead bodies of men, women and children... my dog lay dead... also two of my friends."

It is this imaginative terror with its touch of the grotesque that turned the streets into alien places. Jivan Shinde describes the terror of the unknown in no uncertain terms. "By the time I reached Kamla Park it seemed the gas was over. But by mistake I took the wrong turn—instead of going toward the cantonment I headed through Qazi Camp. There were people everywhere running and vomiting...I cannot tell you what state people were in, almost undressed. I saw an old woman wearing only a sari blouse and knickers. The streets were strewn with bodies, unrecognizable. All night I roamed in my auto picking up as many people as I could. If I had known how poisonous the gas was I would not have gone...it was the stampede of the living and the dead." In all the narratives the memory of that night is seared by the total loss of dignity that rendered the body as alien. In the words of Rashida Bi, death was merciful, for the ones who survived continued to suffer days, weeks, months, years, and a lifetime of torture.

"There Was No Time for Any Emotions"

The earliest attempts to map the course of the poison cloud have come up with differing configurations. Did the gas spread over a well-defined area adjoining the factory or did it follow a more widely diffused pattern? (Grazia, 1985, 12). It is commonly accepted that the gas spread over an area of forty sq km and seriously injured people living as far as five to eight km downwind (Agarwal, Merrifield, and Tandon, 1985, 1). Statistics failed to come up with an accurate record of the number of deaths; worse still, it did not arrive at an accurate assessment of the nature and the extent of injuries.

The images of death began to dissipate and were replaced by other, more compelling images. In the weeks following the night of the accident, people began lining up to receive free rations distributed through a number of government programmes. The programmes soon evolved into long-term rehabilitation schemes. And all this happened while political power brokers insisted that the worst was over, and the official machinery of the government worked overtime to prove that there was no possibility of long-term effects of the gas. It is in this context that the survivor's testimonials take on a poignant urgency. A telling example is Sunil who started hearing voices in his head that were plotting and threatening to kill him. By 1997 he became a certified schizophrenic; it was as though the threat of death had acquired monstrous proportions and had receded into the darkest corner of his mind. Needless to say mental ailment was not registered as gas-related injury. The failure to bring back normalcy in the lives of people began taking its toll on people who were making a desperate bid for survival. Champa Devi's tiny frame shakes with spurts of laughter as she tells me, "You will get tired of our stories. It is not about one night. It is never ending." On the one hand, the rest of Bhopal was trying to cut down the scale of the disaster to a size they could handle. On the other hand, a storehouse of testimonials was waiting to be recorded and disseminated to the world outside. It speaks volumes that survivor groups tried their level best to compile such testimonials and print them for wide circulation. No doubt, such endeavors laid the foundation for future activism, and what is interesting is that information was being dispersed freely among rank holders in the movement. It is equally significant that the academia was much less concerned with oral history as a proven research tool. It points to inherent limitations in our knowledge systems and our inability to grasp the importance of the right to know.

In testimonials taken soon after the disaster, the survivors talk about their sufferings in relation to injuries sustained on their body and mind and the accompanying loss of livelihood. Once again it is the immediacy of their experiences that comes across with powerful intensity; the idea of pinning liability and distributing blame comes later. The shocking revelation that the real culprit was the factory in their midst was accompanied by feelings of anger and despair at the monolithic power of the enemy. When I asked Champa Devi whether she felt angry with the company or the government she gives a philosophical answer: "When you feel so much despair, anger is slow in coming. Please understand, first we ran from the noxious gas, now we were running from pillar to post to get even the smallest thing done. There was no time for any emotions." The objectivity that she is talking about was gained over time, but testimonials provide a glimpse of something more powerful—how strong emotions were getting directed toward collective action.

After Rafique's death Razia Bi had to sell off their watch repair shop at a throw away price. She and many others like her found themselves at the receiving end of dole. The nature of her illness acquired a new meaning. The symptoms were recurrent, and there was no cure for her ailments. Worse still, medical treatment was highly inadequate and expensive. She did not have the means to pay for the treatment: "My daughter developed strange symptoms. She would itch all over her body and get round blue marks as big as a coin. I took her to Hamidia then to Shakir Ali where they told me to take her to Indore. I took her to a private clinic. They told me right in the beginning that Salma's treatment will be long and expensive... at the end of her treatment Salma was only slightly better and I was in debt for Rs 50,000. To keep the home fire going I did all kinds of jobs—sweeping, washing dishes, and every kind of hard labor. None of my children could study. Only my daughter Sajida has passed eighth grade." There was another dimension to the problem; the claims for compensation also failed. "I went to the claim court with my husband's medical papers but the officials said that you have to get 04 forms filled. They told me to come later. I was not able to receive any compensation for my husband's death" (BGIA 1990). Testimonials provide insight into the widespread social dislocation that followed the gas leak and how closely it was linked to the morbidity picture.

The dead you can bury, what do you do with the living? Here is another typical story from the BGIA newsletter: "My husband used to carry cement bags before the gas leak but he hasn't been able to work. He has spells of unconsciousness. He has also become very irritable and sometimes he gets violent." It is this destabilization of the family unit that the testimonials talk about. In this case another horrific dimension is added—the continuity of the birth/death syndrome that makes her womb bring forth the stillborn and the deformed. "My eldest son died after three months. We tried everything to save his life. After that I gave birth to a son. He was born sickly and had strange looking yellow colored eruptions on his neck. When he was about a year old I was still breast-feeding him when he died in his sleep. Another daughter was born to me. She was sick all the time and we lost her too. My living son is not growing properly. He is sixteen years old but looks like he is ten or twelve." What kind of compensation could she expect as her right? "I am the only one in the family to get any compensation of Rs 15,000. We spent much more than that on our treatment. I sold off all my jewelry when my son got admitted to hospital. We borrowed a lot of money. When I told the judge about our children who died he said I had to get documentary evidence."

The newsletter also captures in Bano Bi's words the deep psychological trauma that men suffered when they were suddenly rendered unfit to do any hard labor and sustain their family. "My husband used to carry sacks of grain at the warehouse. After the gas leak he could not do any work. Sometimes his friends used to take him with them and he used to just sit there." The onus of looking after her sick family fell on her. "I had no job and the children were too young to work. We survived on help from our neighbors and other people in the community. My husband had severe breathing problems and when he became weak he had fever all the time. He was always treated for gas-related problems, yet his postmortem report said he had died of TB. Then they told me his death was not due to gas exposure" (1990). Loss of loved ones got entangled in the official web, stripping the body of all dignity. Physical symptoms were disembodied and placed on a measuring scale to determine its medical evaluation as severe, moderate, or no injury. But Bhoori Bi's story tells us that no amount of classification can ignore the intensity of the suffering. "I had pain in my chest, my back and every bone in my body ached. It was so bad I could not walk even a small distance and never could have full nights sleep. I went to so many government hospitals and private clinic. I can't even remember all the places I went for treatment. Most places the medicines made no difference." I realize that in the earliest testimonials the survivors did not talk about the company or the government when they expressed their feelings of being let down. Their complaint was directed against institutions that were closer home. Thus hospitals, doctors, and claim court officials became the main target of their pent up feelings. This emotion was to change over the years, but feelings of hurt, of being betrayed and a philosophical questioning of ones fate are the primary emotions that underlie the testimonials.[10]

Veena Das argues that pain and suffering are not simply individual experiences that arise out of the contingency of life, and she sites the case of Bhopal to show that most often experiences of pain are created and distributed by the social order itself.[11] Clearly the disaster involves scientific, legal, and administrative structures that need to maintain their legitimacy in the face of so much suffering. This was done not so much by suppressing information or through censorship, but by simply using the data in a way that deflected from the original purpose. The idea was to make the suffering visible while hiding its cause. Thus, the use of personal testimonials was restricted. As pointed out earlier, it was mainly used by activists to spread awareness. There was another use that remains largely unexplored—as testimonies in official forums were the need to "prove" damages was paramount. Here methods of classification underplayed the human touch; at the same time, doubts were raised about the veracity of information and its ability to stand up to scrutiny. Survivors were compelled to wear the badge of identification and recognition to enjoy benefits due to them. Bano Bi feels that oral testimonials are worthless in such an atmosphere of deep-rooted suspicion: "We are objects of curiosity. People look at us and wonder is she telling the truth? Once when I was sitting on dharna a young journalist thrust his mike under my nose and said mockingly, can you please tell me what really happened? I told him what is the point? If I tell you the truth you would not believe me. He was quite flabbergasted."

With time the details of any disaster begin to elude us; so has been the case with Bhopal. The survivors were soon to discover that their immediate grief was getting dissipated in controversies that were political in nature. They were being asked for "paper proofs of victimization" (Fortun 2001, xvi) so that they were soon buried under piles of official papers, and they were in need of middlemen who could act as interpreters. All this happened along with distortion of facts, misrepresentation, and suppression of information. It is in this context that we need to understand how women's body became the site of contestation between systems that deliberately underplayed the long-term effects of the gas, and people's testimonial, which was not considered a viable way of pinning responsibility.

"Nobody Knows If the Trauma Will End"

Nowhere are testimonials imbued with a greater sense of doom than in the narratives of Tulsiram and Narayani Bai, both inmates of the MIC ward in Hamidia Hospital. Tulsiram narrates, "I was a permanent worker at the textile factory. More than six times I was rushed to the hospital from the textile mill. The officers at the mill told me to tender my resignation since I could not work efficiently. Before the gas leak I never used to be absent from duty, you can check the records. There are fifty people in the MIC ward; all are in a very bad condition. The fellow in bed number sixteen is going to die soon." Narayani Bai explains, "This is the sixth time that I have been admitted to the MIC ward. I have been here since the last month of 1985. When I feel a little better the doctors send me home but I can't stay there for long. Before the gas leak I had never seen the inside of a hospital. And now I have spent most of the last five years on this hospital bed" (BGIA 1990). Inside the hospital room, which has become the death cell, the survivors have nothing to look forward to—no hope of cure or restitution or of compensation for damages done. Clearly what stares us in the face is the impossibility of using knowledge rationally and with humanity, because scientific discourse in collusion with those in political power continues to suppress and deny the real nature of toxic hazards in a chemical ridden world. It is they and not the survivors who persist in telling lies.

It was confrontation with lies almost daily that first started the stirrings of protest. The women I spoke to look back with hindsight at the growing consciousness of having been wronged by a system. They all tell me that it was women who shifted attention away from their personal sufferings to the need for collective action. In the words of Hazra Bi, "We who hardly left the threshold of our homes first felt the need to go out and protest. For how long could we sit at home and mourn for the loss of our dear ones? There was no house in the mohalla where somebody or the other had not died or was seriously ill. We knew we were raising our voices against deaf ears. The gas had made us run unclothed on the streets. We were now marching, demonstrating on the same streets." Bano Bi pipes in, "You can say we felt the need to do something to change our circumstances. None of us were born fighters or had any idea of how to fight for our rights; you can say it was all need-based. There is something else I want to say. Today we are doing so much talking; we have also learnt to go out into the streets and shout and scream. Then we did not open our mouths. God willing we are waiting for the day when we can stop talking again, for such a day will bring us justice and put a full stop to our sad saga." Both Hazra and Bano Bi were right—for a while the survivor's demands did not go beyond the need for immediate relief, but this was to change in the months that followed. By the time Bhopal was celebrating its first anniversary, a full-fledged resistance movement led by women had already taken shape.

Claude Alvares in an article aptly titled "A Walk through Bhopal," which he had undertaken in 1986, shows how life regained normalcy and a place like J. P. Nagar was once again a bustling slum (in Weir 1986, 90). There is however one significant difference. Bhopal survivors now know that their newfound identity as "victims" of an industrial disaster had brought them momentary fame. Before the accident they had suffered continuous ill health from poor sanitation, malnutrition, unhygienic water supply, and poor housing. But none of these conditions merited any special attention from the government or the political representatives they had voted into power. Now they had certain entitlements that were rightfully theirs. Rashida Bi talks about her rights in no uncertain terms: "It took us a while to understand that what the government was giving us was not an act of charity. They made us feel like beggars. But we had no choice then, everything had been destroyed that night. It is only now that I realize how much humiliation we suffered. Today my attitude is very different; I say to my fellow activists fight for your rights and ask the authorities to punish those who took it away from us in the first place. You can say I have become bold."

Alvares draws attention to an important difference between post-Hiroshima Japan and post-Bhopal India (93). Japan was quick to recognize that the problem of nuclear exposure could extend over several generations, so that research and relief had to be coordinated on a long-term basis. In the case of Bhopal just the reverse happened. Experts from different professional fields, who were called upon to advise the government refused to admit that the effect of the gas was long term and could affect the second generation. It was the ultimate lie about Bhopal. In the concluding section of the chapter, I draw attention to horrific images of death and deformity that haunt women's testimonials. It is a grim reminder of how far the reality of what happened on that night has been misrepresented.

Aziza Sultan's description of the night becomes sinister at the point where she begins talking about the final assault of the gas on her body: "I was two months pregnant at that time. I had a miscarriage right in the middle of the road; my body was covered with blood. I was unable to control the bowels and the faeces ran down my legs." Many of the other women are reticent to talk about an experience that is deeply personal. Young girls who were infants on the night of the disaster are too shy to talk about their bodies. Here is a testimonial that I found in the records of the Sambhavna Clinic, which only carries the registration number; I realize how important anonymity is in a society that is going through the throes of social change. "I have been having terrible problems for the last three years. I get periods once in four months. I get irritable, have abdominal pain and I cannot concentrate on anything. There is pain all over my body. For days before my periods I writhe in agony like a fish out of water. I am sad most of the time. I do not know how, but I feel that my health problems are my fault and I have to bear them. I do not know for how long. I am told not to mention my problems to anyone, but it is the truth."

I leave the readers with images that were widely disseminated soon after the disaster. I am compelled to add that none of these gut stirring, first-person accounts could be used in any official forum to give the survivors what they needed most—a proper compensation or sense of justice being done. Ritu Sarin writes in the magazine *Sunday*—words that can only be described as prophetic. "Travelling in the ambulance which carries cord blood samples, placenta and ailing children to Hamidia Hospital, one learns that four to five children are dying everyday only at the Sultana Janana Hospital...There are shocking tales of mothers who have lost their offspring or who are bringing up deformed infants, the shocking accounts given by the junior staff of hospitals, midwives and nurses who insist they have never seen any birth-and-death cycle of this kind before...And nobody knows if the trauma will end with this generation or the next" (July 28–August 3, 1985).

In 2000, Tim Edwards and Andy Moxon, two researchers from UK, came to Bhopal and met Dr. Ganesh of the Jawaharlal Nehru Cancer hospital. Here is an extract from their conversation, which is published on the Bhopal Web site.

> The name of Dr. Ganesh's project is "Genetic Risk Evaluation of MIC—Clinical and Cyto-Immunological Studies of Population Exposed in Bhopal." He explained that the subjects of the photos he was about to show us were born to parents heavily exposed to MIC. The cases had come to light in government hospitals over the previous few years, and Ganesh had exclusive access to them. He had mapped out diagrams of the family history of each subject. There were photographs of chromosomes attached to each of these case files, and Ganesh pointed out ominous breaks and abnormalities within the material. We were then shown about thirty photos—taken from 2000 onwards—of young children born within gas-exposed families. The images revealed birth deformities, the majority of them so monstrous, so disturbing that I kept revisiting them in my mind's eye for weeks after....There were genital distortions, followed by gross limb deformities (one girl held up a foot five times larger than the one on which she stood—another flexed fingers that protruded from her shoulders), and tiny babies with hyecenchephalitis, whereby the skull swells and bloats, throwing the body out of proportion, and squashing down the features. Finally there was a boy with doughy skin, lying in what looked like an incubator, looking past the camera through a large, single, milky eye situated near the middle of his forehead. It was a relief when the photos ended. Ganesh said he did not have the resources to collect more case studies but he knew that there were many more out there. Apparently the Director of the hospital wasn't giving Ganesh much support on his project; not only that, he didn't really want outsiders to know about Ganesh's research.

The plethora of images of women aborting as they run, fetuses kept in laboratory bottles, monstrous births, mother cradling a deformed child, and organochlorines in the breast milk of mothers is a stark reminder of the way in which trade secrets, classified information, and levels of control in a bureaucratic system have been operative. The process began almost instantly from the time the first gas leak was reported inside the factory.

"I Learnt the Biggest Lesson of My Life"

It has been argued that victims of industrial disaster face permanent victimization because of their socially structured position of disadvantage (Shrivastava 1992, 142–143). They do not have access to instruments of justice or to political power. They are busy continuing with the daily struggle for survival. In later chapters that look at activism, we see how Bhopali women were able to utilize the disadvantages as tools for their struggle. They developed what can best be described as a self-help kit. The tools were innovativeness, self-reliance, sense of solidarity, and healthy contempt for official channels of power and bureaucratic systems. They invaded public spaces and used people's power as a strong weapon. Feisty, gallant, and fearless they raised their voices in order to be heard. Therefore it is not at all surprising that Bhopali women use their stories as tools of empowerment. In the process they have made one thing very clear that Bhopal may have lost its status as a "headline event," but the questions that were raised as early as the morning after the disaster still continue to be relevant.[12]

Perspectives have changed over twenty-five years, with each anniversary becoming a marker of the official time span, and the continuity of the suffering that returns to plague the survivors. The questions have become more searching and specific, overriding the merely descriptive and experiential process of documentation. Champa Devi does not mince words when she tells me, "I know Bhopal has become a sort of lesson for the future. I am happy about that. How else will people remember what happened? But there is also the danger that we end up ignoring individual suffering and the intensity of those who are undergoing pain. We have become good at coining slogans; your students are wearing badges that say more Bhopals should not happen. These badges speak for the rich people who are anxious about protecting themselves."

Both Shrivastava and Bogard take up the larger issue of what lessons ought to be learnt from Bhopal. Bogard raises the whole question of the danger of looking at the event as a freak accident and therefore unlikely to repeat itself. He prefers to see it as a "normal" accident that is symptomatic of a trend in industrial production toward routine technological failure. Such an approach he argues will shake us out of the unsettling sense of powerlessness over our own technological creations. His contention is that when accidents reach the deplorable point of becoming routine that it is time to bring on the wake-up call (1989, 98). Shrivastava's argument is largely about the double-edged nature of disasters; they not only wreck havoc but also provide opportunities for change (1996, 143). Most of the changes envisaged are at the level of laws, regulations, policies, and structural changes. It is interesting to observe that none of the lessons are directed toward the actual amelioration of the continual suffering of the survivors. A technological disaster is clearly looking for technological solutions, so Shrivastava is confident when he writes, "Lack of accurate assessment of losses precludes identification of real victims. The victim compensation system can be abused severely with injustice to the needy. Disaster management can benefit from development of baseline health data and medical surveillance infrastructure to document health effects of disaster" (1996, 144).

It has been noted that the earliest testimonials of Bhopal survivors give expression to the spirit of survival in the midst of grave hardships. What is often not noticed is that it is also the clarion call for changes that are not merely regulatory or at the level of policies, but infiltrate into cultural spaces and create alternate forums for self-expression and creation of awareness. Bhopali women have learnt to occupy this space. Their questions are more direct. Who is the real victim and who is false? The system is being abused but by whom? There is need for surveillance but against whom? Will we be allowed to participate directly in the decision-making processes to bring about change in policies? Will we continue to be at the receiving end of risks that cannot be eliminated?

Bhopal has resulted in intense public debate on the unrecognized hazards in the chemical industry on the whole, but the testimonials are a reminder of how a purely academic debate ignores the real issue of people's sufferings. One of the questions that I put across to all the survivors was whether they knew what was being produced inside the factory. The answers were a collective, "No, we had no idea. It was a modern factory. We thought it made rat poison. We thought it was safe. We were told that it was the pride of Bhopal." Clearly the vicious cycle of hazards is coextensive with the entire framework of modern industrial development. We have already seen how a dangerous production facility was never perceived as threat by the citizens of Bhopal, and least of all by those who stayed in its vicinity. Here again we need to turn to the testimonials to get an honest answer. The testimonials point to the disproportionate levels of vulnerability of the city's poor. It also tells us that the people who lived in the slums around the factory had little choice. In testimonial after testimonial, we see how safety was taken for granted because the slum dwellers simply did not know about the dangers, or worse still they were least equipped to protect their own in the face of danger. They lived in the cocoon of ignorance simply because they were not part of the country's development plans. Literally and metaphorically they lived on the fringes of society.

What makes the story of Bhopal such a fascinating case study is that it does not end here. As the dying masses of people were catapulted into the whirlpool of the unknown, something else happened. Rashida Bi captures the moment with her usual homespun wisdom: "That night I learnt the biggest lesson of my life. I saw people panic, run and fall down dead and unconscious. I told myself I must learn to control my destiny, to know the forces that determine my life."[13] It is this lesson of Bhopal, which is the main focus of the book, and I explore its dynamism and radical content in the chapters that follow.

CHAPTER 3

Bhopal Lives On: The Many Faces of the Continuing Disaster

> Completing the integration of Union Carbide and other acquisitions...we achieved cost synergies of $1.2 billion, significantly improving the profit margins of Carbide businesses and making them globally competitive.
> —The Way Forward: The Dow Chemical Company Annual Report (2002).

> The gas leak from the Carbide factory has left scars on my family and me that will never heal. I hold Union Carbide and now Dow Chemical fully responsible for this disaster. I want Dow Chemical to assume responsibility for Bhopal.
> —Rubina, three years old on the night of the disaster.

> While we (Dow Chemicals) have seen conflicting reports currently being made by various groups and media...we believe it is important for the State of Madhya Pradesh to restart and complete the remediation of the plant site.
> —The Bhopal Reader (2004), 148.

The event of December 3 transformed industrial risk, which had remained more or less a possibility and therefore a mere hypothesis, into the grim reality of a disaster. Described as the Hiroshima of industrial disasters, it left in its trail the official figures of 3,828 dead, 30,000 injured, and 2,544 livestock dead. But statistics belie the true nature of the disaster. This chapter focuses on the events and issues linked to the two decades following the disaster. In this way it draws attention to the many faces of the disaster in the changing national and global context. As pointed out earlier, Bhopal outlived the immediate crisis and continued to plague both the government and the company. It brought to the forefront the brutal reality that corporations in collusion with the state can cause irreparable harm to the most vulnerable section of society. Industrial risk has always been viewed as an inevitable part of enterprise and progress, so that it needs to be contained rather than addressed. The settlement was fallout of the collusion. Profit before people was the ideological impetus that paved way for the disaster to happen in the way that it did. The settlement had a more insidious long-term repercussion. It quashed criminal proceedings against all those who had been accused in the First Information Report (FIR), recorded by the Station House Officer at Hanuman Ganj police station on that night. The FIR was filed against Union Carbide Corporation (UCC), Union Carbide India Ltd (UCIL), and its executives and employees. It is interesting to observe that the settlement order stated that UCC and UCIL were to pay $470 million in compensation to the "Union of India as claimant and for the benefit of all the victims... and not as fines, penalties or punitive damages."[1] Clearly the settlement gave sweeping civil and criminal immunity to the corporation, eliminating their legal liability.

The widespread protest that followed forced the government to review the settlement. Although it upheld the validity of the Claims Act by applying the doctrine of parens patriae and declined to reopen the settlement, the October 1991 order revived criminal proceedings against Warren Anderson and the Indian accused. The Claims Act was the ultimate red herring used by the state and the corporation to hide its need to "settle" matters with each other while claiming to act on behalf of the people. It forced the victims to accept the government as their advocate, while in reality a Supreme Court settlement went against their interests. To underplay its own complicity in causing the disaster, the state officially aligned itself with the victims. It affirmed the regulatory role of the state and sought an executive action to overcome judicial complexity. At the same time, it made policies and the decision-making power of regulatory bodies beyond scrutiny. Under the blanket umbrella cover of protection, the survivors had to lock horns with the various regulatory bodies that kept multiplying with the passage of time. Ironically, these official bodies were brought in to protect the victims, and they were meant to work toward rehabilitation and compensation. The notion of justice was conspicuously missing, so was the idea of restoring rights and any long-term planning to get the people back into the national mainstream. Instead, the survivors were pitched in opposition to larger development plans, so that restitution was part of short-term, emergency action that was not meant to derail the unimpeded growth and prosperity of the nation.

But the legacy of Bhopal created ripples across nations. It raised questions that needed answering. The spread and reach of transnational chemical industries, the impunity with which corporations were being shielded, and the imperatives of privatization, liberalization, and globalization in the post-nineties leading to the twenty-first century, were the many collective issues that helped to keep Bhopal in the limelight. How different stakeholders responded to the continuing nature of the crisis is a primary focus of this chapter. In the process, attention is shifted from the actual accident to the dynamics of what happened subsequently, and how the survivors had to contend with forces of change in the socioeconomic and political context. This chapter is more factual than speculative and provides an update on the background, leading right up to present times.

The Corporate Inheritance

In February 2001, UCC became a wholly owned subsidiary of Dow Chemical Company, completing its vanishing act with minimum fuss. UCC's corporate identity and all its business were fully integrated with that of Dow.[2] The acquisition cost was $9. 3 billion and was hailed as a strategic business decision (Doyle 2004, 426). It made Dow world number two, and by 2003 its annual sales touched $33 billion with 3,500 products in 183 companies and employing as many as 46,000 people. A new vocabulary entered the corporate dictionary. Along with expansion and disinvestments were added the concept of inheritance, but curiously enough it was inheritance without responsibility or the need to compensate, clean up, or face criminal charges. It is in the context of the increasingly transnational character of corporate crime that helps corporations evade laws within national boundaries that we need to understand how Dow continued with the legacy of betrayal and denial that UCC had initiated. It was therefore not surprising that Dow used legal jargon to escape liability. In response to an application filed on August 9, 2004 by Bhopal Group of Information and Action (BGIA) before the court of the chief judicial magistrate (CJM) in Bhopal, Dow put forward the following plea: "It is submitted that UCC even after merger survives as a separate legal entity with its own assets and liability. Dow Chemical (cannot) be made liable and/or responsible for producing UCC... neither can (Dow) be held responsible and/or liable for the alleged criminal acts committed about two decades ago by another distinct juristic person" (cited in *The Bhopal Reader* 2004, 104). Actually the merger agreement between Dow and UCC denied the criminal liability of UCC in the Bhopal case.[3] But Rajan Sharma, a senior US-based attorney representing the victims has stated categorically that in terms of US laws, all of UCC's civil and criminal liability has been inherited by Dow.[4] The Dow-UCC merger was governed by US laws, and it was subject to approval of regulatory authorities such as Securities and Exchange Commission under US law. In January 2002, Dow had to settle asbestos exposure claims against UCC in Texas and West Virginia, US. Clearly there is an urgent need to establish corporate criminal liability as a form of deterrent to check the possibility of waves of corporate crime sweeping across the globe.[5]

Post-Bhopal the state versus corporation debate has become an issue of immediate relevance. The state has the primary responsibility of ensuring the fulfillment of human rights; in cases were there is danger to life or health of the population, the state has to actively intervene in order to ensure swift and adequate restitution of damage. An effective domestic regulation remains the key to ensure that companies respect human rights of local people. What is required is a strong legal infrastructure and empowered well-managed government agencies for proper implementation of national laws, with authority to take punitive and remedial action. Bhopal is a case in point that government agencies have failed in their task. While operating in a protective regime, government agencies failed because of lack of foresight, humanitarian concerns, and rampant corruption. But have things changed in the last twenty-five years? Has the process of liberalization, deregulation, and privatization of State functions changed anything for victims of corporate crime? Sadly the answer is no. If anything has changed, it has led to the further expansion of power for large transnational corporations, with control to more than 25 percent of the world's productive assets. Also for governments of developing countries it is a catch 22 situation. Overregulation can drive away investment and come in the way of economic growth. No doubt, the Bhopal disaster has become the rallying ground for tightening laws for Indian companies, but the impact on multinationals remains negligible. In the case of the Oleum Gas leak in New Delhi, a year after Bhopal, the Supreme Court did come up with the landmark ruling that companies responsible for hazardous activity must face the absolute duty clause to ensure that no harm results from corporate activity, but how mandatory is it for transnational companies?

Absconders from Law

Time and again Bhopal has witnessed the sheer incompetence of prosecuting agencies such as the Central Bureau of Investigation (CBI). As early as December 6, 1984, CBI was entrusted with the task of probing the Bhopal case; it seized most of the documents on the factory premises. In December 1987, a good three years later, CBI finally filed the charge sheet against the main offenders, for offences committed under different sections of the law in connection with the industrial disaster in Bhopal. When the settlement was amended, Anderson was already an absconder. It is interesting to observe that while filing the charge sheet, CBI did realize that Anderson's presence would be required in India, but it chose not to contact Interpol for provisional arrest of Anderson at any point of time. The state police had allegedly let off the man, who had flown into Bhopal within days after the disaster to fulfill his "moral" responsibility. At that point of time, the case was outside CBI's jurisdiction and therefore did not merit consideration in future action. Right from the beginning, CBI's plea had been that the case was dependent on highly scientific and technical evaluation of events. In all fairness, the government of India (GOI) had taken care of this factor by constituting a team headed by Dr. S Varadarajan, the Director General, Council of Scientific and Industrial Research (CSIR) to study the scientific and technical aspects of the disaster. The report was submitted in December 1985 with a backup report in May 1987. Endorsing the findings of the CSIR Report, CBI's own charge sheet stated that the accused persons had joined in acts of "omission and commission" resulting in a disaster. Yet CBI weakened its own case by losing out on time.

Justice V. R. Krishna Iyer coined a new term "Bhoposhima" to describe the disaster.[6] He said the need of the hour was "dynamic jurisprudence" and "humanism of law" that provided redress at a scale and speed that was commensurate with the enormity of the catastrophe. Instead, investigating/regulatory agencies became useless, paralyzed apparatus of the government. On the one hand, burgeoning technology was giving corporations more power than what they chose to exercise responsibly. On the other hand, government agencies were called upon to deal with a situation that went beyond the crisis format. When a disaster becomes continuous the arithmetic of how long and at what cost becomes operative. No one is quite willing to take total responsibility and therefore putting off things and using routine procedures become the way out. It was only after all the available options for bringing Anderson to trial had been exhausted that a nonbailable arrest warrant was issued against him on April 10, 1992. The company claimed that they did not know about his whereabouts, but the UK based *Daily Mirror* tracked him down in Hampton outside New York (Cited in *The Bhopal Reader* 2004, 95). When asked whether he felt any responsibility for so much suffering, his reply was "no comments." None of this sleuth work could have really helped in booking the man, since extradition process is the only course that is available for execution of nonbailable warrant in a foreign country. Accordingly, CBI moved the Ministry of External Affairs (MEA) to initiate proceedings against Anderson. The request was sent to the US government in September 1993. Questions were raised in the Lok Sabha seeking explanation for the government assurance that matters were under examination. Finally the Committee on Government Assurances decided to examine matters and presented their report in Parliament on February 27, 2003 demanding an Action Taken Report (ATR) from the government. In its concluding remarks the committee's indictment of government agencies was severe: "The Committee, particularly in the background of emerging liberalization/globalization when transnational corporations and foreign companies are being invited to set up their units in the country, wants to caution the government that it has now become incumbent on their part to send a message world over that offences of the type committed by UCIL plant at Bhopal will not be allowed to be repeated. For that, government should come out with concrete plan of action along with proper legislation. The Committee hopes that Union government, even after the inexplicable inordinate delay, will now promptly bring to book all the culprits."[7] In May 2003, GOI did send its request for extradition of Warren Anderson to the US State and Justice Departments. On July 13, 2004, US government rejected India's request for extradition on technical grounds of nonframing of criminal charges against Anderson in the ongoing criminal case in the district court in Bhopal. Today the extradition request, which involves so many agencies of the government, lies in cold storage.

The prosecution against the Indian accused has not fared any better. After readmitting criminal charges the case was split between the Indian accused who were available for trial and the absconders UCC, UCE, and Anderson. In September 1996 in response to petitions filed by the Indian accused, the Supreme Court reduced charges from "culpable homicide" under s. 304–2 IPC and punishable by ten years of imprisonment to "death due to negligence" s. 304-a punishable by only two years of imprisonment and/or fine. Usha Ramanathan in an essay titled "The Law 20 Years After: Significant Absences" draws attention to the many gaps in the law regarding industrial disaster.[8] She points out that the laws governing criminal "conduct" of corporate directors and managers have not evolved significantly. Yet post-Bhopal the notion of absolute "offence" in which someone is always responsible has been partially inducted in the 1987 amendment of the Factories Act 1948. This was especially seen in the way the definition of an "occupier" as someone in "control of the affairs of the factory" was amended to "anyone of the directors" of the company. The idea was to hold accountable someone who made decisions rather than a front person designated to take the raps. Absolute offences face the strict liability regime, and the very fact that a situation exists can constitute an offence. And also there are discovery procedures set out in the law in case an accident does occur. However these are regulatory laws. As such criminal law attempts to steer clear of corporate crimes; a lesser offence is far more likely to get convicted. The dichotomy is most apparent when we see how the charges against the Indian accused were diluted from culpable homicide to negligence. Ramanathan is quick to point out that the knowledge of the harm likely to be caused by the accused in their role as corporate managers was watered down, even before it could be judicially established that the decisions made by them constituted criminal conduct. It is interesting to see that the 1987 amendment absolved the designer, manufacturer, importer, or seller of plant and machinery after the plant was handed over to the user, with the undertaking that "if properly used" no harm would ensue. Clearly statutory law in India shows the state's ambivalence on the issue of multinational corporate liability.

The need of the hour was to bring the criminal case against Indian officials to its proper adjudication by appointing a single judge to preside over the entire matter and expedite proceedings. It was only as recent as February 6, 2006, that Keshub Mahindra and other Indian accused have presented their statements before the CJM in which they have denied any role or knowledge of the disaster. Twenty-five years down the line, every single entity accused by the court of law roams free. Both Warren Anderson and the other accused have become notional of the impunity enjoyed by corporations. From the original charge sheet to the corporate game of disinvestments and changing identities the case for justice is still pending.

It is not surprising that the absconders have found other, more innovative means to slip out of the yoke of accountability. Here is a case in point. Once the company and its executives were declared as proclaimed offenders, the CJM directed the parties to appear or have the UCC shares in UCIL attached under s.82 Cr. PC. In response, UCC announced the creation of the Bhopal Hospital Trust in London and endowed its entire shareholding in UCIL to the trust. On April 30, 1992, CJM refused to recognize the creation of the trust and proceeded to attach the shares. In December 1993, the trust approached the Union of India with an offer to sell the attached shares of UCIL to raise money for building a superspecialty hospital for Bhopal survivors. The Union of India filed an application in the Supreme Court for enforcement of UCC's obligation to build such a facility. On February 14, 1994, the Supreme Court permitted the attached shares to be sold. In the year 2000, the Bhopal Memorial Hospital and Research Center (BMHRC) had become operational; since then its history of corruption, mismanagement, and institutionalized discrimination against the gas victims deserves separate analysis in a later chapter on medical rehabilitation.

Voluntary Codes and Responsible Care

The Union Carbide/Dow merger had one salutary side effect. It brought the company into greater focus given the plethora of information—mostly Public Relations (PR) managed and company propaganda—now placed on Web sites and therefore, instantly available . Information technology came with its own brand of utility and risks. A new corporate code was framed. It was still talking about shedding responsibility, but with a more futuristic stance. Thus, www.unioncarbide.com tells us that UCC did not retain any "liability or interest" in the factory site since the shares were sold to MacLeod Russell (India) Limited of Calcutta, who now retained exclusive possession of the land under lease from MP government. Distancing the company even further from any responsibility, the state government assumed control of the site and its remediation in 1998. Instead, the company announced a more immediate task at hand. As representative of the chemical industry, UCC was now ready to prevent more Bhopals from happening in the future. The new responsibility involved a three-point programme that includes improving community awareness, emergency preparedness, and processing safety standards. Picking up the cue from where UCC left off, Dow made claims that while it "had no responsibility for Bhopal, it has never forgotten the tragic event and has helped to drive global industry performance improvements" (www.responsiblecare.com). The term Responsible Care was coined to give direction to the corporate talk about self-regulation. It was no coincidence that GOI, as representative of the developing nations, was simultaneously talking about the need for encouraging foreign investment and creating amenable conditions for companies such as Dow to come to India. It was truce time with both state and industry talking in unison.

Responsible Care was a voluntary initiative and a closer look at the definition reveals a number of loopholes. It is a vision of the future that envisages ethical ways of management of chemicals worldwide that will benefit society, economy, and the environment. Economy precedes environment and the emphasis is both subtle and emphatic. The idea is to talk in general terms by shifting attention from the specifics of Bhopal. Responsible Care heralds a shift from national regulatory authorities to a global management initiative. Clearly Dow needed to focus on image building. Through the nineties, public distrust and fear of the chemical industry had reached an all time high. This was further fuelled by aggressive and widespread community-based campaign against toxic exposure. Dow made every effort to overcome bad publicity. It did so by power brokering and political lobbying. Corporate sponsorship and giving donations to government regulatory bodies became common practice. Paradoxically enough, while the chemical industry has always been under the regulatory spanner, it has also been the source of information for safety data on products. Taking advantage of this dependence, Dow aggressively sponsored studies and exercised control in the acquisition and release of data. With governments downsizing its role in academia, corporations have played an active part in the funding of scientific research and education. In the United States, chemical companies are known to give billions of dollars to universities and foundations for agricultural research.[9]

There is the other face of reality behind the public image and the rhetoric. Responsible Care does not set higher standards for the chemical industry that can be objectively and openly verified by the public or by independent scientists and government regulators. It is a public relations effort that depends on feedback from polls and focus groups. The stated ideals of Responsible Care are in direct conflict with chemical industry's advocacy against further regulation. Self-regulation is the smokescreen that hides the conflict between community-right-to-know with the industry's opposition to greater transparency. More importantly, Responsible Care cannot put enough pressure on companies to voluntarily clean up or undertake proper restitution work at the community level through direct involvement and dialogue with people. But the "other" face of Dow is the "real" face of Bhopal.

It takes a click to navigate another Web site called "The Truth about Dow." Here we are given a rap sheet on Dow's history of poisoning. Parallels can easily be drawn with Bhopal. Thirty years after the Vietnam War, people still continue to suffer the health affects of dioxin poisoning from Agent Orange defoliant, which Dow supplied to the US military. We are now talking about long-term effects of toxic poisoning that pass from one generation to another. In Michigan, dioxin contamination stretches twenty-two miles from Dow's plant in Midland, along the Tittabawassee River to Saginaw and beyond. We are talking about impact on human beings, animals, flora, and fauna. In the Myrtle Grove Trailer Park in Louisiana, Dow produces vinyl chloride at a plant resulting in toxic waste disposal problems for decades. In the twenty-five years since Bhopal gas tragedy happened, we know much more about Dow's chemicals and how they are accumulating in the bodies of ordinary people across the globe. We are now talking about the chemical body burden that makes mother's milk the most contaminated human food on the planet. The awareness of one's body being used as a chemical storage site carries its own psychological significance. The legitimate claims for reforming product line, safe storage, transport, and disposal of waste have to go hand in hand with medical monitoring, cleanup, and compensation for poisoning. The obligations are both legal and moral and are part of people's demand that emanates from claims belonging to the community. The words of Rubina have been quoted at the beginning of the chapter She was three years old on the night of the disaster; she has no understanding of Union Carbide as the original offender, the legacy she is burdened with belongs to Dow alone.

Dow accepted UCC's legacy on the grounds that everything had been settled. But settlement did not address the three vital issues of lost livelihood, health care, and contamination of the factory site. Besides, criminal charges are still pending, with Dow having acquired the dubious reputation of protecting an absconder from justice. On January 6, 2005, the CJM in Bhopal, following a petition by activists group, ordered that Dow Chemical Company, Midland, Michigan be made party to the criminal case, given the fact that UCC is a fully owned subsidiary of Dow. Slowly and steadily we are moving toward extending international obligations beyond United States to include international organizations and private enterprises. International enforcement mechanisms remain weak, and therefore national laws continue to be the most important means of ensuring legal accountability, but the Amnesty International Report (2004) clearly underlines the need for an international human right's framework to act as a catalyst for national law and regulations. This is more so in the context of how business activities are measured by different standards of labour, environmental, criminal, commercial, and corporate laws (Ibid. 80). Therefore, a need is increasingly felt for universal benchmarks that can regulate corporate conduct.

A lot of background work went into preparing the necessary political climate for such changes. The Permanent People's Tribunal held the third session on Industrial and Environmental Hazards and Human Rights in Bhopal from October 19–24, 1992. In its report it talks about the need to shift attention from the policing power of the state to institutions and social processes that are not traditionally subject to human rights scrutiny. It says categorically, "Human rights standards have too often been narrowly interpreted to exclude from their purview the anti-humanitarian effects of industrialization and environmental damage... Industrial and environmental hazards cannot be appreciated without some reference to engineering, clinical medicine, and epidemiology. For too long specialist knowledge's have excluded lay people from decision-making. The Tribunal has resolved, in an attempt to fill a gap in the international judicial order, to provide a forum for linking technical data with people's rights" (14–15). Corporate logic refuses to see this link and therefore tries to set aside the Bhopal gas tragedy as a one-time event, whose lessons are futuristic. There is a pressing need to use radical and innovative methods of analysis that places Bhopal firmly in the larger sociopolitical canvas, in the context of both the history of corporate crime and national and international forces and how they operate.

The neglect of people in Bhopal gets metaphorically transferred to the factory site that lies desolate and forsaken with the rotting structure signifying the abandoned dream of development and progress. But the image is misleading. The place is a toxic hotspot that has the power to create conditions for a "second" Bhopal of mammoth proportions. The next section takes up the issue of environmental degradation and contamination that highlights the "continuing" nature of the disaster. What makes Bhopal such an important case study is that environment incorporates the denial of basic human rights, which includes environmental pollution, the body burden of chemicals, and the violation of the sacredness of life itself.

Environmental Degradation and the Legal Wrangle

More than four hundred gas survivors gathered at Jantar Mantar in New Delhi from June 18 to 23, 2004, to launch a hunger strike that would bring to public notice the need to revaluate the causes and continuing aftermath of the disaster. "This is a legal wrangle with far reaching consequences for policy makers and activism in Bhopal," said Satinath Sarangi of Bhopal Group of Information and Action (BGIA) and one of those on hunger strike, "therefore it is of paramount importance that the government concedes to the demands." Like everything else in Bhopal the legal wrangle over who cleans up the contaminated site has a long history. I will do a brief recap on the issue of contamination and how it has victimized the survivors twice over.

Way back in June 1989, UCC finalized a "Site Rehabilitation Project— Bhopal Plan" for decontamination of the plant site that contained huge quantities of Sevin and Napthol tarry residues and solid wastes dumped in the solar evaporation ponds. The National Environmental Engineering Research Institute (NEERI) was to undertake the task under the supervision of Arthur D. Little & Co. appointed by UCC. In 1990, NEERI submitted its first report that stated that there was no contamination of the groundwater in and around the plant site. This denial was part of the more systematic attempt to describe the Bhopal disaster as an accident caused by human error. We have already seen how the middle-class imagination has always tried to underplay the disaster and its long-term effects. Surprisingly, a fascinating pictorial book that I picked up in the "Series for Beginners," titled Introducing Environmental Politics, does not even make a passing reference to the Bhopal gas tragedy. Clearly, the manner in which Bhopal has been defined, as an industrial disaster, does not bring in issues of environmental politics. Yet in essence that is what Bhopal means, a continuing disaster that has damaged the body systems of men, women, and children and has caused serious ecological imbalance. While the cocktail of deadly chemicals and pesticides has continued to act slowly on the body, the communities living in the vicinity of the factory have been drinking poisoned water, breathing poisoned air, and growing their vegetables on heavily contaminated soil. The accident on that fateful night was only a small indicator of a much larger process of environmental degradation.

While defining an industrial disaster, we are no longer just talking about the acute effects of a single exposure to chemicals. We are looking at a situation where mass production of chemicals is causing widespread pollution.[10] In 1962 Rachel Carson's classic *Silent Spring* had brought to the notice of the world the potentially devastating effects of DDT and other persistent pesticides, which she describes as the "elixirs of death." But as "elixirs" can they remind us that human pesticide exposures are involuntary, unknowing, and unwilling? What makes the study of Bhopal pertinent, as a global signifier of toxic poisoning, is the crucial link between acute and chronic toxicity, and the fact that both can happen simultaneously. The story of Bhopal's toxic legacy predates the disaster to 1979, when UCIL started manufacturing the pesticides it had previously been importing. As a by-product of its expanded operations, hazardous wastes were being produced. UCIL dumped these wastes in tanks and pits at the plant site, as well as in three solar evaporation ponds (SEP) constructed on the leased property some 800 meters north of the factory. The ponds covered an area of approximately fourteen hectares. In 1981 and 1982 several cattle died as a result of exposure to poisonous water in the SEP. According to an internal UCIL document of 1982, the company was aware of leakage from two of the ponds, and it was notified as a matter of concern. In 1983 farmers in the neighborhood of the SEP were experiencing a drastic reduction in the fertility of the soil due to the overflowing of the SEP into their fields in the rainy season. Two tube wells dug near the solar ponds had to be abandoned because the water had an obnoxious smell and taste. After the 1984 disaster, the plant was closed down and did not resume normal operations, so that no effluent was added to the SEP. In the immediate aftermath of the disaster, the focus was on health consequences of acute exposure to MIC. Little attention was paid to the condition of the factory site, and the more pressing need to investigate the nature of contaminants other than MIC that was present not only due to the accident, but also in the course of the routine operation of the plant.

The NEERI study was undertaken only because UCC had a legal obligation to return the land to the state of MP in compliance with the terms of the lease. The land had been leased on the condition and stipulation that upon termination or voluntary relinquishment of the lease, the land would be returned to the state in the condition that it was leased and suitable for use prescribed by the zoning regulations. Again, in a curious lack of political will, the state government took back the land in September 1998 in a condition that was far from satisfactory, thus allowing the company to go scot-free. In a beleaguered attempt to do its duty to people living in the vicinity, the state government put up notices to warn people against drinking water from hand pumps. However, it did little to provide alternative supply of clean drinking water. Several environmental studies conducted from 1990 to 2002 have testified to the fact that more than 5,000 metric tons of toxic wastes and chemical by-products remain indiscriminately dumped, buried, or disposed of on the former factory site. Also offsite wells and hand pumps have disclosed that subsurface groundwater contamination had become widespread and pervasive affecting the drinking water supply of more than fourteen residential communities near the factory.[11]

Clearly there were three phases to the Bhopal accident. Prior and post-December 3, 1984, Bhopal has witnessed long-term chronic exposure to severely toxic synthetic chemicals and heavy metals, with serious consequences for the health of the exposed population. The overall contamination of the site and immediate surroundings have resulted either from routine processes during the operation of the plant, spillages, and accidents, or continued release of chemicals from materials that remain dumped or stored on the site. The issue of persistent contamination, which was separate from the actual disaster, was addressed in fresh class action litigation filed in the court of the Southern District, New York on November 15, 1999, by Sajida Bano, Haseena Bi, and five other victims directly affected by contamination and claiming damages related to common law environmental claims. The appellants were seeking monetary and equitable relief for personal injury and property damage suffered by them and persons in a similar situation. The MIC leak and the continued damage caused by contamination were two distinct and separate events. Environmental contamination in tort law is termed as a nontraumatic event that continues to cause damage everyday if it is not remedied. Because the two events affected the same population, that is, the residents living in the vicinity of the plant, there was overlap in the persons affected by the gas leak and contamination. The settlement had not addressed the contamination issue, so the process of justice could be reopened.

Judge Keenan dismissed the class action claim on grounds that 1989 settlement covered all claims. In 2001 the class action claims were remanded, but Keenan dismissed the suit once again in 2003 on grounds of limitation. On

March 17, 2004, the court of appeals asked Keenan on remand to consider the claims of Bano Bi and others, arising out of damage to property. It also expressed willingness to consider direct remedial operation, to be undertaken by UCC, provided Union of India had no objection. This was in keeping with the norms of sovereignty of the Indian state. The Indian law is in consonance with environmental remediation and the "polluter pays principle" that asserts that the costs of remediation and clean-up and losses sustained by those affected are to be borne by the offending corporation. After considerable pressure was put on Ministry of Law to change its earlier stance of linking contamination with settlement by the hunger strike, GOI submitted a memo before Keenan stating that it had no objection to decontamination undertaken by UCC at its own cost. The letter submitted to the New York court supported the survivors' litigation and clarified its position that the previous settlement of claims "had no bearing on or relation whatsoever to the environmental contamination issues." It was a major step forward. More than anything else it offered the possibility of linking the question of legal redressal to scientific discourse. The technical report on Population Based Long Term Epidemiological Studies (1985–1994), (June 2004) brought out by the Indian Council of Medical Research (ICMR) stated that the normal "epidemiological triad" of information comprised of "agent," "host," and "environment." But in the case of Bhopal very little information was available on agent and environment and therefore studies concentrated on the "host factor" based on mortality and morbidity data. The report admitted that pertinent questions regarding the exact nature of the toxic gases, their biological effects, including long-term genetic and teratogenic effects, as well as the clinical course of the morbidities suffered and the residual permanent disabilities were asked, but not conclusively answered. By raising the issue of clean up of contamination, agent and environment could become the focus of the scientific survey.

Environmental Issues and Political Action

The story of environmental pollution brought Bhopal firmly back into the global debate. We cannot talk of livelihood and economic rehabilitation without addressing the question of access to clean air and water. There can be no equity without ecology. Environmental rights incorporate within its broad category the right to information, consumer rights, prevention clause, precautionary principle, and polluter pay's principle. We are also talking about the interests of local community when it is pitted against corporate activity. The Bhopal Principles on Corporate Responsibility has an important clause.[12] States must ensure that corporations are liable for injury to persons, damage to property, biological diversity, environment beyond the limits of national jurisdiction, and global commons such as atmosphere and oceans. Liability must include responsibility for environmental cleanup and restitution. States must fully implement precautionary principle so that corporations have to take preventive action before environmental damage or health effects are incurred. States must also establish national legislation to use resources in a sustainable manner. Bhopal Principles were clearly a fervent bid to create an international instrumentation on corporate accountability that was enforceable and universally applicable. But a debate or a memorandum has to be part of a political platform in order to be effective. This section shows how environmental issues became the basis for political action in Bhopal, so that creating awareness fulfilled the purpose of directing such actions.

On August 10, 2006, the appellate court in New York once again rejected claims by Bhopal city residents seeking compensation from Union Carbide for environmental contamination. Without ruling on whether or not Union Carbide ought to do environmental remediation, the court observed that any order directing Union Carbide to clean up would run into technical problems "because of the impracticality of a court-supervised clean-up project on land owned by a foreign sovereign." In the same order, the court also rejected the appeal by Hasina Bi for seeking reinstatement of claims for property damages and remediation of the Union Carbide plant site and contamination of groundwater. The court cited lack of legal tenure over her property. According to the ruling, "the record reflects that Bi resides illegally on government-owned ground. She therefore cannot sustain claims for trespass or private nuisance under New York law." In the months to come the issue of who will eventually pay for the clean up of tons of toxic wastes abandoned by an absconding company became a live issue. However much the decision might have seemed like a setback to the Bhopal survivors, Union Carbide was not out of the fray. Yashwir Singh, the then Director, Bhopal Cell, Ministry of Chemicals spoke on behalf of his ministry when he assured the Bhopal activists that the "GOI is not party to the U.S. Court case. We have approached the M P High Court seeking that liability is fixed on the polluter. According to our rules, the polluter will have to pay." These sentiments were to prove misleading in the conflict of interest that was played out.[13]

On the one hand, what was increasingly emerging was an integrated vision of the responsibilities and tasks pending before the government and the corporation. It was very clear that over two decades later the list of things left undone was staggering. More than 100,000 people continue to suffer chronic and debilitating illnesses; survivors are still awaiting economic and social rehabilitation; plant site still awaits clean up; no one has been held accountable for the gas leak. On the other hand, there was increasing talk about "fairness in a fragile world."[14] There was much debate on the need to integrate markets in a framework of social and environmental regulations and limitations on a local, regional, national, and global level. At the same time, what was being fought out in Bhopal was a ruthless and bitter political conflict involving players at different levels—local/global, regional/national—so that survivors had to confront the hydra-headed monster that represented state and central government and the corporate entity. Importantly, the global context both integrates and dissipates the enemy. There is always the danger that sustainable development becomes a semantic innovation that allows the developers and the environmentalists to participate in the same forum, without destabilizing each other. Economic growth and efficiency are viewed as necessary conditions for sustainability, so that development-as-growth is upheld without really going into the question of development for whom. In the following chapters the focus will shift to the more challenging task of presenting the people's point of view to navigate the elusive core that lies at the heart of any definition of the Bhopal tragedy. Environmental remediation was closely linked to the question of economic rehabilitation and health care, since the disaster had long-term and debilitating after-effects that displaced lives in terms of an ailing body, diminished capacity to work, and breakdown in family and community ties. As we listen to people's testimonials we are compelled to perceive their experience of living out their displacements. Gender politics is brought in to show how vulnerabilities get played out along fault lines that are endemic.

Even as the legal case was being fought out in the Claims Court in New York, the MP state government had commenced on a hasty clean up exercise, initiated by the Madhya Pradesh Pollution Control Board (MPPCB) and the state level Bhopal Gas Relief Cell in preparation for an above-surface containment of the stockpiles of toxic chemicals lying inside the factory. The MPPCB was keen to finish the first phase of the clean up by June 20, 2005 in response to a district high court order. In pictures that were plastered all over local newspapers, workers, including women and children, were seen cleaning up without any of the basic safety precautions in place. Clearly the state government was acting counter to the central government's earlier position that GOI had no objection to applying the polluter pays principle that would make UCC directly responsible for the task of clean up. The time had come for the government to make public its clean up plans and protocols and what mechanism was to be in place to recover the costs from UCC. The need to ensure transparency, accountability, and safety standards were vital issues before both the state and central government. Instead, the police cordoned off the plant and posted armed constabulary, along the broken perimeter walls of the factory. In the first step toward remediation, sacks of chemicals lying in open were shifted to sheds. An officer of the MPPCB admitted that the containment was temporary, with no concrete plans about the restoration of the highly contaminated ground water. The state and central government face-off was clearly meant to dilute corporate accountability. The fact that accountability had shifted from UCC to Dow, now that ownership had changed, did not help matters. If anything, it paved way for an insidious political game that was played out at multiple levels.

On the face of it the state government was going ahead with its plans to contain and transport the surface level hazardous waste. So a tender notice was called to invite bids for transporting the waste to two locations at Ankleshwar, Gujarat, and Pithampur, Indore. With both locations refusing to take responsibility for incinerating the toxic waste, the deadlock situation continued.[15] In 2005 Ministry of Chemicals had urged the MP High Court to order Dow to deposit Rs 100 crores ($22 million) as initial deposit toward cost of clean up, with estimated costs ranging between Rs 400 and 500 crores. At the same time, in 2005 the corporate friendly overtures of the present government prompted business houses in United States and India to set up the US-India CEO Forum, which comprised of a select coterie of chief executive officers (CEO) from India and the United States. The forum carried the mandate to develop a road map for increased investor-friendly, business partnership between the two countries. Taking advantage of the political climate, Dow Chemicals began lobbying hard directly and through the US government, to have the "legal hurdles" on its way to investment in India removed. Insidiously, like most closed-door politics, the grounds were being prepared for another settlement, potentially more cruel and devastating than the first settlement in its betrayal of the people.

The Road Map to the Second Settlement

In April 2007 a note was prepared by the cabinet secretariat toward resolving matters relating to Dow Chemical's possible investment of $1 billion in the chemical and petrochemical sectors.[16] The note stated that "given the scope for future investments in the sector, it stands to reason that instead of continuing to agitate these issues in court for a protracted period, due consideration be given to the prospect of settling these issues appropriately. An important aim is to remove uncertainties and pave the way for promoting investments in the sector." The idea was to present to the cabinet a proposal absolving Dow of all its outstanding liabilities. This was in response to a letter written by Andrew Liveris, CEO of Dow to Ronen Sen, the US envoy, soon after they participated at the US-India CEO forum on October 20, 2006. The letter sought immediate intervention on the part of the Indian government in resolving the Bhopal legacy issue facing Dow. It called for quick action in the remediation of the contaminated site with the support of the government and the industry. The letter stated in no uncertain terms that GOI had taken a position adverse to Dow in the ongoing litigation at the MP high court, and it wanted withdrawal of the application for financial deposit against remediation costs. The letter ended on a note of quid pro quo stating a "common goal to support economic growth in India, including foreign investments that will promote job creation, economic diversification and technology updates."

Acting as mediator between Dow, the finance minister, the planning commission, and the prime minister was none other than Ratan Tata, Indian industrialist and chairman of the Tata Group. In a letter addressed to P. Chidambaram, who was then Finance Minister, he expressed his willingness to set up a Site Remediation Fund or Trust for clean up of the site. He believed it was in the national interest, to allow responsible corporate houses in the private and public sector, to come forward and contribute to the trust. Dow had reportedly indicated its willingness to contribute to this corpus, but insisted that none of this should be seen as arising from legal obligations.[17] It would be fair to recall that the Tata Group, a family-owned Indian multinational with the corporation's flagship company Tata Steel and 2005 revenues of Rs 76,500 crores ($17.8 billion), has a good reputation. As undisputed king of the protected economy, they have played a role in India's development and have used their wealth in manifold philanthropic activities. Many a tale of human rights, labor, and environmental violations have gone unnoticed with Tata's successful public relations strategy.[18] But postliberalization, talks of nation building and corporate responsibility have to go hand in hand with obligations to shareholders. The realities of operating in a globalized environment have begun to catch up with the Tatas', and however well meaning Ratan Tata might be in offering to clean up the mess left behind by a company yielding considerable power, he cannot absolve himself from the charge of taking part in a political conspiracy to deny justice to the victims of an industrial disaster. Given the public outrage that followed once the news was leaked out in the mainstream media, Tatas quickly backtracked on their original bid to play a front role in the GOI-Dow truce.

Mercifully for the survivors, given the pressures of electoral politics and the fact that much is at stake with Bhopal, no government can be seen as opposing people's interest. A lot of it is covered up by popular perceptions on national development. But more importantly no one is quite willing to take the onus for the decisions made. Thus, Montek Singh Aluwalia, the deputy director of the Planning Commission who was mediating with Ratan Tata, went on record to tell the press that he was only playing the role of a facilitator. "Ratan (Tata) wrote to me about Dow in my capacity as the chair of the Indo-US Economic Dialogue Committee and I have forwarded his request to the Ministry of Chemicals and Fertilizers (MOCF). I can only play the role of a facilitator here as neither am I an expert nor am I authorized to make any such recommendations," he said to Outlook in a telephonic conversation.

The danger of a second settlement is still not over. If realized in its stated form, the second settlement would be nothing short of a naked attempt to circumvent the normal judicial process. It happened despite the fact that Dow Chemical was fined $325,000 by the United States Securities Exchange Commission in February 2007 for having paid at least $200,000 in bribes to Indian officials, including senior officials in the Ministry of Agriculture. The bribes were paid to expedite registration of pesticides, including Dursban that has been prohibited for domestic use in the United States owing to evidence regarding its toxicity and effects on children's health and mental development.[19] An investigation by the CBI into the bribery case is currently ongoing, and Dow Chemical is under enquiry.[20] More importantly, a settlement would amount to a second victimization of people who have already paid the price for systemic failure, inbuilt in an ideology that puts profit before people. The question is what has changed since 1989? Is it possible to work out an out-of-court settlement that is conclusive and fair, allows for people's participation, a comprehensive and accurate estimation of liabilities, and the guarantee that all the conditions of the settlement would be honoured to the last detail? If not, then the second settlement, for all its talk about national interest is missing the point. The proposed settlement attempts to exempt Dow from the "Polluter Pays" principle and established laws regarding legal liability of polluters and potentially responsible parties for environmental remediation, compensation, and health reparations. It gives preferential treatment to Dow by writing off legal liability for solely commercial considerations. The settlement is between "joint tort feasors"—namely, the Governments of MP and India and Dow Chemical. More importantly it excludes Bhopal survivors, the affected people from the political process of decision making. Once again it endorses a closed-door system. Finally, an out-of-court-settlement is both unconstitutional and illegal given the fact that matters of vital importance are still on trial. There is absolutely no ground on which the government could claim that the survivors stand to gain in anyway by this settlement. In the ultimate analysis, the second settlement shows an increasing violent trend that Arundhati Roy describes rather eloquently, "We have a growing middle class, being reared on a diet of radical consumerism and aggressive greed. Unlike industrializing western countries, which had colonies from which to plunder resources and generate slave labour to feed this process, we have to colonize ourselves, our own nether parts. We've begun to eat our own limbs. The greed that is being generated (and marketed as a value interchangeable with nationalism) can only be sated by grabbing land, water and resources from the vulnerable. What we're witnessing is the most successful secessionist struggle ever waged in Independent India."[21]

Quick Fix Solutions

The government came up with a few quick fix solutions, possibly to avoid any charges that the state has become an enemy of the people. Of the $470 million as settlement, UCC contributed $420 million held in a US dollar account, and $44 million or Rs 68.99 crores was given by UCIL and held in a rupee account. The claims court started adjudicating claims in 1992 and the accrued interest was not paid. Over the years, owing to the appreciation of the US dollar vis-à-vis the Indian rupee the sum had grown to $327.5 million. Dow actually made a claim that this money should go toward clean up, so that the survivors paid for their own restitution. After considerable resistance from the survivor groups, the Supreme Court passed an order on July 19, 2004 to allow for the remaining funds to be disbursed to those victims who were entitled to get compensation money based on their previous claim.

A Co-ordination Committee on Bhopal (CCB) was constituted by the central government after the prime minister conceded to the survivor group's demand on April 17, 2004 to set up a body with necessary infrastructure, authority, and resources to monitor the situation in Bhopal. The idea was to create a model for effective, information based, people-participatory response to industrial disasters. Right from the beginning, the CCB was dominated by the government officials and a former medical advisor to the UCC. After much pressure representatives from survivor groups were inducted. Right from the beginning, the functioning of the CCB was marred by nonimplementation of plans. The first meeting was held on June 7, 2006 and despite two follow-up meetings, and plans to set up subcommittees by inducting professionals from outside the government, nothing has happened so far. The committee is mired in the state versus center impasse. The need for an empowered National Commission that can counter a merely bureaucratic, technocratic solution to real, human needs remains an unrealized demand on the part of the survivors.

In 2004 a Supreme Court order instructed MP government to provide clean drinking water to the residents of fourteen affected wards near the factory. Tanker services were pressed into action, but the number of tankers visiting everyday fulfilled 14 percent of the demand, and at least five bastis with poor roads did not get any water at all. During the monsoons most bastis become unapproachable. Promise by the Municipal Corporation of Bhopal (MCB) to provide permanent piped water continues to remain a distant dream. Water from the Kolar reservoir, which is the main source of water supply for the rest of New Bhopal, is the only clean option. But MCB carried on with plans to supply water from borewells from Rasla Khedi that lies north of the Union Carbide factory directly in the flow path of the contaminated ground water. It was only after considerable agitation by the survivors that plans were changed; however, the bureaucratic tangle of getting orders passed continues to plague everybody concerned.

The failure of piecemeal, knee-jerk reaction to the larger problem of restoring human rights, which in turn links livelihood with environmental protection, explains why Bhopal has not ceased to be a matter of concern at the national and international level. The 1989 settlement failed to bury the ghost of the Bhopal gas leak; another settlement can hardly take away from the grim reality of what continues to happen at the ground level. To understand the exact nature of the fallout of systemic failures, we need to look at the ground reality from the perspective of those who were at the receiving end of injustice. In the rest of the book, we therefore shift attention from structural analysis to the more lived experience of social disruption, loss of livelihood, and effects of acute morbidity. We enter homes, the workplace, hospitals, and claims court to understand how oppressive systems operate on a day-to-day basis. It is in this context that we try to explore the "alternative vision" for redressal and remediation that was emerging from the most unlikely constituency—the women survivors of the disaster. Slowly and steadily women had started regathering their strength by drawing on the basic principles of environmental politics, which is to secure community rights over natural resources. Women were fighting to restore the rich cultural life of local communities, with all its diversities, difference of opinion, shared grief, common political platform, and a unifying vision of a life of dignity. Unlike written, official texts with its use of bureaucratic jargon and double-speak this vision is oral, visual, spontaneous, and inspiring.

CHAPTER 4

Women as Bread Earners: Shattered Lives and the Relentless Struggle for Survival

Before the gas I had never seen the insides of a hospital. And now I have spent most of the last five years on this hospital bed. I used to work as an assistant at a day care center and now I cannot do any work. My husband Kaluram also cannot go to his job. He used to carry loads. My son works as a tailor, he is the only one earning in the family.

—Narayani Bai, gas survivor.

The objectives behind ex-gratia payment was laudable but mechanisms to achieve the objectives was not worked out. If only one lady survived in a family of eight, where would she keep cash, how would she protect this amount and how and where would she spend it. These disbursing officials calculated the eligibility of beneficiaries mathematically and went on distributing money.
—Moti Singh was the collector, Bhopal in 1984 and he was the author of *Unfolding the Betrayal of Bhopal Gas Tragedy* (2008).

We felt like beggars on the street. We forgot we were asking for our rights as citizens of a free country.

—Sheela Thakur, Gas Survivor.

An immediate aftermath of the Bhopal disaster was its widespread economic fall out with loss of revenue, social dislocation, and the incapacity of a section of people to earn wages in exchange for labor. A single night snatched away people's ability to work and earn a living that left them on the brink of economic destitution. Given the unprecedented nature of the disaster, it caused severe mental agony to those who lost their sense of social and economic well-being. At the same time, the disaster and the economic rehabilitation that followed, threw into jeopardy the technocratic view of global development with its attendant theory that technology, unencumbered by politics, can remove poverty and inequity in the world. Rajni Kothari in his book *Politics and the People: In Search of a Humane World,* Vol. II (1989) eloquently argues that the seventies was the decade when politics came face to face with the socioeconomic aspirations of the people that challenged the ability of economic pundits and technocrats to provide a framework for development that could deal with these aspirations. In this and the next chapter, I explore the clash between people and development as set against the background of the social and economic rehabilitation that followed the disaster. Most of the gas-affected families lived in poverty-stricken conditions before the gas leak. What the disaster managed to do was snatch away their ability to overcome poverty, so that in the two decades following the disaster, they were left out of the burgeoning socioeconomic and political changes that accompanied globalization.

To rehabilitate the community and bring them back into the mainstream required much more than competent relief measures. It asked for a political process that tried to restore people's democratic rights. So economic rehabilitation schemes had to establish links with activism that sustained a relentless struggle against the sources of inequity. In Bhopal such a process was systematically curbed. People's attempt to ask for their rights was suppressed, and rehabilitation schemes that fitted the technocratic development plans were set in motion. In most cases, short-term schemes that were meant to provide external assistance to raise standards of living and therefore remove poverty were put in place. Many of the schemes failed because the need of the hour was for a different model that could take on more socially meaningful form and was less dependent on populist pronouncements.

Right from the beginning, government had to work in conjunction with voluntary organizations that represented people's interest and could act as watchdogs. Given the scale and magnitude of the disaster, there was urgent need to spread awareness, disseminate information, and carry out community level work. Unfortunately, what happened at the ground level was an increase in the patronage of state bureaucracies and politicians. In reality any sort of bureaucratic decision making that involves emergency planning and policies cannot move top downward, and it has to take roots at the bottom so as to percolate to the lowest level. Otherwise schemes will fail to be implemented. This is precisely what happened. As a result, dissent and protest took roots in Bhopal, accompanied by a sense of deprivation and gross injustice.

Grassroots movement took shape in constituencies that were living through the experience of acute deprivation. Women were in the forefront of such movements because they bore the brunt of poverty. The disaster also shaped an environmental movement, for livelihood issues were closely tied up with ecology. Gas victims and victims of contamination belonging to the working class came forward to take on an administration that had virtually collapsed. Bhopal created space for activism that challenged a technocratic and apolitical view of the development process. The activism was shaped by women who were making their own charter of demands for a genuine alternative to a system characterized by stagnation, institutional collapse, and closure. Oral testimonials are used in this and the next chapter to capture the suffering, protest, and the stirrings of political consciousness of those engaged with the democratic process, and the growing awareness among the victims that things cannot go on like this.

Nature of Disasters

It is interesting to note that definitions of disaster often bring together war, nuclear accidents, and industrial disasters under the same category, given the social and political ramifications of these events.[1] Most disasters are viewed as temporal events concentrated in time and space. But we have to be fully cognizant of the various components of a disaster—physical, demographic, epidemiological, social, economic, and political. Only then can we draw inferences from the physical impact, the social disruption, the economic/political, and deep-rooted psychological effects of the event. But definitions can easily overlook the less visible and quantifiable aspects of a disaster. To begin with, the Bhopal disaster entailed a total collapse of the social structure and breakdown of the family unit. In the course of my research, I found many a case study that is typical of the widespread mental agony that followed social disruption. It is interesting to know how sociological analysis is able to evoke the deeply private nature of social displacement, thus linking it to an important aspect of oral history. A dip into archival sources, especially taken from newspapers and journals, comes up with anonymous accounts of individuals, often used to typify the kind of hardships that an industrial disaster entails. My contention is that oral history takes the anonymity factor into consideration, and yet uses narratives that constantly slip into the personal realm of experience.

The analysis of disaster asks for an intimate understanding of trauma and the kind of suffering it involves. Such cases are manifold. A forty-year-old blacksmith who witnessed the death of his two sons tried to commit suicide. He stopped going out for work and waited with his family for the gas to leak again so that they could all die together. Another laborer could not eat, sleep, or stop his hands from trembling. He had not gone to work for months on end. A twenty-year-old man could not stay in closed rooms, felt giddy all the time, and had sudden outbursts of anger that he could not explain. He was not able to concentrate on his studies. A thirty-year-old housewife had stopped cooking, cleaning, and taking care of her children. She would lie in bed the whole daylong (Chauhan 1996, 50–62). The list is endless suggesting a total breakdown of interpersonal relationships. This is how a child describes the experience of economic hardship: "There is very little to eat. Very little to wear. Papa just doesn't get a job. He has no permanent job. Before the leak he used to work on a boring machine. Now he cannot work on that machine." The trauma, as experienced by the provider in the family, is equally disturbing: "Before the gas leak I worked in the textile mill, in the spinning section. I was a permanent worker and worked there for fifteen years. Now I am not doing any work. From the day the gas leaked till today I haven't done any work. I go here and there in search of work, but no work is available" (in *The Bhopal Reader* 2004, 112–113).

It is interesting to observe how suffering was internalized so that the onus for taking personal responsibility shifted from institutions to the individual. Veena Das takes a sharp look at such a phenomenon and refers to the discourse of power that effaces the reality that suffering is often manufactured and distributed by an unjust society (Das 1995, 139). It prevents the powerless from exorcising their grief. Individuals are compelled to blame destiny or god in order to overcome their own burden of responsibility. In real terms, suffering has the potential to dismantle structures of legitimacy, and in the remaining chapter we see how people's testimonies were able to deconstruct bureaucratic jargon and its claims of compensating suffering. The magnitude of the disaster involved the scientific, legal, and administrative structures of modern society. The cost of litigation and the strain on the administrative machinery was staggering. Bhopal was asking for an innovative and radical bureaucracy. Das shows us how in the Agent Orange case, the courts became a site for symbolically reenacting the Vietnam War and its hardships (141). In a similar way, administrative structures that came up in Bhopal became a site for reenacting the crisis that accompanied development. It not only indicted bureaucratic systems that were meant to deal with the crisis, but also showed how these systems denied suffering, by taking away its concrete, physical, lived reality.

Middle-class commitment to development, in the form of dams, nuclear energy, or Special Economic Zones (SEZ) draws its battle line against a propped up enemy. In the case of Bhopal the modern monster was the recalcitrant victim.[2] Vishwanathan and Sethi argue that much of the debate on development focuses on the slum as pathology and excess. At the same time, the slums were part of the city commons that provided many of the essential services needed by the middle class people. So slums were provided with the bare essentials of water, sewer, and electricity connections. The Bhopal disaster was asking for rehabilitation of a section of society that was already entrenched in poverty and with whom the rest of the city had arrived at an uneasy truce. Here again oral history provides the tool for taking up individual stories, like that of Rashida Bi's economic hardships, and presents it as a typical case study of the social reality in Bhopal. Her story begins much before the disaster. Just listening to her testimonial helps us understand the thin line that divides a disaster from the normalcy of lives steeped in poverty. "I was born into a poor family in 1956. My father did business in fruits and he suffered severe loss, which took our family to the brink of destitution. Our family practiced parda. I was not sent to school. From the age of ten, I used to roll beedis along with the other women in the family, and we used to earn Rs 2 for rolling thousand beedis. Many a time there was not enough food for two meals in a day. I was barely twelve when I was married off to a tailor who came from an equally poor family. I had to continue rolling beedis, otherwise my in-laws refused to give me food. Five years later I had a son who died soon after, because we did not have enough money for his treatment. At the time of the disaster I was homebound without any idea that something so monstrous was going to change the direction of my life forever."[3] The monstrous change of direction that Rashida Bi is talking about was actually the irreversible damage that followed from the total collapse of civic administration. The crisis situation was aggravated by preexisting conditions of poverty and deprivation. The administration viewed it as a problem of law and order, while the need of the hour was for governance and participation that sought to alleviate suffering and bring relief. What followed in the name of damage control only added to the chaos. The state apparatus that had earlier failed to rein in corporate power also failed to take charge of the situation. Rehabilitation proved to be another case of systemic failure.

An Alternative Knowledge Base

A technological disaster has to draw on resources provided by scientific experts, legal experts, medical research, and investigative organizations. At the same time, the immediate aftermath of the gas leak called for massive relief work that involved large-scale voluntary effort. The real need was for technology that was relevant to people's needs, so it had to draw upon indigenous knowledge. The only way that the government could get a proper scientific assessment of the situation was to conduct door-to-door surveys to determine the levels of mortality and morbidity. Instead, what was put in place was an objective method of classification that was rigid, draconian and involved mammoth paperwork. A hierarchical administrative structure was set up to endorse the system. In 1985 a Department of Gas Relief and Rehabilitation was created under the charge of the chief minister. An additional chief secretary designated as Relief Commissioner was in charge of the department. The administrative head was the additional collector, and a Relief Committee was constituted as the apex body to coordinate relief and rehabilitation. This committee included local members of parliament, members of the legislative assembly, the mayor of Bhopal, and representatives of all recognized political parties. It is interesting to observe that sector-wise relief committees that had been set up to do the ground level implementation of programmes were asked to propose names of beneficiaries; clearly such a selection process had immense scope for political bias.[4]

People were asked to fill up forms, show their ration cards, submit photographs, and answer questions that established the veracity of their claims. Given the fact that these people were illiterate, had barely got legal sanction to occupy government land, were migrants and hardly possessed any official documents created a great deal of uncertainty and confusion. Soon after the disaster, hospitals were coping with an emergency situation and had failed to keep proper records of mortality and morbidity. Quacks had come up with ways and means to help false claimants. The enormous administrative burden on the state government created an atmosphere of mutual suspicion. It is interesting to observe that much of this burden was seen in financial terms, and when the government had to officially account for what was being done it spoke the language of expenses incurred. This is how the official Web site of the Gas Relief Ministry sums up the situation (updated on 2007): "Rs 4 crores has been earmarked for economic rehabilitation of gas victims. Expenditure up to May 2007 is Rs 27.05 crores."

To understand government's rehabilitation plans, we need to shift our attention to the voluntary groups and the effort they put in to gather testimonials and collect information. The idea was to create an alternative knowledge base. No doubt a lot of voluntary action was fragmented, often working at cross-purpose, and fraught with tension and exhaustion. However, it was crucial to the democratic process of governance and participation. The administration failed to tap such a knowledge base. Instead, it went on a rampage of repressive action by pitching people against systems. The fact that voluntary action included gas affected people from the bastis meant that the survivors were at the receiving end of such repression. It is important to draw upon testimonials that recreate the trauma of having to contend with coercive action. I choose the most vulnerable section of people, the widows and orphans. Once again, individual stories typify the constituency of victims/survivors. This is what Nanni Bai who has crossed sixty and did not receive pension has to say: "The government is not giving either employment or pension. All the compensation money I received from my husband's death is long exhausted, firstly paying off the lawyer and middleman who got me the compensation and then all the medical bills. How long will it last? How are we expected to live?" (*Amnesty International Report* 2004, 20). Parvati Bai echoes her question. She is around seventy years old and too old and weak to work. Her husband who was a construction site worker died a few months after the disaster, and most of her compensation money went into paying the lawyers and middlemen. She gets a meager pension of Rs 150 per month, not enough to make both ends meet. "It is not enough to even buy me some food," she bemoans. "Often I just go around and ask for food. Some day I will die and the municipal corporation will take my body away. That will be the end" (Ibid., 2004, 69). The story of sixty-year-old Kamala Bai is even grimmer. She is gas affected and lives in Annu Nagar, one of the water-contaminated bastis. She lives close to the railway line in a shack made of plastic sheets and gunny bag. She has cervical cancer and gets her radiation therapy from Sultania Hospital. Her son and daughter-in-law have refused to look after her since they are too poor to take care of a sick member of the family. "I am ready to die," says Kamala Bai, "I feel so alone and sick with no money at all."[5] Clearly systems of oppression work in multifarious ways that cannot be officially recorded.

At the other end of the spectrum were children who lost both their parents on the night of the disaster. As mentioned earlier, in 2003 I had spoken to many of them.[6] In their testimonials they had given vent to their deep sense of hurt and anger at being let down by the state government, which had made a lot of political noise about "adopting" the orphans and rehabilitating them. Sunil, who lost seven members of his family, introduced me to the other orphans. He took me to the Housing Board Colony at Karond, and some of the worst affected colonies like J. P. Nagar, Kainchi Chola, Teela Jamal Pura, and the Oriya Basti to meet the orphans. With his canny sense of what stories I needed, he told me how they were given gifts on every anniversary. "We were photographed with politicians and some of us were even taken to America by survivor groups to depose before the court. As gas orphans we were like exhibits, but we have always been the most neglected people." Sadanand was working as an assistant in a tiny tailoring shop, though his eyes were damaged by the gas leak. He got too breathless to do any hard labor. The Housing Board Colony, better known as the Widow's Colony, suggested the levels of neglect. This is what Sadanand had to say: "Government claims that this colony is for the rehabilitation of gas victims, but just look around you. We don't have proper lighting or water supply. Soon after we moved here, we were handed electricity bills for Rs 8,000. Obviously, we didn't have the means to pay. The employees of the state electricity board, accompanied by the police, raided our houses and removed all the fittings. Many carried away whatever meager possessions we had. The roads have not been paved since the colony was built—it is just dust and rubble. They make a feeble attempt to clean up only when a politician decides to visit. I am told the houses have been given to us on a thirty-year lease. What will happen after that? They will remove us and make a housing society for the rich. It is dirty politics that is responsible for our plight. Elections are round the corner. We have decided not to vote. Whom do we elect? They are all the same." Shahid Noor and Firdous became orphans on the same night and somewhere in the course of their bleak journey they fell in love and married. Noor spoke about broken promises and told me that employment was their main concern. He showed me a copy of a 1995 Report brought out by the Gas Relief and Rehabilitation Department, MP government and an album containing photographs taken at every anniversary with the chief minister.

"Successive Chief Ministers have asked us to come and meet them after we have finished with our education. The present CM we have met eight or nine times to remind him of his promises. This report says that the allocated budget for orphans is Rs 5,00,000 out of which Rs 4,25,000 has been spent. On what? None of the twenty-two orphans have got jobs. We were given a meager sum of Rs 2,000 each in 1995. We were promised medical care and treatment. For a while we were taken by a van to Hamidia Hospital as part of the Indian Council for Medical Research (ICMR) monitoring. We were provided medicines, but in my case it was abruptly stopped because I did not have any specific ailment. But we have so many health problems that range from breathlessness, weakness, palpitation, and low immunity. We were promised education, jobs, and protection by the state but none of the promises were kept. We feel truly orphaned."

In testimonial after testimonial we get the growing sense that the accident had driven people to states of penury and dependence on state apparatus for providing essential relief. It had also torn them apart from traditional structures of community life. What comes across are widespread feelings of despair and cynicism. The testimonials raise an important question on why the development model, and more specifically the institutional and structural framework through which it operates, was so consistently anti-poor. Clearly a managerial, technocratic, market-based development model cannot remove inequity, oppression, or poverty. Increasingly the poor became a burden on the exchequer. Once health care got linked to livelihood, the family became the integrated unit. After the gas leak, multiple earners, including women, replaced the sole male bread earner. Women took on the additional task of caring and nurturing children and other dependents, including the sick and those in need of constant tending. Traditionally, women have played a marginal role in the political process. In the rest of the chapter, we see how the need to reconceptualize the political process brought women's issues to the center-stage. A whole new alternative knowledge base was opened up for scrutiny.

The Gender Perspective

The Bhopal disaster catapulted women into the employment scene, largely in the informal sector where workers received no protections for employment, no benefits, and were given nominal wages. Statistics reveal that women across the globe do unregulated, low skill work that nevertheless plays a crucial role in providing livelihood to poor families.[7] There is a close link between informal work, unpaid household labor and the formal economy. One of the major effects of global restructuring has been increase in the quantum of women's unpaid labor. Postdisaster more and more women were engaged in providing care within the family, along with the additional burden of working in a largely conflict-ridden and administratively mismanaged workplace. In this context we take a look at few such workplaces, like the sewing and stationery centers that were set up with the idea of providing jobs exclusively for women. It was a bureaucratic decision based on certain preconceived notions of a women's role in the family and in the community. Therefore, the larger question of women's agency was narrowed down to a set of relationships that were built on preexisting patriarchal and class practices.

Women do service-based jobs that get linked to the larger responsibility of doing jobs that are critical to human survival such as feeding, clothing, and health care.[8] However these jobs are not valued in market terms. The prevailing stereotypes describe women as passive, docile, and submissive. Women are expected to perform duties that are assigned to them. They are also socialized into obedience and tolerance of power. The disaster created a major rupture that threw their lives and traditional value systems out of gear. At one level, the renewed responsibility within the household only added to the growing dependence on levels of authority. At another level, women were asked to take on the role that is traditionally denied to them—that of the sole bread-earner who is at the helm of the family. It is important to remember that any change in role-playing was at the cost of a ruined household—earning male members were dead or grievously ill, daughters could not be married because of social stigma, and many young girls were deserted by their husbands and sent back to their maternal homes. This in turn got reflected in the need for women to join the city's precarious labor force. Predetermined sexual division of labor went hand in hand with unequal power for women within the household, so each reinforced the subordination in one form or the other.

If health is defined as a state of complete physical, mental, and social well-being, then women's health is most vulnerable. The gender perspective becomes vital in any health debate, for equitable and appropriate health care is possible only in the context of economic and social equality. In other words, medical care and economic rehabilitation have to be gender sensitive and must begin from inside the household before it can move to the workplace. Poverty is a major determinant of ill health and the industrial disaster aggravated the harmful effects of both. As part of the rehabilitation schemes, sewing centers were set up to generate employment for gas-affected women, but these schemes were not sensitive to women's needs. In a market-driven economy, most of the schemes were structured in a way that perpetuated existing inequalities. When a system, built on power relation and influence, gets interpolated with a disaster situation, the most vulnerable section of society is rendered even more powerless. This is what happened in Bhopal.

Women are primary users of health services for their families, so in a sense they have firsthand knowledge of how systems work. But such knowledge was not used to improve systems. Neglecting the knowledge base provided by women was equivalent to neglecting people's perspective. To establish the link between health and livelihood and to allow this awareness to percolate down to the ranks was the challenge that women's activism had to face in Bhopal. In the rest of the chapter we explore the gender perspective, to see ways in which entrenched values were dispelled, by breaking down cultural barriers, unquestioning ways of life, and inherited beliefs. The fact that all this came at the cost of enormous suffering is what made Bhopal a tragedy.

Interim Relief

It was with a lot of fanfare that the state government advertised various schemes for providing interim relief, in glossy annual reports. In recent times they have a fully updated Web site. On paper there was nothing wrong with the schemes, but in most cases the proclaimed results were blatantly false. For instance, families of the dead were to receive Rs 10,000 for every member who had died. In 1987 the certified number of dead was 1,762, that went up to 3,000, but only 848 had got the money. This was largely because the processing of data was yet to be completed and government faced the dilemma of having to decide whether interim cash relief should be given before the processing of data was recorded. The ground level reality was grim. In many cases the identification of the dead had not been completed and the heirs could not be traced. The government had also announced an ex gratia payment of Rs 2,000 for the seriously affected and Rs 100 to Rs 1,000 for those with minor injuries. Later a fixed amount of Rs 1,500 was settled for each affected family, rather than payment per person. Though 18,000 families were expected to fall within the prescribed categories, only 400 families had actually received the payment.[9] Clearly there was a wide gap between planning and implementation.

Even a scheme such as free distribution of ration and food-grains, which is a staple relief measure, ran into problems. The immediate cost to the government was more than Rs 10 crores. While most survivors said that the ration was a big help because nobody was in a position to cook their own food, many complained of the quality, erratic supply, and uneven distribution. In a letter dated January 2, 1985, Moti Singh, the then collector wrote to the sector in-charge: "Temporary ration cards were prepared for only one time ration distribution and as per the decision taken in a meeting at the higher levels, these cards were to be retained in the fair price shop with the representative of the Marketing Federation. 12 kg of food grains per unit per month shall be given free in the months of January and February 1985. 23000 ration cards were prepared and distributed. Remaining applications were rejected for want of eligibility. These ineligible applicants keep on roaming about with a view to manage temporary ration cards by hook or by crook."[10] It was clearly a problem of sheer numbers. Misuse is an administrative problem, but the official approach was to blame the people who were acutely in need of help. The survivors were branded as exploiters of the system. Unable to deal with the emergency situation, government went on extending the scheme so that ultimately free ration was distributed for a very long time. The distinction between short-term relief work and long-term economic rehabilitation was kept out of sight. In his book *Unfolding the Betrayal of the Bhopal Gas Tragedy* (2008) that is fairly candid in the way it spells out what went wrong with the rehabilitation schemes, Singh admits that problems were compounded by administrative delays, inadequacy of data, and political pressure. Almost inadvertently he reveals how scientific research was used for routine bureaucratic tasks. The Tata Institute of Social Sciences (TISS) was asked to do a survey of households so as to identify families requiring long-term relief and rehabilitation. We are told that the survey covered 25,300 families in 30 localities. Clearly data was pointing toward the need for a long-term rehabilitation, but TISS left suddenly without even providing the data that had been collected. Interestingly enough, a computer system had been put in place to feed the data. This set the tone for the kind of adhocism that plagued all rehabilitation schemes. Singh writes, "The authorities abruptly suspended cash relief distribution after having made payments totalling Rs 36.37 lakhs. Nothing further was heard about the scheme. The government claimed that over 5,700 gas victims had received financial assistance before the scheme was shelved" (210).

Long-Term Action Plan

A seven-year action plan (1985–1991) was set in motion, which was then extended to 1999. There was a budget of Rs 164.3 crores to be spent on medical, social, and economic rehabilitation, with money coming from the central government. By 1995 the cost had escalated to Rs 258 crores. In its 1995 Annual Report, state government showed that it was spending Rs 24 crores every year, out of which Rs 19 crores was earmarked for medical rehabilitation, Rs 2 crores was for judicial and administrative expenditure, and Rs 1 crore was for economic and environmental rehabilitation. Clearly economic and environmental rehabilitation was low down in the priority. When I put the question of the state government submitting a white paper on expenditure to Mr Bhupal Singh, former Director of the Gas Relief and Rehabilitation Ministry, his reaction was sharp: "For what purpose? It is easy for the center to throw the ball in our court and hold us responsible for everything. Do they think the gas tragedy is the only problem on our hand? Our responsibility is to provide clean drinking water and proper medical facility to the entire state and not just to gas victims. The whole matter is highly politicized. Can you imagine what kind of pressure we work under?"[11] It was not merely a problem of keeping proper accounts; it was a more invidious power game played out between the state and the center.

Statistics belie the situation at the ground level. Bureaucratic planning refused to see the link between medical care and livelihood. Most women testify to the fact that escalating expenditure on medical treatment pushed families into debt, making them sink rapidly below the poverty line. Poverty, destitution, and acute morbidity became a vicious circle. Meanwhile, public money was being spent on ill conceived, flawed rehabilitation plans that were conceptually long term, but in a realistic sense were not meant to last very long. Once again the gender perspective links the problem to systemic failure. The livelihood schemes were meant to operate in a protected market, catering to the women's workforce. The basic assumption was that the workforce was illiterate and unskilled, without any technical qualifications, and the majority of survivors were already working in the unorganized sector. Women were the ideal choice because semi-skilled jobs such as sewing, cutting, packing, and manual assembly were labor intensive and suited the nonprofit market. Most women I spoke to said that it was easy for them to find employment in the sewing centers for they were familiar with the work and could balance the training with housework. Why was it that a readymade plan failed to generate employment, despite the fact that as many as 152 work-sheds were built in a special industrial zone?

A glance at successive government reports, brought out annually, will familiarize us with the language of public administration: "The economic rehabilitation plan proposes to rehabilitate people in both industries as well as services sector. The foremost need it to train people so that they can acquire new skills and get employment in works not involving hard physical labour. Training facilities, therefore, have to be provided immediately after which they could be helped to set up their own business. There will, however, always be people who may not be able to compete in the open market and such people will be provided employment directly through small public sector units or units run by services organizations." The work sheds were completed in 1991, and work began in twenty sheds. Fifty-five sheds were given to private enterprises. Women were the main recruits as they were seen as more stable and responsible than men. However, no attempt was made to do proper assessment of the situation, keeping in mind the ground reality of a postdisaster situation. In the nineties, new economic policies and greater corporatization threatened employment opportunities for women (Avasti and Srivastava, 2001). Technical innovations meant that men were taking over women's jobs.[12] Such trends had a trickle-down affect on the job scenario for gas survivors. Soon the sewing centers became unviable with a diminishing market, low demand, and general apathy. The government lost its political will to continue with rehabilitation schemes that were not part of the economic calculus of the prevailing market.

The original plan was to provide training for 583 women per year and according to government records 4,080 women were given training. In 1992 a sewing center that employed 2,300 women was closed down without disclosing any official reason. Today, only one center, which produces stationery, is still running with approximately ninety women on its role. There was propaganda of "developing Bhopal as an export center." At the same time, the government's popular manifesto was to uplift "the weaker sections of society." Caught in its own contradiction, the government failed to bring development to Bhopal or work toward justice for the survivors.

Quite obviously things went wrong at the conceptual level. New technologies bring with them a range of problems, which nonunionized women workers are ill equipped to deal with. Paradoxically, industrial growth is often accompanied by growing structural unemployment, and women are usually at the receiving end of such change. In Bhopal the rehabilitation schemes also suffered from bureaucratic short sightedness. Improvement in people's health is contingent upon improvement in the overall quality of life. On the one hand, long lines in hospitals, machines out of order, and inability of doctors to cope with the Out Patient Department rush became endemic. As a result morbidity affected work output and reduced job options. On the other hand, a six-month training programme was not followed up with job opportunities, so women were left with no means to utilize their skills. The need was for cooperative enterprise, which was gender sensitive. Instead, women continued to do petty labor, at piece rate, for which they were paid nominal wages.

Given the rising morbidity and social disruption, there was a pressing need among women to earn extra income to support the family. It made their position very vulnerable. Finally, rehabilitation programmes that were meant to work toward women's upliftment became exploitative. Here is a case in point. A scheme for self-employment of single women was made available with loan facilities. The government put in motion an existing programme under Special Training and Employment Programme for the Urban Poor in MP. The only change was increase in the quantum of loan and relaxation of eligibility conditions. But here again, schemes were floated without considering the volatility of the situation. Elaborate paper work was necessary to get loans, creating a need for brokers and middlemen who exploited the needy women. The sheer number of claimants was not anticipated. Women testify to the uncooperative behavior of bank officials, ranging from officious, unsympathetic, arrogant to down right abusive. Only a few remember encountering someone nice and helpful.

The rehabilitation schemes were brought in to serve a larger political agenda; it explains why they failed to benefit people who needed them most. The schemes had to be economically viable, so government had to ensure proper marketing outlets. But markets were drying up, and women who had taken loans to buy sewing machines found themselves without work and with payments coming in very slowly. Initially the idea was to link up with the private sector and big export houses. But most negotiations fell through for the terms and conditions set by industrial houses were too steep. Clearly the benefits of economic programmes were meant to serve the entire city, so that schools, hospitals, and community centers were built under the general plan for slum improvement. It included better roads, low cost sanitation, street lighting, construction of drains and sites for more housing. It is interesting to observe that government reports refer to normal urban development activities as gas rehabilitation work. A look at the Web site of the Department of Relief and Rehabilitation (as updated in 2007) shows how under the heading of "environmental rehabilitation," money to the tune of Rs 20.55 crores was being diverted for "development of green belts, children's park, constructing roads, pavements, and lighting of streets." Under the banner of general improvement of urban infrastructure, specific gas-related problems were ignored. Even "social rehabilitation" that was categorized as schemes meant for the special needs of women could only boast of one short-term plan: "free milk was supplied to expectant mothers and children up to the age of six through five ICDS projects running 792 anganwadis. On an average 71,280 beneficiaries were provided free milk on a daily basis." Women's testimonials show how ill-conceived and mismanaged such schemes turned out to be. Collectively women speak about harassment, corruption, and indifference to their real needs. They also reiterate their experience of sheer humiliation, of feelings of sadness, frustration, and anger. Many say they have lost hope that things will ever improve.

Unfortunately, when the work-sheds started closing down one by one it was not because they had become unprofitable. A more insidious kind of logic had begun to replace the notion of providing employment and empowering women. The Web site also talks about the setting up of an Industrial Training Institute, in a self-sufficient modern building that was specially constructed for providing training for the unemployed gas victims. By late nineties the focus had already shifted to a male-dominated, market friendly scenario. But the trend was there right from the beginning; the game plan was to cash in on such need-based strategies that began as welfare schemes but were soon handed over to powerful nongovernmental organizations. The idea was to open up market tie-ups and direct selling outlets so that private organizations could step in to provide funding and basic infrastructure. Voluntary organizations such as the Mahashakti Seva Kendra were set up with a revolving fund and big buy order from the Madhya Pradesh Textile Corporation, with the state government providing them with three sheds spread over 1,000 sq feet. Tanwant Singh Kheer, the then state minister in charge of gas relief, went on record to say, "it was high time we put the tragedy behind us and collectively utilize our energy for constructive purposes instead of waiting for doles" (*The Times of India*, February 14, 1997). Economic rehabilitation schemes were being used as means to lull resistance, so that increasingly people began to utilize government schemes for their own benefit rather than oppose them.

Inside the Work-sheds

In this section we shift attention to individual testimonials that takes us inside the work-sheds and gives us a firsthand account of the dynamics of a workplace. In 2007 I met a group of women who had worked in the J. P. Nagar and Bharat Talkies sewing centers. They had gone through the entire gamut of recruitment in the rehabilitation scheme followed by retrenchment. Most of them are now in the autumn of their lives, too tired to look back with nostalgia; those who are part of grassroots movements are more vocal in registering protest; what they all share is their experience of suffering, which shaped their collective identity as victims of systemic failure. One of the things I realized is that the resistance movement in Bhopal draws its strength from local concerns, which has to do with the everydayness of disaster. And this is where oral history plays such an important part in reconstructing an industrial disaster. Someone like Sabra Bi who has not been going for protest marches for many years, because she had to take care of a husband who remained ill for more than two decades and died only recently, was still part of the process of framing a charter of demands because of her experience of suffering, which she shares with other women. "I share the joys and pains of success and failure. I bless everyone who is fighting on our behalf. I am too tired to fight, but I believe in the cause," she tells me.

The levels of political consciousness displayed by these women as they talk about their own collective strength never cease to surprise me. What they share is a growing awareness that they play a crucial role in giving shape to the mediating structures, which carry the voice of the people to the government. Importantly, their moving out of the confines of home into the workplace marks the shift in their role as providers in the family to grassroots workers in the community. The household and the community get indelibly linked in their struggle for justice. It is accompanied by a growing realization that Bhopal disaster is not a one-time event that can be taken care of by short-term relief measures. They also understand that long-term rehabilitation involves a long and arduous struggle for their democratic rights. "Can we expect the government to go on being interested in our plight?" Sabra Bi asks, "Even a mother turns her head away from a child who is crying all the time! But can a child who is in pain stop crying?"

Sabra Bi remembers the time when she first heard about the opening of the sewing centers. "It was largely by word of mouth that I got to know about the sewing center at Bharat Talkies. I remember the centers opened after much agitation. It was only when the political climate became very hot with more and more demands were being made to give us work that the state government began implementing the rehabilitation schemes." Tasleem registered herself at the J. P. Nagar sewing center soon after it was opened, "Some officials came door to door and helped us fill up the forms. I was illiterate so they wrote down what I dictated. I had no experience of doing stitching work, but they said it was all right. The center would give me training. We had a lot of hope." Hazra Bi's experience was different, "When I got to know about the sewing centers I started going there regularly, but they had already filled up the batch of 150 women. The supervisor used to chase me away. I was determined to keep on trying. I had asked for a loan and got Rs 6,000. One day when I walked into the center I saw two of the machines were lying idle. I knew they were lying about no vacancy. I decided to get in touch with the collectorate office. I gave in a slip with all my details. I was told I could not get a job and a loan at the same time. I told the collector you give me permission and I will give you proof of how many men have managed to get a loan while their womenfolk are employed at the center. He said he liked my frankness and recommended me for the job. It was the first time I realized that a sense of outrage can bring its own rewards."

Most of the women look back with pride at their first earnings and the fact that it was hard earned. Bano Bi was a housewife before the gas leak: "My husband was the only earning member and worked in the railway godown. My children used to study in the Railway Bal Mandir, a good school in those days. Everything finished for them on that night. They did resume studying after a while but they gave up, because they had to start earning. When one of my sons failed in class eight we stopped sending them to school. I knew stitching so I was admitted in the first batch at the J. P. Nagar sewing center. I got my certificate after three months. I also got a loan of Rs 12,000. I bought a machine for knitting wool. I made cardigans and shawls and sold them. But one of my sons fell so ill I had to mortgage the sewing machine to buy his medicines. The moneylender gave it away as dowry for his daughter. Later she died and he was repentant and wanted to return my machine. But I never took it back. How can you take advantage of someone else's misery? The work at the sewing center brought steady income. I had much more skills than what they asked for. We were to stitch a set of frocks and knickers. We made Rs 300 per month. The money was given every month. It paid for all the credit we had to take. Sometimes when a woman became too ill to finish her lot of stitching, I helped her out, and we divided the money. We helped each other a great deal." After training they were asked to take their work home. Jubeida Bi fills in the details, "We came on particular days of the week and took our orders home. In one week we were given four bundles and we were paid according to our workload. We had to return the order on time. The supervisor would check the work and scold us if the stitching was not good. This arrangement suited me better because it was easier to work from home. I used to do all the housework through the day and stitch at night. It was difficult, for my eyes had gone weak, and they used to water a lot. But the money was helpful."

Tasleem talks about the comradely feeling the women shared. "We missed coming to the center after the training. It gave us a sense of purpose. Then a society was formed by a group of co-workers who had more leadership qualities. I joined the society. I had to pay Rs 150 as registration money. Shehnaz Madam was heading the society. When the center closed down so did the society and I never got back the money. We trusted our leaders and never questioned them. Most of the time, we were too tired and pressurized to challenge them. We were told that the society would continue giving us orders even after the center closed down. It was based on this promise that we joined. Today when I look back I realize we were cheated because we were illiterate and gullible." Tehzeeb did not join the society started by Shehnaz Parveen. "The society started operating in a shed behind ours. They were collecting money, and I was told the leaders were pocketing all the money. Women who were part of the society used to work on the cloth-cutting machine. There was extra payment for these odd jobs. These women were hand in gloves with the supervisors. After the center closed down all the machines vanished." Tasleem admits that it was tempting to make extra money. "My family had got into heavy debt. My mother-in-law who used to live with us was too ill to do even house work, so there were extra mouths to feed. My husband remains ill even today. I was constantly taking my children and husband to hospital. At one point the burden became so much I gave my younger son to my sister-in-law. She brought him up. What to do? For a major part of my life I have been both bread-earner and homemaker. My earnings at the sewing center helped to pay back all the debt. I am grateful to god for that."

Sheila Thakur explains her own role in forming the society, "I think the society was called Pragati Selai Udyog. My memory has become dim; there are so many things I cannot remember. The supervisors at the center advised us to open such societies for rumors were afloat that the centers would soon close down. After all, what profit was there in making frocks for school children? The orders started coming down and women had to return empty handed. It was during lunchtime that we started discussing the possibility of becoming more self-reliant. The supervisors gave us direction and the center started providing us with the cloth for cutting, which was then distributed for stitching. Some people got us orders for stitching railway uniforms, sacks for carrying fertilizers and hosiery work. The center gave us loans and we started sending our products to state government outlets. We were doing good work and it helped a number of women. I think Shehnaz Parveen became greedy, and the whole society got a bad name. I was given a salary of Rs 750 and though I was filled with doubt I could not speak. Later there was a police raid and a truck full of goods was caught near the bus stand. Shehnaz was arrested and she died two years later because she was not able to face the disgrace. I think she was not a bad woman. She was just misled by the suppliers."

Noor Bi feels that such societies were dangerous and led to the centers being closed down. "We were asked to follow the instructions of those in power. Some of the women acquired supervisory power and they were the ones that hired and fired. After the center closed down the government decided to give it out to private people. A jute center was opened at the J. P. Nagar sewing center, but none of us were employed. Women were brought in from elsewhere and we were left high and dry. My sewing machine, which I bought on credit from relatives and repaid in small installments, became useless. Whatever little skill I had learnt was totally wasted. Later I sold my machine for a few measly rupees." Tehzeeb says they had some inkling that the center would close down "because the orders started diminishing. We were just told there is no supply and it would come next week. Soon the weeks went by, and one day we were paid our last dues and told that we need not come to the shed to pick up our orders. It was a big blow. Besides, nobody told us what had happened. Hazra Appa tried to mobilize the women to come for demonstrations, but nothing came out of it. I do not remember anybody really taking up our cause."

Hazra Bi is more vociferous when she recalls how bitterly she felt let down. "Women lost out in everyway. Take my case. After the disaster the family harmony was broken forever. We had to live with our separate nightmares. How can I ever forget the evil moment when I rushed out of the house and in the melee I left my middle son behind? When I realized what had happened one and a half hours had already gone by. I rushed back like a mad woman but the police had already cordoned off the area. We were taken to the factory where a few doctors were rushing around giving medicines. Suddenly I found my son lying on a cart, unconscious, foaming in the mouth. He survived but he has never been the same again. I was so preoccupied with this son that I could hardly take care of the others. My husband left me because he could not cope. He lost his self-esteem for he could not earn properly. When I got the loan money he felt this was ready money at hand. He took it away and left me. Since then I have been a single parent, and when the job was snatched away I felt a lot of bitterness and despair. There has been total destruction from all sides. The loss of job only added to it. We were not given a reason for the closure of the center; it is a denial of our basic right to know why the system keeps punishing us. I think I know why they asked us to take work back home. They did not want to give us any job security that comes with belonging to a workplace. First they told us it was only training, no jobs. Then they turned a few sheds into production centers. Those employed with the stationery center had a workplace. We had nothing. Our work was stalled on the false pretext of no supply. The work-sheds became dysfunctional but the machines remained for at least two months while the stock was being cleared. Then overnight the machines were removed. Big locks were put on the sheds. For us it sealed our fate. The year was 1993 and since then we have not been given any other jobs."

Listening to Hazra Bi brings up the pertinent question of whether the issue of economic rehabilitation made Bhopal a localized event, which concerned a section of society with more entrenched interests. Given the nature of the disaster, specific institutions like hospitals/medical care, judicial system/legal redressal, and media/modes of representation came under the scanner. In the next chapter

I turn to the stationery center, the only surviving work-shed, where the first all-women-worker's union was established. The workplace became the site for activism. I also take a close look at some of the major survivor organizations that came up. Bhopal ceased to be a local issue and called for international attention. More and more people had to step in to take charge of the situation. A need was felt for professionals, intellectuals, and people with progressive mindsets rather than just technocrats. There was urgency to create a think-tank that transcended ideological dogma and populist clichés. A knowledge bank had to be created, a documentation base that was not unrelated to political process. Intellectuals had to rub shoulders with activists and the ranks of mass movements. The immediate task was to overcome the deep insensitivity of the middle class and a closed-door bureaucracy. Bhopal provided a constituency of activists—an eclectic, mixed, dynamic group—drawn from different parts of the country, and bringing with them the forces of change that was innovative and transformative. Women like Hazra Bi, Bano Bi, and Sheila Thakur were part of the process of transformation, and their empowerment began from inside the work-shed.

Voluntarism and Empowerment

Through the nineties a mixed sort of voluntarism started taking shape in Bhopal. A lot of it was done in coordination with the government and with the help of development-oriented voluntary agencies. Such agencies kept away from politics and hardly played a mobilizational or confrontational role. But another kind of voluntarism acquired a political stance that took up cudgels with the authority. It challenged assumptions on development and implicit faith in markets. Mobilization of people had to go hand in hand with their empowerment. It was this kind of struggle-oriented voluntarism that enabled people's activism in Bhopal to walk the fine line between local and global. It is interesting to observe that women had a big role to play in providing the insight into the situation at the ground level. Their narratives act as impetus to oral history and the way it can present reality from below. Voluntary groups like the Bhopal Group of Information and Action (BGIA) were actively bringing out newsletters, which were distributed at the community level, and provided the all-important feedback on how rehabilitation schemes were working. Here is one such newsletter that came out in April/May 1987, Issue no. 10 & 11. This is how it describes the situation. Its irreverent tone sets the mood for people's participation in challenging bureaucratic systems: "For this issue of our newsletter we wanted to prepare a report on the rehabilitation programmes being conducted by the government. On April 4th 1987 we submitted a list of queries concerning rehabilitation programmes to Parvesh Sharma, the additional collector in charge of rehabilitation. Ten visits and more than a month later we were told that he could not give us any information because he did not have clearance 'from the top.' So we got information from the 'bottom' and present it in this issue." A photograph of an abandoned work-shed in Dwarkanagar is accompanied by a news item, which says, "Three work-sheds in different stages of completion are situated near Hamidia road. These large buildings (floor space 150 sq meters) on which an enormous amount of construction material has been spent are now being used as garbage dumps."

We have already seen how policies for economic restructuring reproduced the same inequalities that women suffered under existing patriarchal assumptions. In the context of the disaster the restructuring became part of damage control. When women entered their new domain, their skills, abilities, and wages were calculated by pregiven market rates. Could women challenge systems through scattered resistance, confined to a narrow workplace? The next chapter will show how women got together to retrieve their sense of a place, which made them come together to share their joys and sorrows. In exploring the connection between voluntarism and empowerment, we understand how women's issues became a powerful tool for activism to mobilize support at the grassroots level. Women were forthcoming in joining the people's movement and they were more than ready to bring their experience of hardship out in the open. Women's issues brought into focus the need to develop concrete economic alternatives based on notions of social equality and participatory processes. It opened up a debate on economic subsistence and its link with environmental issues and the focus on the body burden of chemicals and its devastating effect on the new generation. The woman's body became the site of contestation that drew attention to issues of marginalization and the need to integrate excluded voices and local matters. The women of Bhopal were able to draw attention to the marginal space they occupied and how physically distant it was from the core of the nation.

CHAPTER 5

"We Are Flames Not Flowers": The Inception of Activism

> We are women of Bhopal we are flames not flowers
> We will not wilt before your corporate power
> With our brooms in hand we're gonna sweep you away
> Cause we'll fight for justice till our dyin' day.
>
> —Terry Allan (Copyright, 2003).

> Survivors organizations and their supporters have achieved much...most government relief and rehabilitation measures have been made possible by their legal and extralegal interventions. Credit is also due to them for introducing, in a city without any history of militancy, a culture of popular protest outside the political parties in Bhopal. It is mostly because of the persistence and grit of the survivors organization that the continuing disaster in Bhopal continues to receive attention.
>
> —Satinath Sarangi, interview in *Closer to Reality* (2004).

In a newsletter aptly titled *Bhopal We Will Never Forget*, Issue 6 & 7 (Nov/Dec 1986), brought out by Bhopal Group of Information and Action (BGIA) to commemorate the second anniversary of the disaster, the reporting on the ground level situation is frighteningly candid. "The government's relief and rehabilitation remain so many castles in the air. Fully two years after the event government has become, if possible, even more fanatical about secrecy than it ever was. We wanted to review all aspects of the disaster in this issue. The question was how? With unmitigated hostility and suspicion towards BGIA, collecting information continues to be hazardous. We wrote letters to all the chief officials in charge of gas relief with a detailed list of questions on government action and planning. Not one responded." It was in the face of repression, apathy, and willful distortion of facts that activism began to shape an alternative perspective that could fearlessly challenge entrenched attitudes and points of view. As the newsletter goes on to claim, an eloquent voice was rearing its head: "We decided, therefore, to let the gas victims to speak for themselves. This would be the best way of conveying the nature of their suffering, the most revealing and comprehensive means of understanding their condition. Physical suffering is unabated. Perhaps most devastating is their anguish at their helplessness. Their chief source of pride, their work, and their ability to provide for themselves has been taken away from them. But their voices are eloquent as ever. Any hope for proper and long-term relief and compensations seems possible only as a result of such eloquent struggle." The fervent appeal of the newsletter is to the common future that links everybody to the struggle: "But how long can a deprived and debilitated community struggle? Gradually, hope is likely to give way to despair. When that happens, industry, government and the general public shall write 'finished' to Bhopal and march on relentlessly till another one is let loose. We must not let that happen." The rest of the newsletter scrupulously records the voices that shape the struggle for justice. Oral history provides the tool for documenting this struggle as it went through its different phases. As systems became global, the fight for justice also drew its strength from international support. In this chapter we trace the movement as it went through its tactical journey from local to global.

To begin with activism in Bhopal was linked to workplace that grew out of the perilous circumstances of a postdisaster situation. We have already seen how the government came up with livelihood schemes that catered to available models for development. The schemes were framed with women in mind and their role within the traditional family system. Since the household was seen as an undifferentiated unit with the man as the natural head and therefore prime beneficiary of rehabilitation, any sort of developmental intervention was not meant to address issues of inequitable distribution and the need for rights and empowerment. The idea was to delink livelihood from any kind of activism. Community development planners have always felt comfortable with programmes that reinforce the traditional social order (Ramaswamy 2000, 2–15). In 1974 a commission was set up to study the status of women. Two reports were brought out in 1988 from its findings, *Shramshakti* and *National Perspective Plan for Women*. It is interesting to see how certain employment categories were reinforced for women; as "marginal" workers they worked for less than 183 days per year, and women's work was largely "invisible" despite their vital contribution to economic activities. But the 1991 census showed that women were the prime movers in the informal sector. According to Ramaswamy, women took the lead in all kinds of self-employment schemes that ranged from street vending to home-based productions. As a result, development initiatives could no longer ignore women's contribution and their concerns. It was also in the eighties that there was an "exponential growth of grassroots women's collectives—mahila samitis (women's society), self-help groups, savings and credit groups, women's co-operatives...and federal bodies of grassroots initiatives" (4). It was this contradictory pull between traditional roles and growing awareness of the potential for realignment of power equations that emerges clearly in the case of Bhopal.

In Bhopal, the economic rehabilitation schemes were meant to tap women's skill, knowledge, and capacity to work with available resources in a poor household, without disturbing the status quo of women's social identity. However, the violent social disruption that followed the gas leak added to the volatility of the situation. It became necessary to link livelihood to questions of altering the power structure of the society. Grassroots pressure groups were formed with a large baseline of women who were in the forefront of any protest action. More and more women felt the need to come out in the public forum and register their protest against rehabilitation schemes that failed to help the gas survivors. They also felt the need to create space for women's issues. Paradoxically, in Bhopal this space was created at the time when the workplace was snatched away from women, with the closure of their work-sheds. Therefore, women's issues had to be raised without integrating them in larger organizational perspectives. In this connection, I show how two major survivor groups came up in Bhopal. Both started from within the context of the workplace but had a much wider reach. A section of women belonging to the various sewing centers created a survivor's organization, Bhopal Gas Peedit Mahila Udyog Sangathan (BGPMUS) that went on to play a major role in the grassroots movement in Bhopal. Meanwhile the stationery center saw the creation of the only all-women gas-affected worker's union in Bhopal, the Bhopal Gas Peedit Mahila Stationery Karamchari Sangh (BGPMSKS). The workplace was used as a platform for raising issues that merged with the wider struggle for justice. Importantly, issues of local interest became relevant at a macro level, and a women-led movement began to acquire a wider reach. Not surprisingly, both BGPMUS and BGPMSKS are the two earliest survivor groups that continue to be active even today.

Women's activism in the context of the Bhopal disaster can best be described as the transformation that accompanies the centripetal move from home to workplace to the streets, in search of collective strength, leadership potential, sharing of experiences, democratic process of decision making, and sustaining of the collective. It was not an easy journey and there are ample instances of both success and failure, as seen in the backdrop of changing affiliations in a conflict-ridden field. The focus in this chapter is on grassroots initiatives of women that worked toward political empowerment by linking livelihood to health care and the need to be educated on rights. Traditionally, women are seen as raising "women's issues" that separates them from mainstream developmental concerns. Bhopal has subverted this attempt to segregate women and men by showing how women take on major battles that concern society at large. By linking livelihood and health care in the context of an industrial disaster, Bhopal women draw attention to the larger battle against corporate crime in the age of globalization. What makes the clash so intriguing is the uneven turf that pitches survivors against monolithic power structures and the need for a gendered understanding of the conflict. As mentioned earlier, women are more than willing to share their experience of oppression and feeling of subordination. This I believe is the underlying strength of oral history and its use in studying man-made, industrial disasters. At the same time, what I trace in the rest of the chapter is their personal journey as they transcend the self to become part of an organization, and a social movement that goes beyond individual experience to address wider socioeconomic and political issues.

Community Activism and Daily Hardships

I provide more voices, drawn from archival sources, to show how community activism grew from hardships faced daily.[1] It is interesting to observe how a new category of "unemployed workers" becomes predominant. As each one of them talks about their experience "before" and "after" the disaster, it becomes a crucial yardstick to redefine interpersonal relationships within family and the larger community. This in turn becomes part of the identity formation as gas victims. Naraini Bai: "I used to work as a laborer. Now I can't do that. After the gas leak I have worked for only eight or ten days. I get breathless, I feel dizzy, my head aches. When I rest, I feel slightly better. When I get back to work I feel sick again." Gomti Bai: "I used to make a thousand bidis a day. Now I don't make even 500 and my head starts to reel. My legs ache when I sit for long. I feel giddy. The tobacco makes me cough a lot. I did not cough before. I feel breathless." Gyana Bai: "I can't make baskets properly now. I work on one bamboo for two days and make baskets on the third day. Before I could strip the bamboo in a day and make four baskets. When I sit in the sun to strip bamboo, my head reels and darkness comes before my eyes. I go in and lie down and my eyes burn." The voices of men and women merge, but clearly for men the repercussion of what they could do earlier and failed to do now had serious physical and psychological implications. The sample of textile workers, railway porters, and those doing menial service jobs can give a clear picture of the grimness of the situation. Gopilal: "Since the gas leak the textile workers have lost the capacity to do work. Even with little work we get breathless. In the spinning and carding section there is a lot of cotton dust. The number of deaths occurring among textile workers has gone up. In our union when a worker dies other workers pay Rs 1 from their salaries toward a death fund. Sometimes we pay Rs 4 in a month. Many workers left the mill since the management is bent upon intensification of work. If the workers refuse to do such jobs they are suspended. Who does not want to work and earn money?" Mustaq Ali: "At the time of the gas leak I was on duty at the railway station. I got back to work eight days after that. I cannot lift the amount I used to. Every month I am sick for fifteen days. Before the gas leak I used to run from one carriage to another. Now I am breathless, because of this my earnings have suffered badly." Santosh Singh: "I used to work as a waiter in the Union Carbide canteen. I used to get Rs 500 per month. Ever since the gas leak I have not been able to get any employment. I have got myself registered at the employment exchange but I have not received any offer till now."

As mentioned earlier, activists gathered such testimonials under hostile conditions. The idea was to use the indigenous database for spreading awareness and nurturing feelings of solidarity. It explains why many of the voices express anger, resentment, bitterness, and the strong will for survival. But there is also a strident demand to fight systems. It is not surprising that the majority of voices belong to women. Both Barkat Bee and Dulari talk about their strong desire to break down the entire factory with their bare hands. But what Sumati Bai is saying is more interesting. "I participated in a number of protest marches. We had gone on a procession to Kamala Park and there the police beat us all up badly. They hit me on my hand, and till today, a year later, I can feel the pain. We felt we ought to punish Carbide by ourselves, that is why I participated in the procession." Laxmi Bai joins other voices to say, "I feel Carbide is responsible for what has happened. Both Carbide and the government must be punished. The government is colluding with Carbide. I have not voted after the gas leak. Before I used to vote for Congress. Now each and every party must be beaten with shoes." Many of the women I have spoken to look back with satisfaction to the period of time when they were motivated and inspired to join grassroots organizations. They all admit that being part of groups gave them a sense of direction and helped them overcome feelings of hopelessness and despair.

Women's activism was issue oriented and need based, and therefore a lot of it was pragmatic and anchored in interpersonal relationships that tied the home to the workplace. The women I met take on their multiple roles with great ease, so identity formation can be fluid, diverse, and fragmented. Traditionally, men have thrived in electoral politics and have enjoyed greater opportunities in formal, institutional space. Women survivors discovered that at the local level there was ample scope for taking up initiatives on micro issues. We will see how such dynamics worked out within the Stationery Union and Mahila Udyog Sangathan (MUS). The women survivors of Bhopal were able to participate in the formation of a civil society that had a rich and complex associational life that was continually created and recreated through experiences of daily life. Before focusing on the two women-centric groups, it is useful to draw attention to the social, political, and cultural dimensions of a protest movement that came into place the morning after the disaster.

Protest and the Battle for Survival

The history of agitation in Bhopal began on the morning of December 3, 1984, when more than 1,000 people from the nearby bastis marched toward the factory, ready to set it on fire. At that time nobody knew which gas had leaked or who was to be held responsible for the ghastly event. In the days that followed it was this kind of spontaneous protests, mostly leaderless that made people agitate in front of government offices, hospitals, and relief camps. A lot of wrath was directed against American bosses of the company, so that "Hang Anderson" became a common slogan. But the main demand was for help to keep people alive, to count the number of dead, and to give the survivors a sense of direction on what to do next. Agitations were mostly directed against the total administrative collapse. At the same time, communities were coming together to protest, and leadership was beginning to take shape at the grassroots level. A small number of people played a role in taking collective decisions, and on December 16, 1984, hundreds of people marched to the governor's residence. And this happened despite the rampant fear and chaos that prevailed all around. Within a week of the disaster, groups with leftist leanings founded two organizations that played a major role in shaping the initial phase of activism in Bhopal. The groups Nagarik Rahat and Purnavas Committee (NRPC) (Citizen's Relief and Rehabilitation Committee) and Zahreeli Gas Kand Sangharsh Morcha (Poisonous Gas Disaster Forum for Struggle) clearly indicated the dual task of "sangharsh" (struggle) and "purnavas" (rehabilitation). Unfortunately both the groups got dismantled in no time and as we shall see, many more affiliations and breakaways groups were formed with different kinds of ideological orientations and work agenda.

One thing was clear, Bhopal had brought in people from outside, from different walks of life, with degrees of commitment and varying ideological and political affiliations, and they were asked to work in close coordination with an affected community for whom protest and the battle for survival was part of the basic struggle for existence. It is important to note that nothing in Bhopal happened without a struggle. Oral history had to take up the all-important task of foregrounding this struggle by drawing attention to middle-class involvement and its close association with the survivors. It had to walk the fine balance between an anti-technoscientific approach, a narrow human-interest angle, and the use of discursive apparatus for spreading the message of "no more Bhopals" in the twenty-first century, with its middle-class bias. Did oral history succeed in bringing to the forefront a far more subversive use of history from below? This could happen by drawing attention to rehabilitation and compensation as politically loaded terms, requiring organizational skills and agitational methods that helped to bring out in the open, the issues of immediate relief, health care, livelihood, human rights, women's rights, corporate accountability, and the environmental rights of the poor. The idea was to focus on the "pressures" of activism thereby reconstructing its history from the people's perspective.

I spoke to both Satinath Sarangi and Anil Sadgopal about their involvement with Morcha and their experience of being part of the initial phase of activism.[2] Sarangi was a founder member of BGIA that came up in 1986, and it was characterized by working from outside. "A great deal was wrong with the Morcha. Part of it was ego battles and the need to justify ideological positions. But I think the main problem was difference of opinion on how organizations should be structured. My solution to that was middle-class people have to go. Middle-class people have a privileged position in terms of their education, contacts, and skills. Once they are in leadership positions their power becomes unbridled and unchallenged. That is why I felt middle-class people should give support from outside without having a formal leadership position. Second, democratic organizations cannot come through rhetoric; it has to come through practice. I agree there was the dilemma of secrecy and effectiveness; if you want something to be decided fast, then the decision has to be taken quickly by a few people at the top rather than all the people. Today I believe that even if we have to wait longer it is worth taking a collective decision through democratic participation." Sarangi minces no words when he says he was thrown out of Morcha because he had differences with how the main functionaries operated. "In BGIA we were never more than four or five people. We decided we will work from outside people's organization, and help in different ways, keeping our background in mind, and that we will not present ourselves as representatives of the victims. As long as there is power it will continue to corrupt the minute we exercise that power. The only way to avoid it is not to have a system that is a clone of the dominant system. It is always easy for one top down organizational structure to deal with another top down organizational structure. BGIA played the role of getting information, generating studies and spreading information that will help people decide on what they should do."

I met Sadgopal, a founder member of Morcha, in 2003 at the Gandhi Peace Foundation in New Delhi. He told me he had long disassociated himself from Bhopal but the memories were still vivid. "The Morcha emerged within a few days of the gas disaster as almost the first organized response by the local citizens. Only three of us—Satinath Sarangi, Sadhana Karnik, and I—came from the Kishore Bharati group located in the neighboring Hoshangabad District. This, however, did not affect the local image of the Morcha since we belonged to Madhya Pradesh and had a history of social action in Bhopal. However, the Morcha members had come together from heterogeneous backgrounds and did not share a common ideology, not even a common perspective. A broad Marxist orientation of several of us was not adequately concretized to be translated into a meaningful political strategy. The seeds for Morcha's disparate ways of functioning and the later fragmentation were present from its inception itself." Sadgopal is able to analyze the situation in hindsight. "The Morcha debated how to interweave the immediate need for medical relief and rehabilitation into a long-term political battle. We exposed the scientific disinformation spread by both the Union Carbide and the Indian scientific agencies, acting almost in tandem with each other. This was reflected in our demands presented to the chief minister after almost 10,000 gas victims had *gheraoed* (lay a siege) his residence for almost a week in January 1985. The issue was the continued danger posed by the stored poisonous chemicals in the Union Carbide factory. The chief minister promised to get this matter investigated by a senior scientific team of the central government. We instead demanded that the Morcha be allowed to send its own scientific team inside the factory to conduct investigations since we don't trust the government scientists. When the chief minister refused to accept this demand, the negotiations broke down. Interestingly, the breakdown was not on the issue of relief and rehabilitation but on the credibility of the government in revealing scientific facts regarding the safety of the people. In continuation of the siege, the Morcha organized a demonstration at the gates of Union Carbide's R&D set up. Here, the Morcha demanded that the central government should withdraw the income tax exemption given to Union Carbide for R&D work since it was engaged in developing chemicals with potential for use in chemical warfare. Soon after, most of the Morcha leaders, including myself, were arrested and imprisoned. Many of the action plans we entered into were almost suicidal. Look at the *rail roko* agitation (stopping trains from moving), for instance. Some of us felt it was too premature, but the announcements had already been made. We went ahead and the impact was mixed. Arrests followed, along with clampdown and repressive action. We lost mass support that had appeared spontaneously during our siege of the chief minister's residence. We got unprecedented support. Truckloads of food were sent from the city to keep us going. This public mood vanished rapidly after the repression that followed in the wake of the *rail roko*."

Sadgopal recounts a memorable action: "It must have been in April, 1985 when more than 300 women marched to the DIG Bungalow hospital holding bottles with urine sample in their hands. They were shouting slogans: *'Hamaare peshaab mein thiocyanate ki jaanch karo.' 'Batao kitna jahar hai hamaare andar.'* ('Measure thiocyanate in our urine.' 'Tell us how much poison is in our bodies.') Clearly, the women were concerned about how the persisting poison might affect their pregnancies and the unborn babies. This became the basis for a popular demand in Bhopal since the urine thiocyanate levels provided a scientific basis for claiming continuing medical treatment from the government and also compensation from Union Carbide. This is precisely why both the government and the Union Carbide turned hostile to the demand. In June 1985, the police pounded on the Jan Swasthya Kendra's clinic and confiscated the clinical records of the gas victims along with the urine thiocyanate data. Eventually, it took a Supreme Court order to get the records released. The DIG Bungalow women's demonstration was a result of the power unleashed by combining scientific knowledge with people's movement. The context of reproductive health provided further synergy and turned this into a new dimension of women's movement in Bhopal. This pedagogy was learnt from the work of Kerala Shastra Sahitya Parishad (KSSP) that pioneered the people's science movement in India. Again, the Morcha lacked a collective appreciation of the pedagogy and lost the opportunity of energizing the Bhopal struggle with the valiant spirit of the emerging women's power and people's science."

Most conflicts in activism are generated along the fault line created by a need-based strategy versus a rights-based strategy. It was no different in Bhopal, and perhaps explains the strength and weakness of the movement. Most of the group leaders in Bhopal, when asked to comment on why there was split in the organizations, offered interesting explanations.[3] Notable was what Alok Pratap Singh, another founder member of Morcha had to say: "All of us had experience of working with mass movements, and we had a similar experience before Bhopal where we had used the Mohalla Committee structure in which certain educated people were identified and given responsibilities. We as outsiders had our limitations, we could not participate in the movement perpetually, and the local people had to take the lead because they were going to take it forward in the long run. It was evident that local people could identify and offer solutions to local problems. There was nothing unusual about the situation in Bhopal. If outsiders had come only to do research then it was all right, but if they had come to help the people and work to change the situation, then you should not hesitate to participate in people's problems. You should not back out when the occasion requires intervention. The victims looked up to us for leadership because we had created hope in the first place and it was unfair to shirk responsibility. Anil Sadgopal and others were debating questions like 'who are we to lead?' My point is we have to lead because we have taken the role of helping these people, and we have organized them, we have formed committees in thirty-two bastis, it was our baby, it was our moral responsibility" (tape 33). He recounts the major protest action on January 12, 1985, in front of the CM's office, where frontline leaders were arrested, leading to confusion among the rank and file and leaving the strong team of 3,000 women from the bastis totally vulnerable to police repression. Listening to his side of the argument, we realize that the real battle was between unequal power structures and the nonavailability of any proven method of mediation. "All the leaders were detained in the control room so the rally headed first to get them released and then toward Vallabh Bhavan. The CM Motilal Vohra had already fled to Delhi. The chief secretary called in a delegation of twenty-five people for discussions. He agreed to direct the collector to meet with our demands such as surveys and medical care, which were the most basic demands of the people. There was lot of dissent among us. Some of us were demanding much larger things that were not in the purview of the chief secretary or in the immediate radar of the people who were waiting outside. We were being overambitious. When we came downstairs to talk to the people we saw a sea of footwear, there had been a lathi charge on the people. This was very bad for the victory we thought we had achieved. We later learnt that the police was instigated by some outside activists...after this incident we lost a lot of supporters" (tape 33). Here was a classic case of the kind of differences that were to surface time and again, creating rifts in a movement that depended on external leadership, political backing, experts in various fields, and the strength of numbers that comes with mass mobilization.

At one level, any urban infrastructure will demand proper health care, education, and job opportunities. At the same time, urban conflicts arise from the question of who has more rights over urban infrastructure, and correspondingly, who enjoys more rights over natural resources like clean water and pollution free air. Without a shift in power equation, the poor will never have enough rights over resources to improve the quality of their lives. Government relief programmes in Bhopal were need-based so they could not restore dignity of life. More importantly, the cause of the disaster was not properly investigated so no attempt was made to redefine notions of development in the light of what had gone wrong. A need-based strategy further marginalized the survivors by projecting them as obstacles to development, thus increasing their vulnerability vis-à-vis the unaffected population. They continued to live out their lives of destitution and constraints, which was already imposed on them due to their lack of rights, entitlement, and political leverage. Clearly Morcha played an important role in opposing development plans that tried to mitigate poverty without reinforcing rights and opportunities. Therefore, its historical importance cannot be ignored. Did its breakdown signal a change in direction for the movement? Volatile circumstances were brought on by the head on clash between agitational methods and state repression. It was to shape the direction that the campaign for justice was to take in Bhopal. Realignment of forces took place at a more fundamental level. These changes were largely issue based, so that a sharp division between short-term and long-term demands began to rear its head. Organizations tried to mediate this gap in a way that influenced the history of the movement.

Organized Opposition and Vested Interest

It is important to keep in mind that most man-made disasters call for political management of the crisis by the establishment. Any sort of opposition is viewed as disruptive and antiestablishment. The key phase of early activism in Bhopal has to be seen in this context. The accident happened three weeks before the national parliamentary elections, and it was important that the ruling Congress party acted promptly by suing Union Carbide Corporation (UCC) for damages on behalf of the victims.[4] Such a move paid rich political dividend; Congress won state legislative assembly and national parliament seats in MP. In 1989 after Rajiv Gandhi arrived at a court-ordered settlement with UCC, Congress lost the elections and was replaced by the Janata Dal (JD)-led coalition government with V. P. Singh as prime minister. Singh had campaigned on a social justice platform, and his government decided to appeal the settlement that had been reached by the previous government. In a populist move, the JD government decided to announce an interim compensation of Rs 200 per month, till final terms and conditions of the settlement had been decided. Though such a need-based strategy was politically expedient, it was an administrative blunder. Gas victims were increasingly made dependent on short-term relief measures. Medico-legal documentation that would prove their status as gas victim was put under extraneous political considerations.

Right from the beginning protest was met by repression that was meant to break the sustaining power of activism. Short-term relief measures caused antagonism and divisions in the community that prevented them from uniting in the face of state terror tactics. A number of voluntary organizations played a limited role of aiding relief measures. Once they completed their tasks they pulled out of Bhopal. Some like the Self-Employed Womens' Association (SEWA) and the Mahila Chetna Manch tried to open training and production centers, but they were too small in size and covered only a fraction of the affected community. Government backed those organizations that were not confrontational, but little work was done consistently for a length of time. Jobs were routinely assigned and schemes folded up whenever government-dictated criteria were not fulfilled. As a result, a lot of help proved to be adhoc and purely temporary. An opportunistic, charity culture inundated Bhopal with its own variety of vested interest and corruption.

Tara Jones draws attention to the government's attempt to exploit the division between the Carbide workers and the slum dwellers (1988, 72). This had more serious repercussions. Trade unions and both the communist parties, the Communist Party Marxist (CPM) and Communist Party of India (CPI), came forward to strengthen their traditional, political base among the industrial working class. But Bhopal was not a copybook case for a national working-class movement. Trade Union Relief Fund (TURF) for Gas Victims was formed by several trade unions in Mumbai, but its intervention was largely in the context of UCIL's attempt to sell off the plant. Unfortunately, the established trade unions that were affiliated to political parties failed to go beyond sectarian concerns to launch an agitation that supported the claims of gas victims, especially the daily wage earners living in the slums. Carbide's own union was asking for alternative employment for the workers. TURF put forward its demand to hand over the factory to the workers and start soya-based food production, which would be run on a cooperative basis by gas victims and workers.[5] On June 14, 1985, 400 workers broke into the plant to begin a sit-in protest over job losses (Jones 1988, 78). In July 1985 the factory was finally closed down. In December 1985 UCIL made paltry cash settlement with the workers to end further demonstrations. This is how Kailash Nagda, the former president of UCIL Union describes the situation in the BGIA newsletter (December 1987): "More than 100 permanent workers of the UCIL Bhopal plant are still unemployed. All workers are from the gas-affected bastis. They do not want jobs that take them away from Bhopal, as they cannot avail of the special medical care meant for gas victims. Also they have been offered very low wages, half of what they used to get in Union Carbide." A special bureau was set up by the state government to help UCIL workers to get jobs. But it was one of those ill-fated schemes that soon closed down, but not before it had divided the community by turning the basti people against the workers.

Actually the Bhopal disaster offered crucial lessons in what can go wrong with activism. Too many groups joined the fray, bringing in their own agendas and vested interests to an already conflict ridden arena. But it was only those with sustaining power that remained behind. The Bhopal disaster brought to the forefront risks that are inherent in hazardous industries. The gas leak was only the tip of the iceberg. Exposure to hazards and the victimization that follows are not merely confined to the workplace, but are directly linked to the communities at risk. The loss of life, the range and scale of morbidity, and the degradation of the environment and its impact on lives were frighteningly widespread. How was activism to begin envisaging the rational possibility of remediation and proper compensation? Besides, there were larger questions to grapple with. Are risks, benefits, and burdens equitably distributed? Are remediation plans seen as technical solutions without considering the right to life, health, and livelihood? In all fairness NRPC and Morcha created a niche that debated many of these issues. They rejected establishment ideas of voluntarism. To that extent they had enormous potential to link remediation with empowerment and participation. But they played a more confrontational role. In their eagerness to oppose government schemes, they did not back up their critique of governmental programmes with viable, alternative plan of action. What they did was useful in the long run. Members of Morcha used their personal contacts to get nonparty radical groups such as Eklavya, Delhi Science Forum, and Medico Friend Circle to collaborate with them and form a think tank for grappling with such vital issues as environment, science, and health care. But clearly Sarangi's notion of "extending help from outside" had its own problems. Groups were plagued by internecine clash, autocratic modes of functioning, dogmatisms, and attempts to catapult local issues onto national concerns. For instance, the Rashtriya Abhiyan Samiti (National Campaign Committee) was formed at the end of the national convention that was held in Bhopal in February 1985, where sixty-five organizations from different parts of India participated. The idea was to carry on a campaign at the level of the subcontinent by raising issues on Bhopal in various forums. Later, this sort of networking helped in organizing national protests, but at the same time, there were practical problems of disagreement and disputes between different groups.

The government retaliated by coming down heavily on outsiders. They were branded as professional agitators from outside Bhopal, with CIA links and links with UCC. Morcha had started a health clinic in May 1985 called Jana Swathya Kendra (People's Health Clinic), with the purpose of administering sodium thiosulphate (NaTS), a recommended detoxicant. The clinic kept detailed records on the impact of NaTS. The clinic was raided and closed down in June 1985, followed by mass arrests of doctors and health workers and confiscation of all documents. The arrests were done as preventive measure, since a massive protest rally had been planned the following day. The idea was to criminalize protest and brand activism as disruptive and violent. Once again the idea was to alienate the activists from the survivors. What Morcha successfully did was challenge the government monopoly over technical knowledge. But at the same time, it failed to understand that mass mobilization had to take into account the individual components of a community with their specific problems and limitations. Besides, it failed to put in place a system whereby leadership can be handed over to the people; thus it perpetuated the process of delinking rehabilitation from the political process of restoring people's ability to control their own lives. But it was just this sort of self-help lessons that were being learnt at the grassroots level. In the next section I link activism with grassroots organizations formed by the survivors themselves with some help from outsiders. The focus was on survival by valiantly defying systemic attempts to destroy life and identity. After the dismantling of Morcha and NRPC, a few dedicated individuals remained behind to carry on with the struggle for justice. Not only did the campaign take on new directions, but it also grew from strength to strength, with more and more women joining the fray.

The March for Justice

It is not at all surprising that the story of the Stationery Union sounds like a modern-day tale of surviving all odds with its quotient of heroics, surprises, tears, and laughter. As we listen to voices from within its folds we realize it has epic qualities that defy literary norms. I recall what Sarangi had said to me about people's participatory role: "Living in Bhopal is a political education. You can talk about linkages between government and multinational corporations in theory, but here it is evident, happening before your eyes in the most glaring way. One day the chairman of the company says something in the US, next day the Indian prime minister echoes what he is saying, and the very next day the chief minister makes a similar statement. A big part of education is when you make the connections. When connections are made people realize what is happening is not an aberration but the rule. But political education has to change into political action. In Bhopal what we do is take over spaces—political space, social space, cultural space. We make the terrain our own by reclaiming territories that have been taken away from us. It is this taking over of lost spaces that I call the creative part of political action." Given my own background as a fiction writer and a teacher of literature, it is the "creative" part of activism that holds my interest. I am interested in discovering new ways of looking at the subject position of people whose history is otherwise ignored. Mostly we concentrate on circumstances and external factors that loses out on what is hidden from view. Oral history can penetrate that all-important space where historical events link up with people's stories. Therefore, archival material is used to strengthen the base of the testimonials. At the same time, we are compelled to see how official methods of recording negates the voices of people. My effort is to make us "listen" to some of these "muted" voices, an effort that is no less literary than it is political. I believe it enriches historical analysis and vividly recreates the ups and downs of the campaign.

Champa Devi Shukla recounts the inception of the Stationery Union as one such reclaiming of rights over the workspace. In November 1985 hundred women from severely gas-exposed communities were selected for training in two centers for production of office stationery such as file covers, writing pads, registers, and notebooks. The stationery shed was part of the welfare measures undertaken by the state government to impart technical training and provide employment to gas victims. "Out of the hundred women, fifty of us were Hindus and fifty Muslims. It laid the grounds for communal harmony. At the end of three months of training, the District Industry Center told us that our training was over, and now we had to return home and start our own business. We decided to take up matters in our hands. Rashida Appa and I were chosen by the other women to represent our cause. We decided to register our protest in front of the chief minister's office. We were so new to things that it took us an entire day to find the place. We sat there for three months from morning till evening shouting slogans, singing dirges, and drawing attention to our plight." Following this protest, commercial production of stationery items started in March 1986 under the control and management of the MP State and Industries Corporation, and the women who had received training were given jobs at piece rate. "For eleven long months we reported for work, but there was nothing to do. We were asked to take home Rs 6 as monthly payment; we all refused." In August 1987 the Stationery Union was formed and registered in Indore. "We paid our lawyer from the money raised from members. We chose a name that highlighted our identity as women workers. We took up issues of adequate wages, better working conditions, and our basic rights as factory workers. At each step we had to fight an indifferent administration." A 1988 official directive recommended that the Factory Act should apply to the stationery production center. "We started getting monthly wages in place of piece rate. From Rs 150, our wages were increased to

Rs 250. But we got to know that the center had made a profit of Rs 4 lakhs. In May 1988 we started a major demonstration and sit-in followed by hunger strike in front of the Secretariat that lasted for more than twenty-seven days. At the end of our action the Stationery center was made a unit of the government printing press. It was our first taste of victory. But we soon got to know that the workers in the printing press were being paid Rs 2,400 while we were getting a measly sum of Rs 532. When we protested we were told that as gas victims we should not have any more expectations. This was adding insult to injury. In June 1989 we started on a padyatra (march on foot) from Bhopal to Delhi. We had no idea how we were going to cover the distance, or how long it would take us, and what hardships we would face. It was a foolhardy decision but we were desperate. We wanted to place our demands before the highest authority in the country, the Prime Minister Rajiv Gandhi."

I met the women of the Stationery Union to get a firsthand account of the padyatra. They have vivid memories of the long and arduous journey, though the significance of the event has paled in comparison with so much that has happened since. "In the history of the campaign it will go down as an action planned, executed, and completed successfully by a bunch of novices who had little experience of activism," Rashida laughs. "Come to think of it we had hardly planned anything. When we were on our dharna at Vallabh Bhavan I felt that our actions were not having the desired effect. I told Champa didi we need to do something that makes us more visible. Let us go to Delhi and place our demands before the PM. We had no money to go there so I said let us walk!" Bhagwati Bai who has been with the Union right from the beginning adds, "We just joined the padyatra because Appa told us. We believed in her and Didi and we knew that being part of the Union was for our benefit. We realized that without collective pressure nobody was going to listen to us. We had no idea where Delhi was!" Rashida clarifies, "They believed in me at a time when I was just beginning to understand things. For example, we knew that we were grossly underpaid, but we knew little about the Minimum wages Act. The management would constantly try to strike a deal with us by increasing wages marginally. We had no demands on what posts to ask for or what roles we were to play. We were just happy to be removed from piece rate to fixed wages. But while we were planning our padyatra we decided to be smart. Through the media we warned the CM about our impending action, and we warned him that if anything happens on the way it would be his responsibility. As a result the state officials arranged for a team of doctors, a water tanker, and police team to accompany us." Jameela who was only eighteen at the time of the padyatra talks about the political fallout, "We were hoping Moti Lal Vohra (CM) would call us back. He did send someone to meet us after we had covered some distance. The official told us we were being foolhardy given our physical conditions, and that our demands would be met if we returned to Bhopal. Appa and didi were adamant. They said give it in writing."

Abida, Shakeela, and Umrao join Jameela in recounting the hardships they faced on the way. Jameela: "We were seventy-five to eighty people, with over thirty children and twelve men, mostly family members who wanted to come along. In the beginning we covered not more than eight to ten km in a day. But as we walked we felt angrier and our energy level went up. Soon we were covering twenty to thirty-five km per day." Abida: "When our feet felt sore we tied it with leaves. Most of us felt giddy and some fainted and had to be taken care of by the doctor. We had to ask for food in villages. We started early to avoid the sun." Shakeela: "The villagers were very cooperative. We had no pamphlets to give them. But we explained our plight to them. They also shared their problems with us. It was a learning lesson to see how the poor live." Umrao: "There was lot of bonhomie among us. Most of the time, we had to sleep on the roadside. We kept close as a group and we took turns to keep guard. We heard frightening rumors about dacoits in the Chambal Valley, and a very nice policeman accompanied us for the entire stretch. We spent a night in a school building. When we parted ways at the district border, the policeman said to us with folded hands that if he had the power he would give us all our demands. Things were different in Dholpur area in Rajasthan. There the commissioner was rude. It was a low point in our journey when we had nothing to eat or no place to rest. We cooked our food and literally begged for assistance." Bhagwati Bai sums up the hardships faced: "We had so little money. Some of us sold our ornaments to raise some money. It took us a while to get out of debt. We were not paid our salaries for three months after we returned. Even the women who had not participated in the padyatra had to face disciplinary action. Thirty-five of us had to be hospitalized because of severe stomach infection. Yashoda was five months pregnant and she aborted in Agra. Ask Chandrakala how her husband had sold all the utensils and mortgaged many things. Munnu Bai's husband beat her black and blue because he was suspicious of her staying outside home for so long."

The padyatris reached Delhi after thirty-three days. Bhagwati and Savitri Bai look back on those days with bitterness. Bhagwati: "There was nobody to meet us when we reached Delhi. We had been marking the distance on the road posts, but our walk to India Gate seemed the longest. We stayed there for nine days. This was long before cell phones and computers, so we had no means of communication. We got to know that Rajiv Gandhi was not in town. We felt utter despair. Suresh Pachuari (member of parliament) came to meet us. He asked us to go back to Bhopal. We will come there and get your work done he said." Savitri Bai: "If I remember correctly Devilal (once deputy PM), who was passing by stopped to ask who we were. When we explained he did listen and donated Rs 2,000, but nobody did anything. There was another padyatra in 2006, but most of us never joined. What is the use? To date we have not been made permanent so none of us will have retirement benefits. I think it is better to fight in court. But at that time we had a lot of enthusiasm in us, a kind of red hot burning sense of injustice in our chest. That was enough to make us walk miles." Bhagwati adds, "We got to know later that Rajiv Gandhi said he was sorry he never met us in one of his election speeches. Well, what to say? If he felt remorse then that is good. But today we know that media is more alert, especially with TV news spreads fast. Every government fears bad reputation."

Stepping Out of the Workplace

I look around at the stationery shed. The place has a dilapidated look. Outdated machines are lying dormant and women are sitting in groups and chatting; work hours are regularly interspersed with prayer times. A few bundles of stationary papers are lying around, and some women are cutting, pasting, numbering, and putting them in piles. I am told that the tempo from the press comes everyday for delivery and pick up. The stationery work-shed is a clear example of how rehabilitation schemes have failed to increase job prospects or to cater to a larger section of the community. What has failed? In the course of my fieldwork, I also visited another shed in the Industrial Area in Govindpura run by the M. P. Mahila Kalyan Samiti (Women's Welfare Society). This Samiti was started way back in 1975 in the International Women's Year for providing employment to needy and destitute women. It was in 1986 that the Samiti opened a workshed for women gas survivors, and I am told that the moving spirit behind the enterprise was Vimla Sharma, the daughter of the, former President of India, Dr. Shankar Dayal Sharma. The place is bustling with activity and is engaged in doing assembly job for transformers, supplied to the BHEL a major public sector enterprise. The plant supervisor gives me two interesting bits of information. The workshop also takes in women who are not gas survivors and the numbers are not constant. Besides, nobody is permitted to indulge in activism during work hours. "We don't have control over what they do outside, but if we hear rumors then the worker is fired," she tells me.

There is no doubt government started rehabilitation schemes with the idea that it would be taken over by private enterprise and nongovernmental organizations. The work-sheds were temporary stopgap arrangements like most other rehabilitation schemes. Also the bureaucracy relied on the fact that with employment being generated activism would get quelled. The fact that Stationery survived, despite being perceived as an economic burden on the welfare state, is an indicator of its real strength. The members of the union have spearheaded the most consistent battle against the very systemic failure that has reduced the shed to its present state of neglect. Rashida and Champa talk about the biggest challenge they posed to the state industrial corporation. They filed a case in 1990 for "equal work equal pay" in the MP State Tribunal, Jabbalpur. In September 1998, the Tribunal dismissed the case on the grounds that the petition was not sustainable under the Tribunal. "Imagine," Rashida bi retorts, "they tell us eight years later that this was not the right place! The Tribunal directed us to the State High Court and two years later we were told this was also not the right place! So the case was filed in the Labour Court in Bhopal in 2000." On December 19, 2002, the Bhopal Labour Court gave a decision directing the state government to appoint the women employed at the center to permanent posts as Junior Binders, with effect from April 1998. The court ordered that the women should be paid arrears due to them. "We celebrated by dancing nonstop on the streets," Rashida says with deep sense of irony, "but we should have known better. Though the court order clearly said that the decision had to be implemented within a month, the state government went on to make an appeal in a higher court. What about arrears for the fourteen years we wasted in going from one wrong forum to another?"

The Stationery Union was characterized by activism that straddled employment issues and the larger struggle for justice. The women tell me that the period from 2000 to 2002 was very crucial for the movement. The stationery became part of a coalition that came to be known as the International Campaign for Justice in Bhopal (ICJB) that took formal shape in 2004. As an international body, dedicated to the task of campaigning for justice—both legal and economic—in Bhopal, it evolved a structure that worked on the principle of a worldwide coalition of some twenty people's organizations, nonprofit groups, and individuals who could draw on the strength of new communication technology, especially Internet and the possibility of collaborative work with other organizations that were actively involved with the fight for justice world over. The idea was to get the survivor's organizations in Bhopal to play a leading role in the international network. The movement had clearly geared itself to put pressure on monolithic, powerful adversaries like Dow Chemicals, the US and Indian governments in the context of globalization. The focus of the movement was on cleaning up the abandoned chemicals on the site, while ensuring adequate health care and proper economic rehabilitation for the survivors of the disaster and their children. It is important to understand how the Stationery Union shaped itself through such a coalition. From the women's testimonials it becomes clear that the transition was not smooth and a breakaway union was formed. The conflict was on familiar grounds of needs versus rights, but an added dimension was the emerging question of leadership, clash of interests, and international aid.

During the discussion on campaign history and the part played by leadership, Rashida Bi explains why under her leadership the union felt it necessary to pitch their strength behind the coalition, and its concern for widening the demands beyond the immediate needs of the rights of stationery workers. She makes it very clear that Stationery Union joined other organizations whenever the need arose, "We would join rallies and dharnas whenever we were called. It is wrong to say that we were only concerned with stationery demands and activities.

During the fifteenth anniversary we tried to come together for strategic reasons. But we did not believe in the men lead groups, so we kept our affiliations limited to court cases and legal petitions. In 2000 Greenpeace came to Bhopal and after that we joined hands with Sathyu bhai. He told us about the problems of water contamination. Since 1990 this issue of people drinking toxic water has been gathering momentum. When I heard about this issue I realized that activism had to fight a much bigger battle. What has happened in Bhopal has already happened, one needs to join forces to stop it from happening again anywhere else in the world. The fight is not just for gas survivors and their compensation, but a fight against the fault of companies that knowingly spread toxics across the globe. To save the world from this, the struggle in Bhopal has to spread across the world. Compensation is a limited issue and limited demand" (tape 29).

Listening to a member who had been part of Stationery Union right from the start and a close confidante of Rashida and Champa Devi, we nevertheless sense a tension between decisions taken unilaterally and collective decisions arrived at through a democratic process. Most grassroots organizations in Bhopal continue to be plagued by the problems of leadership, which is largely based on the personality cult and the question of winning trust and loyalty of the group. The member uses an interesting simile to describe the influence that leaders like Rashida and Champa had on the women, "When one spark comes out it does not take much for the paper to catch fire, in the same way Appa and Didi would come and raise issues and ask us to take it up. The answer would be yes and we would take it up. All the women would come along. When Appa and Didi went abroad and won an award the women had difference of opinion. They felt that this was only self-promotion and everyone should equally share the prize money. I believe the women were wrong. They did not see the other side of the picture that Appa and Didi had reached such a high level of success, which they could not have done on their own. They had earned stationery a good name. International support is good. Support and solidarity is a boost for our cause. It is wrong to think that Appa and Didi have left stationery behind in working with other groups" (tape 23). However, in interview sessions that were not recorded on camera many of the women felt that issues had got diverted from the primary demand of the Stationery Union for permanent jobs and postretirement benefits for the workers. An underlying grouse was that both Rashida and Champa were too busy with other work to pay attention to the daily needs of stationery, and they had got the opportunity to improve their economic conditions and lifestyle, while most of the other workers continued to wait in vain for government redressal. It is interesting to know how international support emerged as a controversial issue with all the other groups that were interviewed. There was a lot of discussion on the ethics of getting monetary aid from outside and the need for transparency. But the real issue is more complex. We are looking at the dialectical tension between the different kinds of demands and how they were to be prioritized and then placed before the government and other international forums. The clash was between short-term demands that were likely to be met, and the long-term fight for justice that did not bring tangible results.

There has been a lot of politicization of how groups have gone on to frame their agenda for the struggle for justice and chart their own course of action. Morcha had broken up under the pressure of the crisis situation, but two decades later groups have continued to break up, with leaders leaving one group to join others. In 2005 the Stationery Union broke, to form a separate registered union that was named Bhopal Gas Peedit Mahila Stationery Karamchari Morcha. The leaders of the new group, when spoken to are dismissive of any real differences. Member: "True that if all the organizations work together it will benefit the overall movement. But the fight even with them working separately is the same. The issues remain the same and if organizations want they can come together" (tape 26). Another member: "We are now in the majority. We take up causes that are linked to Stationery Union. But we do take advice and are in contact with the BJP. They come and join the Stationery Morcha to show their solidarity, but their involvement is limited to just that. My colleague and I too join their rallies to show our support" (tape 25). For the majority of women who have joined the breakaway group the problem is more emotional. We trusted Appa and Didi is their collective complaint, and we gave our life to this union and did whatever they asked us to do, but the two have moved on and forgotten us. Do leaders take care of this emotional quotient when they plan their agenda is a question that is left unanswered. The groups share a history of collective action and all the people interviewed recall events with tremendous pride. The decades acted as watersheds with the movement changing course with increased demand. Needless to say, women played an active role in shaping such changes.

The year 2001 heralded major changes in the direction of the movement. With Dow Chemicals taking over Union Carbide and water contamination becoming a matter of grave concern, the grassroots organizations felt the need to take up larger issues of bringing the absconding company to court, providing better medical care and environmental rehabilitation. Despite all the internal differences, the Stationery Union found itself lending solidarity to bigger and bigger actions. In February 2002, they protested in front of the Mumbai office of Dow Chemicals. In April 2002, they again stormed the Dow office. And in June 2002, along with other organizations they sat on a hunger strike in New Delhi, demanding for Anderson's extradition. The hunger strike lasted for nineteen days. Champa Devi, in a personal conversation with me, sums up the conflict faced by activism in the present-day scenario as both emotional and political: "We are living in changed times and our protest too had to change directions. Appa will agree with me, it was in the production center that we all realized the extent to which we were being denied the rights and benefits that regular employees are entitled to. At one level, our problem was confined to the workplace. And today when I look around I see how much the job scene has changed. There are so many opportunities for anybody who has the guts to go out and grab what is offered. But we, the gas survivors, have been pushed out of the race. How can we remain silent in the face of so much injustice? It is through the union that I was given a forum to see my own sufferings in the perspective of the larger suffering of the people of Bhopal. I am now committed to fight for justice. I am now part of a people's movement that helps women understand their rights as political beings. You can say I have gone beyond my workplace."

The Formation of Grassroots Organization

MUS has been one of the seminal organizations that played a major role in spearheading activities connecting livelihood to larger issues of justice. It grew out of the concerns voiced by women in the sewing centers, and it mostly offered to mobilize women from outside by organizing demonstrations on different issues and hiring attorneys to fight the case against Union Carbide. MUS and the Bhopal Gas Peedit Nirashrit Pension Bhogi Sangarsh Morcha (Forum for Destitute Women in need of Pension) had more than 100,000 members within the first two years of its formation. The weekly meetings in Shahjani and Neelam Park became legion. Women came in droves and broke the stereotypes of traditional Indian women by discarding their veils, making fiery speeches, and hurling abuses that would make a sailor blush! It was cathartic and offered a free space for politicization that came with sharing information and actively planning out street actions. Women brought their infants with them, thus extending their traditional roles outside the home. Emancipation was shaped out of tradition in a way that subverted age-old customs. But in the words of Sarangi these organizations came to resemble extended Indian families with its share of patriarchal norms and lack of democratic functioning. Though women formed the backbone of the organizations, men were at the helm dictating modes of functioning and controlling the finances. However, it was both pragmatic and necessary to allow few women to grow in strength, by keeping them in the forefront of the movement. It was equally important to use their resources for mobilization and to focus on issues that concerned women.

MUS was led by charismatic men like Jabbar Khan, in association with Irfan Khan and Nawab Khan, who became leaders of women, but only insofar as women dominated the public space by virtue of sheer numbers and becoming cheerleaders and spokespersons. Both Irfan and Nawab Khan were to leave MUS because they felt sidelined. Women proved to be more loyal. They gained bargaining power on different aspects of activism without really sharing equal space. A few of the women who continue to play a major role in MUS were interviewed on video. They traced their involvement with the group and raised a number of issues that linked with activism in the present day. But it is interesting to observe that most of the women had no issues with giving men the edge in leadership. They admitted that their lack of education meant that they had to trust what Jabbar Bhai was saying. They felt secure in a set up where the head of the family called the shots. I realized that the problem of dependence on different constituencies was endemic in the Bhopal movement. Given the complexity of a technological disaster, and the fact that a maximum number of survivors were not literate, or had limited access to scientific knowledge, meant that survivor's organizations had to evolve a two-tier level of leadership. Responsibility was divided between men and women who shared in the strategy planning at one level, and immediate mobilization at the other, by utilizing different kinds of expertise and work capacity.

When fissures began surfacing in survivor's organization it was not so much over the men/women divide, but a more fundamental conflict of interest. Both Irfan Khan and Nawab Khan who broke away from MUS to form their own group that later became part of the ICJB coalition have interesting insights to give on the nature of the disagreements that kept cropping up. Clearly, changing affiliations and forming of breakaway groups based on issues that became the need of the hour was a common feature of the movement. Irfan talks about his involvement with activism before the gas leak: "In 1977 I joined National Textile Corporation and after training in Bombay I began working in the mill. I got into an altercation with my supervisor for lack of work and I put up posters saying 'I am not given enough work and I cannot support myself with the pay given'. The INTUC trade union intervened and my work was increased. After this I started working with INTUC. After Indira Gandhi's assassination, a peace march was organized by NGOs. I worked with them. Soon after the gas leak, I along with some other people from my colony and surrounding areas gathered and formed a committee, the Mohalla Sudhar Committee. We conducted a survey of those people who had died. We divided ourselves into groups and went from house to house surveying for deaths, illnesses and other losses" (tape 14). Nawab Khan was a tailor by profession and had a shop in New Market that ran into losses due to his prolonged health problems following the gas leak and had to be closed down. He borrowed Rs 5,000 from the bank and bought a pushcart to sells shoes but hooligans looted it and he went into severe loss. "I had also started writing for newspapers for a living since I had a good command over a number of languages including Hindi, Arabic, English, and Farsi. My wife died in 1989 due to prolonged gas-related ailments. I became aware of the campaign because my wife used to attend Jabbar Khan's meetings and she kept me updated. I joined Jabbar and was with him for five years. I was Irfan's friend. Irfan and Jabbar fell apart for some reason and separated. Irfan told me that these people were selfish and greedy and we should start our own group to fight for the poor. We started Mahila Purush Sangharsh Morcha" (tape 4).

Jabbar Khan's joining of MUS offers an interesting insight into how the movement was getting strengthened by men who were locally from Bhopal and brought their own experience of hardships, personal loss, poverty, and the trauma following the gas leak. In that sense they were not looked upon as outsiders. Jabbar takes a lot of pride in his working-class background, the fact that he had worked in a brick kiln, pushed handcarts, and started working at the age of twelve, which came in the way of his getting a college education. A strong affinity for doing social works gets linked to class factors. It explains the impetus for a lifetime commitment and sacrifice for the Bhopal cause. Jabbar is dismissive of the educated, English-speaking outsider who comes to Bhopal and hogs the limelight. He also gives a lot of premium to those who qualify as true victims of the disaster. He feels that they can understand what gas victims really need. The women in MUS are categorical that with Jabbar bhai's inclusion in the organization proper unionization began. Member (MUS): "My husband was a driver and the family lived on his income. His hands got paralyzed after that night and the income stopped. I was trained in stitching and zari work so I started this to sustain the family. I heard about an organization that was fighting for the poor gas victims. I started attending the meetings. I heard Jabbar bhai speak and he had a unique way of talking that touched my heart and I began coming for the meetings regularly. That is when MUS was giving out forms to the public for membership and people turned up in huge numbers. The idea of MUS came from the women, but bhai understood our problems, and we asked him to join us. Bhai agreed to work with us if politics was kept out of the fight. Then the campaign moved ahead on his guidance" (tape 13). Both Irfan and Nawab claim that they later joined the ICJB coalition under their Mahila Purush banner because they felt the problem of leadership created rifts within the organization and restricted their role. While the women in MUS had no hesitation in proclaiming their loyalty to their leader, the men clearly chaffed under one man's guidance.

The Bhopal movement was witness to a lot of personality clashes and divide between women- and men-led organizations. It was also weaning itself off from party-led movements, so that the distinction between ideological positions and the question of vote banks were getting blurred. The idea of creating a vibrant space for civil society with progressive elements coming together to strengthen the hands of grassroots organization began to take form, and found its final shape through ICJB. The idea was to resolve the one leader format and yet nurture the local organizational heads like Rashida, Champa, Irfan, and Nawab whose main task was to mobilize people from their own constituencies. A lot depended on community level work, which had to be consistent and in keeping with local demands. No group was asked to forego their identity or the mandate they carried from the basti people to the movement and vice versa. However, some amount of tension continues to simmer on predictable lines, namely how are such groups funded. MUS and Pension Bhogi Sangarsh Morcha (Pension) are entirely self-funded and raise their money from a nominal donation from each of its members. The women of MUS are vociferous in denigrating international aid. To them this is equivalent to going abroad with a begging bowl; they take pride in being independent and self-sufficient, which they feel instills a sense of responsibility in its members. According to them, international support is a thin guise for tours abroad, hogging foreign media attention, getting awards that rightfully belong to the more deserving candidate or simply an excuse for self-promotion. They accuse the middle-class intellectuals, which includes academics, writers, filmmakers, and activists for exploiting Bhopal for personal gains.

The Bhopal Medical Appeal (BMA) has a different story to tell on its Web site: "The BMA was launched in 1994, when a man from Bhopal came to Britain to tell whoever would listen about the calamitous condition of the still suffering victims. Our first appeal, which appeared in *The Guardian* and *The Observer* on the 10th anniversary, in December 1994, produced a massively generous response. The task of administering this fund was taken on by the *Pesticides Action Network UK (PAN-UK)*, which also adopted the Appeal as a project, in order that our work could benefit from its charity status, and which has generously given time and loyalty. Our first project was to open the clinic in Bhopal. To this end, the Sambhavna Trust was formed in India to run the clinic. In the Bhopal Medical Appeal 'we' don't ask 'you' to help 'us' help 'them'. We have never accepted funding from companies or corporate trusts. This is our vision, that all of us are equal in an unbroken chain between supporters at one-end and gas survivors at the other. Our sincere thanks to those who have been part of it. The people in Bhopal have a lot to give back to the rest of us. Let's carry on the good work we've begun together."[6] Such an appeal has met with a lot of criticism from survivor groups. While some find the image generated of "needy" gas survivors insulting, others have felt that aid from external sources meant that activism was often "managed" to suit agendas. In an off-camera conversation, one of the founder members of Morcha, who claims to have been wronged at every step, said in no uncertain terms that the Bhopal movement has been spearheaded by a handful of powerful men, who raise issues to serve their selfish ends and use women to promote their own cause. Therefore, Bhopal is a women's movement only in name. However, the speaker concedes that it is a movement that has gathered strength from the courage and commitment of poor, dispossessed people; today, the numbers are dwindling, but the strength has not diminished. Talking to the women of MUS, one senses a lot of anxiety about who gets credit for genuine work. There is the palpable fear of getting sidelined and being ignored by posterity.

It is in this connection that we need to draw attention to another dimension in the use of oral history. Questions have been asked about the reliability of testimonials and what methods can be used to verify facts. This is specially so when we are talking about an industrial disaster, particularly for those stakeholders who continue to promote notions of development and world prosperity. Willy-nilly a disaster points to flaws in a system, and therefore asks for explanations. Blame gets distributed, but not necessarily in an equitable manner. In the raging debate that follows, "truth" becomes a polemical issue. This is what happened in Bhopal. People got mired in the truth-telling process, and what made the situation worse, survivors were asked to prove their identity as gas victims in the absence of proper systems of verification. It made them peculiarly vulnerable. They suffered from a deep sense of anxiety. To be erased from the records became equivalent to being written off from the pages of history. It brings us face to face with an important question that oral history asks time and again. What kind of history do we need to write to tell the story of people who are brutally neglected by society? In the ultimate analysis, we need to understand that oral history like any other form of history is a double-edged sword that remembers and forgets simultaneously.

The movement in Bhopal had to keep tabs on whether official schemes were being implemented. It had to support those who got excluded from benefits by drawing attention to their plight through agitational methods. It had to frame alternative plans for rehabilitation, based on the idea of the community taking up its own rehabilitation schemes, independent of government support. At the same time, it had to ask the government for more schemes. This had to go hand in hand with critiquing the establishment. The contradictions were overwhelming and had the potential to create major fissures in the movement. But the emergent survivor groups had learnt their lesson from the breakup of Morcha: they did not want mere disruptive politics. Most of the outstation activists had come and gone, some remained in touch from afar, but a handful stayed back to become absorbed at the grassroots level of the movement. The fact that they were not gas victims or belonged to the middle class did not matter any more. The trust they enjoyed was hard earned, and groups acquired formal structures that were separate and yet only notionally different, often coming together to make joint statements to the press on common issues that needed urgent attention. A lot of interaction was based on personal bonding and long associations.

Local Concerns versus Macrolevel Issues

It is necessary here to take a closer look at Pension, which is probably the group that is best defined by its local concerns. Is inception and work is summed up by those at its helm. Male leader: "Our organization was formed before 1984 to deal with the difficulties that the benefactors of the social security pension scheme, that is, the old, disabled, and widows faced. We chose this issue because there were labor unions, trade unions, women's organization, youth organization, employees' organization but the old had no organization to fight for their cause. Then the gas leaked and the whole city was in the grasp of the aftermath, so we decided to include the cause of the gas victims into our organizational agenda.

Now we work on both issues" (tape 28). Namdeo, who is at the helm of Pension, gives an account of how the organization works. Regular meetings are held twice a week for feedback on people's demands and needs. The steering committee personally visits three banks in a single day to solve individual problems related to pension. The attempt is to negotiate with authorities, and only when nothing works that direct action is resorted to. He admits to his strong roots in left ideology and belief in revolutionary measures, which over the years had to be modified to meet the individual needs of the old, sick, and illiterate women. Like Jabbar he claims that people's needs are at the heart of the matter and cannot be ignored. Pension's ideological position is clear—it will not sacrifice this need to bring in glamorous issues that are transported from foreign soils. Pension targets the state government, and its old and ailing women sit on dharna for months on end without any media attention. There is a sense of step-motherly treatment and not getting due appreciation for their work, which is shared by the leaders and other members of the group. But Pension is equally critical of government-sponsored organizations: "there are lots of organizations that are government aided, so they do not work at the grassroots level, but are merely formed to get government grants. Their focus is to show immediate results out of the money they get, so they only benefit small groups of people and not the masses. Employment can never be provided through NGOs, there has to be a policy change" (tape 28).

Right from the beginning we have seen how different kinds of voluntarism came up in Bhopal in response to the crisis situation. Given the nature of the chemical disaster the crisis situation never got entirely mitigated, so there were no steady solutions to the problem. The decades act as watershed to mark the changing face of the movement and how this change went on to shape the organizations. The changes were more tactical than ideological, and we need to bring in a historical perspective to get the complete picture. The first decade led to the settlement and the protest that followed. After the dismantling of Morcha, MUS and BGIA kept aside their differences and worked collaboratively on the basis of shared responsibility. MUS was the largest organization of gas victims, and since its inception had grown in strength by articulating the victim's demands through public protest and litigation. BGIA had played a big role in conceptualizing this combination of protest and litigation, making both the trademark of activism. The demand was for rehabilitation schemes that integrated medical, economic, and political concerns; the gender question was brought in to provide the link. Mobilization of women played a big part in strengthening the constituency and putting plans into action. Newspaper cuttings provide ample historical evidence of how organizations worked together to fulfill their goals.

In one of its pamphlets brought out in 1990, BGIA uses the voice of Mohini Devi, an active member of the steering committee of MUS, to explain what role was envisaged for survivor organizations: "We opposed the unholy settlement between Union Carbide and the government. On five separate occasions more than 5,000 women from the Sangathan have gone to Delhi and voiced our opposition to the settlement. We have also filed a petition in the Supreme Court challenging the validity of the settlement and now it is being heard. Earlier in August 1988 we had filed a petition seeking interim relief from the government. On March 13, 1990 the Supreme Court ordered the government to pay Rs 200 per person per month to all the residents of the thirty-six gas-affected wards of Bhopal for three years. This amount is being disbursed but there are a lot of problem in the manner in which it is being done." Here if anything else was glaring evidence of how difficult it was for activism to balance the demand for jobs, proper medical treatment, and processing of claims with the larger battle for legal redressal and bringing the offenders to book. A tug of war ensued between the demand for livelihood and compensation.

MUS was responsible for a lot of action that put pressure on the JD government to address the question of how gas victims were meant to survive in the interim years, before they obtained the final settlement. To that extent getting the Rs 200 per month reprieve was a major step in helping gas victims tide over difficult times, while the question of legal redressal was tackled in court. Many of the MUS women admitted to the fact that compensation as an issue had to be kept alive because it ensured greater participation from survivors. At the same time, a powerful voice from within MUS is able to put its historical role in perspective. Member (MUS): "I feel that we could relate to the everyday problems and hardships of victims. We touched these problems in a way that others could not. The others looked for ways to give issues political twists and attract national and international attention. There was so much attention to prosecuting the company that our demands for jobs, ration, and medicines got dwarfed and seemed incongruous. The canvas was vast and our demands seemed very small, but from 1986 to 2000 we kept to our demands and came out on top. In the public field, it is important to gain and maintain the trust of people" (tape 31). No doubt, survivor organizations had to work hard to gain people's confidence. Success was measured by the size of an organization and how the majority felt they had benefited from the intervention of the group. There was always the danger that survivor groups got entangled in populist measures that played into the hands of electoral politics.

Here is an example of how resistance can get coopted into government policies. The disbursal of the additional sum of Rs 1,500 crores that had accrued from the unpaid interest money was hailed by groups as a major victory. The government joined the chorus to show how it was a major step toward rehabilitation of the gas victims. The infamous settlement had started the trend of passing off a paltry monetary compensation as proper rehabilitation of people who had been victimized by the forces of development and progress. But did the gas survivor really benefit from the compensation packages? For instance, the court order for interim relief was meant to cater to the needs of 500,000 people. In 1990 the BJP was elected to form the government in MP, and they used their Hindu nationalism platform to bring in beneficiaries from their own constituencies. As a result, distribution of interim relief was plagued by corruption, which further divided communities. Such divisions put enormous pressure on people's groups, and increasingly there was difference of opinion on short-term populist moves and larger battles for justice.

At the same time, clash of opinions were kept alive as pressure tactics on the establishment. Collaborative action, community control, and innovative action were the trademarks of a movement that used its diversity to work out multiple levels of resistance. This is what Jabbar mentioned to the student team of *Closer to Reality*, when they went to meet him and put the question of differences in organizations: "I admit there have been differences, but we are not going to put our differences on display for the government to exploit. We all believe that our ultimate battle is for justice to be done in Bhopal. But justice takes a long time. Meanwhile people continue to die and suffer. Who is going to take care of that? We have divided our tasks and no division is without difference of opinion. If you want to write about our differences don't forget to mention this." Off camera there is a lot of backbiting and airing of bitterness and feeling of betrayal, but oral history offers a piquant insight into how alliances between groups changed irrevocably, without breaking up the movement.

The shift to macrolevel issues began in 1994 that proved to be a watershed year for Bhopal. The government had kept a decade as marker for winding up its tasks of rehabilitation in Bhopal. Meanwhile the political, economic, and sociocultural trends were undergoing changes with the firming of globalization. The impact of such changes on the livelihood issue was uneven. Larger questions arose about the possibility of a cleaner, less costly and more equitable development pattern. Bhopal dispelled many popular myths, namely that the poor cause environmental destruction. Clearly the rich pollute far more, given the vast quantities of nonbiodegradable waste produced daily. Economic growth is not an effective remedy for eliminating poverty, unless it takes into account renewable energy, water conservation, and prudent use of living systems. In most families that I visited in the bastis I saw how women played an important role as managers, providers, and distributors of food and other resources within the family. They were able to raise issues of sanitation, clean water supply, nutrition, indigenous knowledge of medicines based on alternative treatment and home remedies. I realized then that the divide between old and new Bhopal was really one of perception. In non-gas-affected areas, survivors are seen as roadblocks in the march toward development. Right from the beginning, all rehabilitation schemes were seen as impediments to economic growth. The fact that these people were given huge subsidies and preferential treatment in the sharing of limited resources caused a lot of resentment.[7] They were seen as crowding hospitals, living off charity in dirty slums, and making demands through agitational methods. Worse still they failed to offer the services that comes cheap in cities. Moreover, they were a constant reminder of what had gone wrong with the development plans. What was most galling about the survivors was their tenacity and rootedness to a place and cause, weighed down as they were by a sense of injustice and their blighted memories of a night of disaster. It was a direct clash of interest between the aspirations of people who enjoyed the fruits of progress and those who got left out.

Bhopal became a contentious political issue because it advocated the need to scale down the corporate driven consumer culture, instead of looking for remedies to raise the living standards of the poor. The focus was on equitable distribution, sustainability, and the need to rein in excess. Bhopal carried the notions a step further by adding the principle of restoration and remediation. It also asked for institutional and legal mechanisms for making such principles operative. What made the problem so acute for the Bhopal survivors was that the affluent were geographically and psychologically placed at a distance from the scenes of destruction. Activism in Bhopal has to be understood in the context of a demand being placed before the rest of Bhopal to respect the rights of marginalized people over the resources of the city.

Bhopal has been defined as a technological disaster but it was asking for more integrated solutions. There is general agreement that resources and living systems have to be shared to sustain the web of life. But where systemic failure has created havoc in the lives of people then mere damage control is not enough. Justice has to be done by bringing the guilty to book. Bhopal has proved beyond a shadow of doubt that systems of knowledge and technology are far from disinterested. The battleground has shifted to a global society where protracted power struggle has been unleashed in remote parts of the world. It is this historical shift in material terms and consciousness that activism had to take into account. The first decade had seen activism take care of microlevel issues. Post-nineties saw the interface of local/global issues that addressed a new generation with new concerns.

The year 2000 saw a new generation of survivors entering the political arena; they carried the body burden of chemicals that created new kind of morbidities and inherited deformities. Women and children were in focus, not only because breast milk that nourished life was contaminated, but also because parents were giving birth to children with congenital defects. Activism was in need of international solidarity and the impetus was for the kind of coalition that ICJB had been advocating. It was time for the campaign for justice in Bhopal to strengthen its visibility in global discourses. But before we understand how grassroots organizations were creating space to widen the scope of their demands, we need to take a closer look in the next chapter at the medical disaster that was unleashed on that fateful night.

CHAPTER 6

"No More Bhopals": Women's Right to Knowledge and Control of Their Bodies

> The chemicals to which life is being asked to make its adjustment are no longer merely the calcium and silica and copper and all the rest of the minerals washed out of the rocks and carried in rivers to the sea; they are the synthetic creations of man's inventive brain, brewed in his laboratories, and having no counterparts in nature. To adjust to these chemicals would require... not merely the years of a man's life but the life of generations. And even this, were it by some miracle possible, would be futile, for the new chemicals come from our laboratories in an endless stream.
> —Rachel Carson, *Silent Spring* (1962).

> Actions must be taken to protect public health even when science doesn't have all the answers to a particular issue. There is a need for strong action on the basis of less-than-definitive science, which also explicitly acknowledges gaps, uncertainties and disputes about the knowledge base.
> —*New Solutions* (Spring, 1994).

As the Bhopal disaster moved from the acute to the chronic phase, it brought to the forefront the tragic dimensions of a medical catastrophe that was linked not only to the accident, but also to the rehabilitation that followed. Like everything else connected to the disaster, the lack of information about the effect of chemicals on the body, severe deficiencies in health facilities, and the compounding problem of poverty led to a crisis situation that brought the state administration to a grinding halt. Overnight, a hapless medical community was called upon to deal with an emergency situation of an unprecedented kind. The unknown factors were overwhelming. For instance, what were the specific antidotes to the poison gas? Methyl isocyanate (MIC) was the major toxin, but what possibilities of impurities (phosgene) or decomposition products (hydrogen cyanide, nitrogen oxides, carbon monoxide) being present in the gas cloud?[1] More than 25,000 people streamed into Hamidia Hospital on that night, but there was no definitive protocol for treatment of chemical poisoning. Patients were given symptomatic treatment; for atropinization of the eye local antibiotics and padding was used; respiratory problems were treated with bronchodilators, steroids, diuretics, antibiotics, and oxygen administrations. Most importantly, in the days to come, no system was put in place for profiling individual cases of exposure, by taking into consideration the variable factors such as age, gender, activity that night, and duration of exposure to the gas. In the wake of the chaos a lot of paper work was left incomplete. The rumblings of the crisis was felt most acutely in the corridors of the Indian Council for Medical Research (ICMR), the apex Indian institute for conducting medical research and studies. Within weeks of the disaster, a research study was undertaken, with 1,000 identified cases to probe into the possible clinical and hematological effects of gas exposure. Twenty-four research projects were started with practically no available data. Research had to be investigative in nature, while taking care of the clinical side, since so many people needed urgent treatment. The findings were based on hundreds of autopsies and clinical reporting done in laboratory conditions that could hardly be described as ideal. Statistics failed to reflect ground reality, and the limitations of any research methodology devised in those circumstances were to become glaringly evident in the years to come.[2]

But the problem was not merely that of crisis management. When we are looking at an industrial disaster, then the process of hazard management gets closely linked to prevention and control measures. The chronic effects of active exposure to chemical poisoning are virtually impossible to prove, except as specific events involving accidental exposure. This is precisely what the medical fraternity tried to establish in Bhopal. A lot of effort went into identifying specific organs that were damaged by MIC. Though MIC was not a new chemical, there was little available information on its toxicology. Quite obviously the company was confidant that MIC, an intermediate product used in a closed-production process, was not likely to cause human exposure on a mass scale. Therefore, there was no available literature on its effect on health and the necessary treatment. In fact, the company doctor went on record to inform hospitals that MIC was harmless and acted like tear gas. Patients were advised to splash water on the eyes and face. Grappling with a crisis situation, doctors in the government hospitals went along with Carbide's claim that the effects of MIC was temporary and would soon pass.

The little information that was available on the toxicological properties of MIC stated that the gas was an irritant to the skin, eyes, and mucous membranes of the respiratory tract. Its reactivity to water could make it penetrate tissues, and absorption through skin was known to occur. Symptom prevalence surveys were conducted by ICMR, and it was observed that people were experiencing acute respiratory, ocular and gastro intestinal distress. Typical symptoms of respiratory toxicity were intense bouts of coughing, accompanied by frothy expectorant, a feeling of suffocation, chest pain, and breathlessness. The effect of MIC on the cornea resulted in severe ocular burning, watering, pain, and photophobia. So lungs and eyes were identified as primary organs affected by exposure to gas. There was prevalence of widespread morbidity with 26 percent given symptoms in severely affected areas as compared to 18 percent in control areas.[3]

In the following days and weeks, government put in place a mammoth medical rehabilitation that was geared toward proving the doctors and the industry right. Even as massive relief operations to remove dead bodies and carcasses of animals were underway, more than 100 medical relief clinics were opened in the premises of Hamidia Hospital, in tents and on the pavements.[4] Junior doctors, mostly interns and residents, ran the camps. They only followed instructions given to them; cortico steroids and antibiotics were freely prescribed to reduce inflammatory conditions and to prevent secondary infections. Strangely enough the doctors did not see the medico-legal importance of maintaining records. So in a sense the immediate post-gas morbidity pattern remained unknown, even as subjective assessment of the situation prevailed. The moratorium that was placed on the medical community to keep findings under wraps did not help the situation. A lot of uncertain data was generated without anyone coming out in the open to take the onus for it. What is even more startling is that there was no effort to create a rational discourse that connected pathological and clinical findings to symptomatic observations. The grim reality emerges only now, after two decades, when doctors are publishing scientific articles based on their early research. Here is a case in point. In an article published in 2004 we are told that the autopsies done on 300 victims revealed severe necrotizing lesions in the lining of the upper respiratory tracts as well as in the bronchioles, alveoli, and lung capillaries. Enlarged lungs, bronchopneumonia, and acute bronchiolitis were also seen.[5] This data must have been recorded somewhere, then why was the disjunction between research and treatment protocol so glaring? As a result in the days/months/years following the disaster, victims continued to die and suffer grievously from acute aftereffects of gas poisoning, simply because of the sheer lack of proper and timely medical treatment. This was one part of the horrific medical crime in Bhopal; the other part was even more insidious.

The government colluded with the company to underplay the long-term effect of MIC. It went along with the claim by Union Carbide Corporation (UCC) that MIC is not hazardous for any prolonged period. Thus, *JAMA*, a medical journal of great repute, quotes James Melius, the Chief of National Institute for Occupational Health, Cincinnati as saying: "MIC gas breaks down rapidly in the presence of water, becoming a relatively non-toxic substance known as dimethyl urea" (April 12, 1985). The attempt was to exclude the possibility of unknown effects, arising not just from MIC but contaminated ingredients, and to deny a mixed pathology instead of the pulmonary theory. The problem with a specific organ theory was that it never tallied with the range of symptoms that were being reported in community-based surveys. Although it was possible to initially blame the emergency situation, things did not improve in the days to come, and the medical community soon found itself mired in one controversy or the other.

The Nature of Gender Discrimination

A major concern after the gas leak was the effect of toxic gases on the fetuses affected by the gas in utero. But in a blatant display of sexism in medical science the reproductive effects of exposure was neglected. The constant underplaying of the effect of the gas on women's body throws light on the nature of the gender politics that was played out in medical science. We are already staring into the future of slow Bhopals happening across the globe. Miriam Jacobs and Barbara Dinham in their edited book *Silent Invaders: Pesticides, Livelihoods and Women's Health* (2004) draw attention to the hazards of living in a chemically ridden world. L. Wayne Dwemychuk, article "Chronic Exposure to Agent Orange in the Aluoi Valley, Vietnam" gives the example of another environmental degradation reported in the Aluoi Valley in Vietnam, where 72 million liters of herbicides were used during the war to deprive the forces of protective forest cover and food. In 1999, analysis of blood samples and human breast milk showed high levels of dioxin. Villages in the area also recorded increased levels of birth defects (150). The fact that the perpetrator of the Agent Orange crime was the infamous Dow Chemicals goes on to strengthen the link between industrial hazard and warfare and the systematic assault on the human body. Clearly, the medical disaster in Bhopal had to be seen in the larger context of the modern malaise of chemical hazards.

Barbara Dinham, in her introduction, talks at length about chronic effects of pesticide poisoning, which were tested in laboratories for carcinogenic effects before being placed in the market (Ibid. 12). She argues that such cases become politically tenuous with the markets putting indirect and invisible pressure. As a result, the corporate sector refused to acknowledge potential health effects. It is in the face of this sort of manipulation and market strategy that there was an increasing need to draw attention to gender-differentiated impacts, such as elevated risks of spontaneous abortions, reproductive problems, birth defects, and the potential gender-related effects of hormone disrupting chemicals. The precautionary approach had to be prioritized, so as to draw attention to the health and environmental consequences of exposure to toxic substances for vulnerable groups like women, children, and the aged. In the case of chemical poisoning, knowing the precise health impact was no longer seen as a precondition for prevention and control measures. Epidemiological research, which has in its purview the use of data gathering tools that are close to oral history methodology, worked toward linking health effects with exposure data; this in turn could be used as a powerful tool to put pressure on authorities. Qualitative methods for evaluating exposure were considered important. Talking to people who were exposed to chemicals and getting their experience on record had become a way of gathering local evidence. It was also an important methodology for understanding chemical hazards.

Rachel Carson's *Silent Spring* sent a warning that man-made chemicals were taking a deadly toll on birds and wildlife. In *The Stolen Future*, a book that the authors described as a scientific detective story, Carson's thesis was carried forward to show how synthetic chemicals that mimic natural hormones or "hormone imposters" were invisibly undermining the human future.[6] As an industrial disaster Bhopal might be one of a kind, but twenty-five years later it had no doubt, become an extension of the kind of slow poisoning that was a result of environmental contamination and the chemical body burden, which was affecting the future generation. Environmental agents are known to act as human teratogens. Experimental studies with animals have shown the mutagenic and genotoxic effects of commonly used organophosphates. The findings suggest risks for human beings, but definite evidence needs to be gathered from epidemiological research of exposed people. The use of pesticides in agriculture normally talks of high risks to those who come under general occupational categories like agricultural workers, farmers, and applicators. Environmental teratogenesis and maternal exposure are usually neglected. Risk assessment remains a vital part of toxicology, but scant attention is paid to gender issues, and their social and political ramifications. A lot of available scientific data is biased, contradictory, and inconclusive simply because it is promoted by the industry that makes and sells the product. Policy makers and regulators have also failed to protect the public from potential hazards by promoting stereotypes about use of chemicals.

The Bhopal disaster brought to the forefront a medical scandal that was direct fallout of the refusal by industry-supported scientists and professionals to acknowledge the link between human health problems and chemical contamination. By denying the brutal fact that MIC had entered the blood stream, which could result in immune deficiencies, chromosomal aberrations, and the possibility of birth defects in the second generation, the government entered into a massive collusion with the corporation. Right from the start, medical science in the case of Bhopal was riddled with subjectivity and speculations, thereby reducing the entire question of knowledge and control of the body into a gray area that nobody wanted to probe. The body became the contested site and maximum violence was directed toward it by the denial of proper treatment. Another kind of violence was unleashed when the ICMR research projects were abruptly terminated in 1994, before definitive conclusions based on proper findings could be reached. This chapter picks up its cue from what I feel is the central thesis of my book—failure of medical research in Bhopal became grounds for the failure of justice.

It also prepared grounds for the crucial phase in activism in which women played a major role. Bhopal brought home the lesson that in the absence of scientific certainty, the precautionary principle had to be developed as a decision-making tool, which in turn brought in gender-sensitive considerations. Only then could market ethos give way to an alternative vision that promoted a more sustainable, health conscious approach to survival in a chemical ridden, modern society. In turn, the development model could take cognizance of threats posed by the possibilities of more Bhopals happening in our backyard. More than anything else there was a felt need for right to information. It was the growing awareness of the right to know and control the body that shaped women's activism and spearheaded their struggle for justice. Most of the women I spoke to displayed a sharp, pragmatic sense of the need to catapult Bhopal into the future to keep the issues alive. They readily agreed that Bhopal had to share a common platform with other powerful, worldwide movements on environment and human rights. At the same time, they had a fierce sense of their grassroots concerns and loyalties.

In this chapter we see how the women survivors of Bhopal were able to carve a unique position for themselves within the local/global dynamics of such movements. This was primarily because their vision linked livelihood with health care, and their primary demand was for a toxin free environment where they could bring up the next generation without fear of sickness and death. It became the clarion call for the battle to fight hazards posed by powerful chemical industries in the third world countries. As we listen to women give shape to their alternate vision of the future, we realize that much of the underlying strength of such a vision is drawn from the real experience of living in poverty and sickness. Importantly, oral history offered tools for forging a vital link between the ideological framework and its practice.

Evoking Collective Guilt and Stereotypes

I visited Bhopal in July 2003 to interview doctors who had been part of the original investigating teams and could look back at the direction of events. They spoke bitterly about red tape, administrative and political interference, and the experience of working in hostile and difficult circumstances. They blamed the central government, the state government, the health ministry, and the parent body ICMR for unilateral decisions, secrecy, banning publication of vital data that could have nailed the offending multinational. Many of them expressed a "collective guilt" at having been part of a system that went wrong, so that a statement like, "My tongue is crusted with lies," sounded touchingly personal and representative. The doctors raised many unanswered questions addressed to the establishment they had worked for. All of them wanted to know what ICMR had done with the years of research, after the data was summarily taken away from Bhopal.

Once I was back in Delhi I visited ICMR, and met the man who heads the ICMR Bhopal cell at The Institute for Pathology, Safdarjung Hospital campus. Dr. Sriramachari, who was additional director general of ICMR at the time of the disaster, had been entrusted with the task of bringing out—in his capacity as editor-in-chief—the three-volume consolidated report on medical research done on the Bhopal gas tragedy. It was divided into "An Epidemiological Report," "A Toxicological Report," and "A Clinical Report." The first volume *A Technical Report on Population based Long Term Epidemiological Studies* came out in 2004, just before the twentieth anniversary of the disaster. According to Dr. Sriramachari, questions were being raised in parliament and the constant pressure was on ICMR to bring the report before the public. The clinical report was released almost four years later and the final toxicological report is still pending. Sriramachari does not mince words when he tells me that medical science failed to tie-up loose ends in determining the effect of MIC on the body. But he is equally convinced that under the circumstances he and his colleagues tried their level best to do what could best serve the victims. "There was considerable scope for doing pathbreaking research," he tells me, "but the extenuating circumstances came in the way." As he shared his experience of "the nightmarish days" he provided an interesting insight into what those circumstances were and why things had gone wrong.

In the following section I juxtapose three different approaches to the problem of medical rehabilitation in Bhopal. The documentation center in the Sambhavna Clinic provided me with a plethora of written texts, which included research projects undertaken by nongovernmental organizations (NGOs), scrupulously maintained newspaper cuttings, and letters to and fro between survivor groups and the health department of Ministry of Bhopal Gas Relief and Rehabilitation as well as official records that have been procured through the sustained use of Right to Information (RTI) as tool of activism. I also draw on oral testimonials, interjections, and perceptions of "what happened and why" that are both speculative and interpretative. This helps me "view" the impact of the disaster under the microscope so to speak, and also from the perspective of those who were working at the ground level. Last but not the least I bring in the oral testimonials of people who were at the receiving end of systems, in order to get the "whole" picture. In management parlance, getting the stakeholders into the loop enables you to get a fairly typical picture of an event, which helps in arriving at neat and conclusive definitions. But right from the start Bhopal kept on eluding definitions. Listening to testimonials one begins to understand the thin line that distinguishes scientific facts from popular opinions, and the problematic categories of "true" versus "false," which is one of the demons that plagues oral history methodology. In this chapter I tackle the problem and try to arrive at possible explanations. As I listened to doctors who were in charge of the medical scene in Bhopal from the night of December 3, I was left wondering why truth was so elusive in their case.

Dr. N. P. Misra was Dean of Hamidia Hospital in 1984, and in his own words took immediate charge of the crisis situation, "The first problem was that of numbers. My team treated 170,000 patients in one day. The second problem was lack of information. UCC informed us that the gas was not toxic. They insisted that most of the casualties were result of panic created by people running and inhaling gas. I tried to organize bulk supplies of medicines. I rang up colleagues and civil surgeon friends in neighboring towns like Sehore, Raisen, Hosangabad, and Vidisha and asked them to send supply of medicines and necessary staff like nurses and ward boys. I called up local chemists and asked them to pool in their stocks. Payment, I assured, would be made later. Subsequently I was accused of taking steps without prior government permission. I feel this attitude was unfortunate. 17,900 patients were admitted and treated in an 850-bed hospital. Tell me honestly, can the role of doctors be underplayed in the Bhopal gas tragedy?"

But Misra is far more guarded when I ask him about the kind of research that was set in motion by ICMR, "I am afraid research had to take a backseat because we were too busy managing patients in the initial days of the tragedy. ICMR stepped in five days later. The then DG told me that money is not a constraint. In all fairness ICMR cooperated with us at various stages. I felt that investigations should be of international standard so I used my personal contact to send coded samples to Germany, United States, Canada, UK and ICMR never refused permission. But as head of Gandhi Medical College I had constraints. There was always restraint on publishing data in journals. In 1986 the American College of Chest Diseases invited me to address their annual conference in New Orleans, but the government refused. I was called at the Conference of International Labor Organization (ILO) at Pittsburgh but my presentation had to be vetted by ICMR. I was asked not to meet the media or talk to anyone." Clearly Misra felt miffed by circumstances that prevented excellent data from being published. He spoke at length about conflict of interest in the corridors of power. It was interesting to see how highly personalized infighting was touted as the cause for research being stopped. "Dr. Ramalingaswamy, the DG of ICMR was very enthusiastic. 'I am giving you a drop in the ocean,' he told me, 'you can make the ocean.' After he retired others who took over were jealous. We tried to be as innovative as possible. In the Institute of Industrial Research in Ahmedabad an inhalation chamber was set up where monkeys were exposed to MIC, and experimental research work was done. I was aghast to read in the newspaper that some ICMR bigwig said that the work done was sketchy. Such a statement merits an apology. When I recently met the present DG at a conference I told him, 'Newspapers have reported that people connected with the projects are all dead. But I am alive and willing to help.' But he was not forthcoming. You have to understand, there were four groups operating in Bhopal, politicians, bureaucrats, administrators connected with the department of health and the community of scientists. The first three groups were powerful and wanted to suppress us. After the projects were terminated a person came to take away all the data. We gave back everything. It should go on record that excellent, dedicated work was wasted."

Dr. Misra continues to treat gas victims today in his own clinic, but he adds, "Do not be taken in by the huge rush in the gas relief hospitals. There is no way of knowing the true from the false cases. You see each one of them is given a card that entitles them to free treatment. So families flock to the hospitals and hordes of relatives jump into the bandwagon." This opinion was echoed by most of the doctors I met. Dr. H. H. Trivedi, who also runs a private clinic that treats gas victims, puts much greater emphasis on the larger social problem that ensued after the gas leak. "Till we take cognizance of this we will continue to see the suffering of the gas victims as humbug. I am not too sure the ICMR research addressed these social issues. The scientific findings were being given to judicial officers so that the court could come to a rational judgment for determining the category and extent of suffering." When I ask him to elaborate on this he tells me categorically that matters of compensation does not concern him as a doctor. "The problem as I see and understand is that research did not help in treatment. This was the biggest failure. At that time we had no options, but years later we still continue to give symptomatic treatment because by now the lungs have got permanently damaged with fibrosis and cannot be rectified." He agrees that UCC should have known of the antidote. "I am sure about one thing that any knowledge from any part of the world would have been useful to save human lives." Talking to many of the other doctors I realized that the real problem was that of stereotyping medical science as being value neutral.

The Bureaucratic Approach

Soon after the disaster the government created a propaganda machine that highlighted plans that were futuristic and based on the development model for national growth. In this section I have tried to put together information from various texts, both oral and written that was being circulated in the public domain, to show how numbers were used to play a semantic trick to give the sense of how much was being done for the rehabilitation of the gas survivors. Year after year the Madhya Pradesh (MP) government came out with a yearly report that was commemorative in nature and was circulated widely as propaganda material. Thus we are told that existing hospitals had been expanded to make space for gas victims; beds were added, more doctors and attendant staff were employed, medical equipments and supply of medicines were increased, and a special budget that kept on multiplying was set aside for treatment of those affected by the gas. Soon after the disaster a fully equipped 60-bed MIC ward was established in Hamidia hospital. The fact that it continues to be operational even today speaks more than any statistics. The idea of coming out with facts and figures was clearly meant to show that a bureaucratic structure with a budget allocation of Rs 7,702,980 (1986–1987) had been put in place. Here again the information was structured in a manner to create an ideal situation. A central MIC cell in the office of the Chief Medical and Health Officer (Gas Relief) became operational with a doctor who was in charge of documenting all the treatment that was being provided in different gas relief hospitals. The ICMR had also established a Bhopal Gas Disaster Research Center (BGDRC) for long-term research to be carried out in the future. Reality was starkly different. Given the magnitude of the disaster, changes had to be brought in overnight and old systems had to be modified to make place for the new. As a result, the bureaucratic structure was groaning under enormous pressure. Sadly, there is nothing in the available literature to indicate how many projects had become nonfunctional or were closed down. The real urgency of the situation was kept out of sight, so that oral history was the only tool to uncover such statistics. It was here that survivor groups, often inspired by the mass participation of women, came to play a big role. Unfortunately, much of this information has not really found its way into academic discourse. Thus in an important sense, oral history can bridge the gap between specialized knowledge and material collection that is geared toward activism.

The government propaganda machine took care to give out information in little packages so as to "contain the crisis situation" (in bureaucratic parlance) and keep the media at bay. Meanwhile survivor groups started making their contacts through doctor friends in government offices. The Bhopal Group of Information and Action (BGIA) newsletters gave the inside story. Thus we know that a new disease complex was identified and the term "Bhopal Toxic Gas Disease" or BTGD was coined. The key phrases were "comprehensive health care system" and "constant medical surveillance." The government surveys, which were concerned with gathering epidemiological data, played the vital but limiting role of looking at the sociomedical aspects of the disaster. It was used for mapping Bhopal into the fifty-six wards obtained from the Municipal Corporation, out of which thirty-six wards were gas-affected, while twenty wards were unaffected. This in turn was the basis for demarcating areas as severely, moderately, and mildly exposed. There were thirty-two identified symptoms. It is interesting to note that these registered cohorts served as database for drawing subset, which could provide the samples for other clinico-epidemiological studies. The baseline had been created for massive research to be carried out on a war footing. What really went wrong?

Perhaps the most problematic area in the management of patients was the clinical aspect of BTGD. Doctors uniformly agreed that they had to carry on with standard clinical practice as per the advice of the working manuals brought out in 1989. As one of the doctors said off the record in his interview, the use of these manuals was made restrictive, and mostly they never reached on time or were unavailable. Clearly the system could not take the pressure of sheer numbers, which as reported in newspapers was above three to four thousand outpatients daily. The follow-up for radiological investigations was equally difficult, given the fact that not many laboratories were available or operative. At one level, the advice for standard clinical practice was knee-jerk reaction to the crisis situation. At a more insidious level, the government was trying its level best to underplay the magnitude of the disaster. Why the government never got out of the crisis mode begs many more questions, especially that of lack of political will.

A crucial area in health care was mental health but here again a manual, which was meant to develop appropriate care programme for different forms of mental distress, was not brought out till 1987. It remained the only publication till 1994, despite the fact that doctors have admitted in interviews that the fallout of mental trauma had taken on epidemic proportions and refused to disappear with the passage of time. In 2002 Srinivasa R. Murthy brought out a report on the *Mental Health Impact of the Bhopal Gas Disaster* as part of Fact Finding Mission set up by the Other Media, New Delhi. BGIA and Medico Friend Circle (MFC) Newsletters provide a disturbing insight to the situation. They point to the lacunae between research and service needs that were identified as short term and long term. Short-term perspectives that looked at reactive psychosis, anxiety depression reactions and grief reactions, were not distanced from long-term perspectives that looked at psychological reactions to chronic disabilities. There was an urgent need to bring out publications on long-term morbidity that was not carried through by the ICMR.

The 1987 supplement on *Scientific Studies on Bhopal Part A* was perhaps the only published document that entered the public domain and catered to a wider, general readership. It covered different aspects of morbidity. But here again, like most research done in academic institutions, the publications were meant for niche audience and restricted readership. Therefore the needs of a crisis situation were not addressed. Though the research done (article were received between August and November 1985) clearly indicated that follow-up studies were necessary, no *Part B* was published. In some vital areas such as lung function studies there were indications that separate reports would soon be submitted. In new areas of immunological, mutagenic, and genotoxic studies, it was clearly stated that analysis was still underway and studies would be repeated after six months to one year. But any findings from further analysis went unreported. It is interesting to observe that a purely academic matter carried serious political implications. It would be worthwhile to take as example an area of research that was more urgent than others; in this case it would be lung function research.[7] To get immediate result, samples had to be drawn from outpatient and inpatient sections of Hamidia Hospital. Severe constraints prevented the hospital staff from using larger samples drawn from a wider population, despite the scale and immensity of the disaster. Observations had to be made in a limited way through symptoms that were most apparent such as severe cough, expectoration, and breathlessness. The absence of data on the preexposure lung function status was compounded by the unavailability of more detailed tests that could explain why symptoms were often found to be grossly out of proportion to the degree of lung function impairment. A greater time-gap had to be given to establish the ultimate fate of lesions. So long-term follow up alone could have determined the evolution of the "lung disease" caused by the gas. But it was precisely the "evolution" of a new disease complex caused by exposure that research in Bhopal wanted to deny. Therefore, what began as constraints of research conditions in the acute phase continued to remain so with the passage of time, and no one addressed the real problem at hand.

Here again it is interesting to note how BGIA was able to fulfill its role of vigilance. A sustained effort was made to bring on board specialists from different fields, particularly doctors from different parts of India and abroad, to do in-depth analysis of the medical scenario.[8] A quick look at what was happening at the level of bureaucratic crisis management offers an interesting picture of the political dynamics of the situation. The Bhopal Gas Disaster Research Center (BGDRC) was set up in Bhopal in August 1986, under the directorship of the late Dr. M. P. Dwivedi. It was to act as a local coordinating unit between the state government and the center and other scientific institutions across the country. The idea was to use the services of scientists and experts from different fields. Different Project Coordination Committees were put in place, monthly meetings were held, and Principal Investigators were asked to review targets, and to discuss problems, if any. Out of the eighteen ongoing projects nine were completed. Many were pilot projects or had very short-term specifications. Doctors who were on such committees, have on promise of anonymity said that on paper future planning of studies was clearly underlined. The two areas of study that were marked as important were toxicological studies and cytogenetic studies on chromosomal aberration, with reference to women who were pregnant at the time of the gas leak so that chromosomal abnormalities could be correlated to subsequent pregnancies. The Project Advisory Committee (PAC) was entrusted with the task of giving suitable recommendations for continuing or modifying studies. In most cases the advice was to design a suitable protocol or to present a comprehensive report. And whenever a particular aspect of research was completed, the advice was to transfer the assets to another project where these may be utilized. The PAC did not envisage winding up of projects.

In 1988 five new projects were recommended and passed by the PAC. They included a study on organic brain damage in adults, on the mental and intellectual development of children, on the involvement of the nervous system, a preliminary study on fertility, and finally a research project for observing the thiocyanate levels in aqueous humor in the toxic-exposed population. But doctors express cynicism when they say that ICMR had begun to distance itself from the BGDRC by allowing the latter to take up sole responsibility of one major project on *Long-term epidemiological studies on the health effects of toxic gas exposure through Community Health Clinic*. In a sense the epidemiological study was to act as a broad umbrella cover to bring in and restrict various sensitive areas of research. The doctors admit that they failed to make many of these connections at that time, and it is only with hindsight that they realize how the attempt was to keep important findings under wrap. Some of them were willing to come on record to speak about the situation.

Further Testimonials from Doctors

I met Dr. Nalok Banerjee, officer-in-charge of the Center for Rehabilitation Studies (CRS), Bhopal, which is a separate cell of the Gas Relief Department and was instituted in 1989 for all administrative purposes. At present its sole activity is to carry on with the Epidemiological Research Project that remains the only surviving scientific project. Its broad-based nature enables it to include assessment and management of chronic patients and a few sprinkling of ophthalmic, immunological, and cytogenetic studies. Again the study of woman's health is conspicuously missing. The only other project that is continuing to date is the cancer registry at Gandhi Medical College. Banerjee briefs me on the history of BGDRC. He says it was an extramural Research Center of ICMR and under its aegis specialized laboratories were set up in different departments of Gandhi Medical College. Thus an immunological laboratory was set up in the department of pathology, a genetic laboratory in the department of anatomy, a toxicological laboratory in the medico-legal institute, and sophisticated PFT laboratory was developed in the department of medicine and pediatric. In 1994 the ICMR expressed its inability to continue with research in Bhopal and instructed the MP government to do so under BGDRC. A fund of Rs 5 crores was earmarked for research activities in Bhopal and the accrued interest was to help in continuing with the projects. A formal handover of all the staff of BGDRC and the existing infrastructure to the state government was completed on April 27, 1995.

When I asked doctors in Bhopal why ICMR closed down research, and whether the reasons were scientific or political, the reactions ranged from cynical to skeptical to bemused, while some professed total ignorance of the cause. Dr. N. R. Bhandari, who was then the medical superintendent at Hamidia Hospital, felt that scientific research was mired by the constraints of a policy decision on the part of ICMR to stop publication of any data. "We were told not to talk about findings, or give any lectures on the scientific aspects in seminars and other forums. I was invited by US doctors for a series of six lectures in various universities, hospitals, and naval center for which they sent me air tickets. I was refused permission by the then health secretary. CM Mr. Motilal Vora overruled and gave permission. The secretary contacted Ministry of Chemicals and got a nod to cancel the trip. The scientific world from other countries wanted firsthand information about the toxic effects of the gas, but a bureaucrat was deciding everything. It was a colossal waste of data and money, and scientific material which was unparalleled was never published." The then director of the Gas Relief Department, a bureaucrat, professes total ignorance of why systems became nonfunctional, "I am not a medical man and I do not have a clear understanding of the medical aspects of research. All I can say is that it was a unilateral decision on the part of ICMR to close down research. The CRS continues with surveys in certain areas only to accommodate those who were originally employed. Our attempts to contact ICMR about publishing the research findings are met with no response."

When I ask Banerjee what kind of research was being done by the CRS he responds cynically, "The projects were terminated and not 'handed over' to the state government as ICMR would like to claim. Why didn't ICMR handover research to a medical college? The labs that were set up in CRS are no longer operative because of lack of manpower. I have been made officer-in-charge, which gives me neither administrative nor financial rights. Since 1994 we did not get any financial or technical help from ICMR. So whatever research we have undertaken is against all odds. Recently, as per instructions of the government of India (GOI), ICMR has come forward to carry out clinical research to understand the causative factors behind high morbidity pattern observed in long-term epidemiological study, which has been continuously carried out by our center."

As early as 1990, ICMR was winding up at its own end. Thus a proposal was mooted to give BGDRC a permanent status, but somewhere along the line such a move got scuttled. The long-term epidemiological study was to continue up to 1994, with a decade being used as watershed in a way that was arbitrary and quite unscientific. To handle the huge amount of information that had been gathered a Data Base Information System was set up in Gandhi Medical College, and it was handed over to the BGDRC in 1988. The idea was to enhance the proper management and time bound analysis of data. In 1990, 290 MB of data on various clinical and demographic characteristics of toxic gas victims and control population was available. Banerjee laments that the projects were closed down abruptly "before conclusive findings could be arrived at. The only findings—and they were half-baked—were put in the annual reports of the BGDRC. ICMR has now decided to carry out genetic study. According to me medical research should continue till the morbidity pattern comes to normal level or is comparable to control population."

Dr. Prashant Pathak, who was part of a team that was looking at the prepubertal and postpubertal growth assessment of children exposed to toxic gas in utero and having delay in language sector of growth, spoke with a deep sense of anguish. "In our case the PAC was meeting to consider a proposal to extend our project by five years. Imagine the irony, even as the meeting was underway the DG directs for termination of studies! It seems the PAC members were kept in the dark! What was the reason for termination? We were looking at children born between December 1984 and September 1985, so an average child then was five years of age. We needed to study them till they were fourteen/fifteen. We lost contact with the children and the families. It was painful. There was no plausible reason for termination that we, the members of the scientific community, were aware of. Several questions had been raised on cancer, immunology, genetics but none of the queries were answered properly. Perhaps the reason for termination was not scientific at all but administrative."

It was in 1990 that listings of specific persons linked morbidity were handed over to agencies like Department of Gas Relief and Rehabilitation, MP and Directorate of Claims, Bhopal. For many of the doctors to whom I spoke it was the linking between medical science and compensation that was the root problem. Dr. Rachna Pandey was a postgraduate student at the time of the disaster. She worked with the investigating team in a junior position, and after the termination of the project she got a part-time job at the claims office. "I know what a racket it was. Soon after the termination we went to the Health Secretary, Mr. V.G. Nigam and told him so much equipment was lying around, research should continue. His reply was, 'MP is a poor state. It cannot afford research.' All energy went into compensation claims. We worked part time on a contract basis for three months and were paid Rs 25 per file. We had to complete twenty-five files per day. This was not research of any kind, set guidelines were laid down and there was no documentation, no keeping of records. The files were meant to be used in court and I remember many false claims." When I ask her to comment on whether failure of research was also failure of justice, she does not answer. "If the projects had continued path breaking facts would have emerged. But now all one can have are speculations and postulations, which are only figures. Real and fake facts have got so mixed up that no retrieval of original data is possible. At best we can have piecemeal data that can be put together as part of a jigsaw puzzle, but we cannot get the real picture." Many others echoed the idea that research on

Bhopal is no longer possible. Such an opinion also came from a rather surprising quarter.

As mentioned earlier, The Bhopal Memorial Hospital and Research Center (BMHRC), a 350-bed hospital was built after the Supreme Court passed an order to sell the confiscated company shares and invest the money in a gas relief hospital. It is a sprawling, building set in a lush landscape. The administration is run by a board of trustees, none of whom have any involvement with medical care of survivors. It has modern systems, including a "smart card" that keeps the OPD records of a gas patient, and it can only be assessed by the computer system of the hospital. The gas victims are treated free but general patients must pay. It is essentially a referral hospital, and eight outreach clinics have been set up in the bastis to deal with the crowd. I met the then director of the organization. According to him, 5 crores were allotted for the research wing of the hospital and some areas like psychosocial and cardiovascular were narrowed down for study, but research in the sense of testing out a hypothesis, was never possible in Bhopal. It was largely documentation of damage that was done, not scientific research in the strict sense of the term. When doctors came to Bhopal to be part of the ICMR project, it was just a posting, and they were following government dicta. Some might have got involved but most worked routinely. He admitted to the fact that ICMR has asked him to come to Delhi and check out the pile of data, but he had no real interest in the Bhopal issue.

Future Research in Bhopal

I put the question of future research to Sriramachari. He admits there is a crying need: "There has to be a reappraisal of the Bhopal disaster. All findings must reach their logical conclusion. The lessons of Bhopal have to be learnt." Is the epidemiological survey sufficient? He is reluctant to answer. "I am trying hard to bring out the reports, but there are barriers that I have to face. I am an old man now and after me no one will be interested. But the truth ought to come out. There should be a permanent National Research Institute in Bhopal. The MP government should take it up." I point out to him that my research has shown that as early as 1988 there was talk about the need for setting up a Chemical Disaster Research Institute as part of the eighth Five Year Plan. Why was such an idea discarded? He does not answer my question directly. After 1994, he tells me, the ban on publications was lifted. Sriramachari was able to present his papers in several forums and had written copiously on the subject. I discover that he has a fairly clear idea of the role that ICMR can still play. "It may be necessary to set up a team to undertake accurate onsite data collections and environmental and biomonitoring in environments at risk. ICMR should set up an appropriate 'think tank' to search and scout promising and emerging areas of research at the global level. The leads generated by ICMR's own research efforts in Bhopal need to be pursued, especially the implications of possible S-carbamoylation vis-à-vis disturbances of cyanide metabolism." He waits patiently for me to note down the technical details. He lends me a copy of a paper on "Bhopal Gas Tragedy: An Environmental Disaster," which he presented at the Fourth Sir Dorabji Tata Symposium on Acute Respiratory Disease held in March 2003 at the Indian Institute of Science, Bangalore. It contains in a nutshell the pathological findings based on the autopsies that he and Dr. Heeresh Chandra conducted soon after the disaster and the basic findings of the toxicological studies that were done. "It is the closest we came to finding out what happens when MIC comes in contact with the human body. Unfortunately there were gaps we could not answer for." When I ask him why the toxicological studies were not published by ICMR, despite the fact that I had read a succinct account of it in an anonymous paper called "Health Effects of the Bhopal Gas Tragedy" (April 1986), he is noncommittal. "That paper was prepared by me and Dr. P.K. Ramachandran for advising American lawyers defending the Indian case. It was finally brought out for internal circulation without our names because others wanted to take credit for it. When you have worked in Bhopal you have seen the worst side of human nature, vanity, corruption, negligence, apathy. The scientific community was ridden with jealousy and ego battles. How can you establish scientific facts in the face of this?"

Sriramachari did offer to explain some of the scientific facts. According to him, the pathological changes that take place in fatal cases of chemical exposure were not well known or described in "forensic" pathology in 1984. While it was immediately known that MIC was the main chemical involved, serious questions arose regarding the nature of the chemical compounds involved. "Forensic" observations of leftover residue of approximately 12 tons in tank 610 indicated the possible role of breakdown products of MIC such as HCN, CO, reactants such as methylamine, dimethyl urea, and a series of polymerized compounds. Sriramachari provided graphic details on how 311 bodies were brought in on December 3, 1984, 250 on December 4, and 60 each on December 5 and 6. Approximately 50 percent of the bodies were subjected to complete autopsy. The histopathological findings showed cherry-colored discoloration of the lungs, the target organ. Bodies brought in after one to four months showed extensive pulmonary edema and after one year it showed fibrosing alveolitis. In his own words, here was proof of the adage—"the dead speak to the living"—a golden rule of pathology.

The scientific community in Bhopal was facing a situation that was unique in the history of chemical disasters. A man mellowed by age and philosophically facing the truth that "we are all answerable to god," Sriramachari speaks with conviction, "I will tell you not only the successes but also the failures. My late friend and colleague Heeresh Chandra and I realized the importance of coordinated histopathological and chemical analysis of tissues. Since the time of the Bhopal disaster, many institutions across the globe have undertaken animal experiments on inhalation toxicology of MIC. But Bhopal was a case apart, of a single lethal exposure to MIC. Success and failure went hand in hand in a lot of research that was undertaken in Bhopal. The issue of recurrent cyanide toxicity in Bhopal will remain a mystery. But carbamoylation studies on the victims of the disaster have provided evidentiary information in the field of forensic toxicology and given an insight into the possible 'biochemical lesion' following inhalation of MIC. UCC was unwilling or unable to provide any information except that on interaction with aqueous tissue surfaces MIC would convert to relatively innocuous methylamine. The toxicological studies were able to postulate a working hypothesis that at least a part of MIC had crossed over the alveolar-capillary barrier. On entering the bloodstream it interfered with the exchange of blood gases and caused characteristic 'cherry red' discoloration of the blood and the internal viscera, especially the lungs.[9] You have to remember that scientific facts had to be proved in a surcharged atmosphere. We were working against all odds. Rampant disinformation from Union Carbide, makeshift labs, getting the data sent across to labs in other parts of the country, and waiting for results. Do you think it was easy to arrive at the kind of conclusions we wanted to reach? Just making a lot of noise about thiosulphate injections, as a section of activists were doing was unscientific and populist. We wanted to bring things to its logical end. Research cannot go on forever. You cannot go on giving injections indiscriminately when it is no longer needed. We were studying every aspect. It was like a thread running through the beads. The process was delicate." Today he looks back with regret at how the links and connections were snapping all the time.[10] He is willing to admit that it was failure of research with devastating consequences, though he is quick to add that the fault cannot simply be brought to the doorstep of the scientists.

It is interesting to observe how failure of research methodology got disconnected from the entire question of possibility of future research. It perhaps explains why the issue of reopening research by ICMR was viewed as a political matter. The doctor heading the Non-Communicable Disease (NCD) of ICMR was categorical in his statement that ICMR did not close down research and it would be willing to open doors to any area of research that is considered necessary even today. The then dean of Gandhi Medical College felt that all research had perforce come to a halt because of lack of state funding. It was clarified that the Cancer Registry was still operative and was continuing to gather data through a system of registration. It was quickly added that the registry was looking generally at all cancer patients in Bhopal, for how long can gas victims claim special status? The HOD of the Department of Pathology, Gandhi Medical College was more vociferous in his claim that all research, which is looking at long-term effects of MIC, was humbug. "We are going to come out with our findings soon that there is no effect of MIC anymore, unlike what some NGOs claim. The effect of fibrosis of the lung, for instance, is a natural aftereffect of an accident. It is not a new disease. You cannot link it up with MIC now."

Sriramachari's insight was more futuristic and philosophical: "See, a research of this kind can only be done by the government for it alone has the resources and manpower. It is unfortunate that the political will is missing today. There is much to be done. ICMR had defined the cohorts. All that is needed is to enumerate people as traceable and nontraceable. The next step would be to redraw morbidity patterns through authentic history taking, so that vulnerable areas like TB, COPD, hormonal, menstrual, and reproductive health can be identified. Today there are noninvasive techniques. Why not use them for follow up? There were two kinds of damages, organic and functional. Look, we need to thank the almighty that in many areas the organic damages were less than what we feared. The body has its own way of healing. But functional damage has remained. We cannot wish that away."

The Nature of the Conflict

Reading through the mammoth *Interim Report on Sodium Thiosulphate Therapy of the Bhopal Gas Victims*, written by Anil Sadgopal and Sujit K. Das in May 1988, I realized that there was a need to sharpen our understanding of the conflict, and how deeply embroiled it was in the systemic failure that plagued Bhopal. A committee was constituted by the Supreme Court to act as independent machinery after the state government failed to submit an appropriate scheme for detoxification of the gas victims. As a constituent group it was highly representative and ought to have worked very effectively in ideal conditions. ICMR was represented by Sriramachari, BGDRC by Dwivedi, government of MP by Director of Health Services, Dr. A. K. Handa, Dr O. P. Sharma, the Dean, Gandhi Medical College, and Heeresh Chandra, Director of the Medico-Legal Institute. Sadgopal and Sujit Das were minority members.

According to the *Interim Report* the committee was torn apart by strife and total refusal on the part of the majority members to allow for independent recommendations by the minority members. Confidentiality was imposed on entire deliberations, meetings were not held regularly, and simple queries went unanswered. So much so that the committee was unable to agree upon a unanimous interim report, and separate majority and minority reports were submitted to the Supreme Court. What were the grounds of conflict? Could science use the argument that it dealt with matters of high precision, time bound (Sriramachari: "the cells lapse within a cycle of 120 days, so I was racing against time"), empirical and therefore demanding conditions of confidentiality to make unavailable *all* scientific information? In the case of Bhopal, what the scientific community failed to do was to work out a system that would override the "atmosphere of conspiracy." A proposal was made to set up a National Medical and Rehabilitation Commission for the gas victims with twenty members, but such suggestions went unheeded. The then Head of the Ophthalmology Department, Gandhi Medical College at the time of the disaster puts it rather tellingly, "Increasingly it became a matter of who pays and how much. I mean both in terms of liability and compensation. Research gets mixed up with all that. It is then that suspicion and distrust about findings and data become rife. For what purpose will it be used? It is then that the process of clamping down starts. Nobody is willing to stretch out their neck and take the onus."

Sadgopal insists that there were a few like him who were willing to take the risk. He remembers vividly the harassment, the police raids, the four-hour grueling interrogation, the arrests, the demonstrations, and the abuses targeted at them, which ranged from being "Carbide men to antinational because I was married to a foreigner." At the same time, activism too saw itself as mired in a kind of role-playing that was thrust on it. It took up the case of sodium thiosulphate because the immediate goal was to use the findings of research for therapeutic purpose. It had a larger purpose as well. The Directorate of Claims (government of MP) had selected urine thiocyanate level as one of the medical parameters for characterizing the gas victims and assessing their morbidity status. The activists feared the worst that there would be gross underestimation of morbidity status. So their demand for scientifically designed investigation was accompanied by charges of incompetence and corruption that was hurled at the majority members of the committee. It vitiated the atmosphere and made any kind of negotiation volatile and full of dead ends. When it came to supporting such claims with factual data, a lot of it came across as unspecified and nonverifiable. UCC and media fanned the cyanide controversy because cyanide was commonly known, while in reality MIC was far more lethal as a toxic gas. We also notice how research was sitting in uneasy proximity to the political fray. Clearly the majority members of the committee would not enter into a dialogue of this kind. They did what they had both power and position to do, ignore the minority report, so that many valuable suggestions were lost.

But the Interim Report managed to do something valuable. It challenged ICMR's exclusive position by positing a number of research projects undertaken by smaller NGOs. What was the nature of the dangers that the persistent toxins in the human body might pose at a later date by increasing teratogenic (fetus deforming), carcinogenic (cancer forming), and mutagenic (genetic) risks for the gas-affected population? These were some of the questions that the report was asking, which were deliberately side stepped by ICMR. Individual studies were taken over by smaller groups sometimes with excellent results. In the last section of this chapter, I shift attention to testimonials drawn from women/men, who were suffering the consequences of what the medical community was compelled to accept, that MIC had entered the blood stream, and was causing multisystemic damage that was not just affecting the reproductive health of women, but also the new generation that was being born.

The True Legacy of the Disaster

A full-page advertisement that came out in *The Guardian* (December 3, 1994) as part of the Bhopal Medical Appeal (BMA) carried a simple heading, "Thousands of our children were not so lucky. They survived." Here if anything else remains was the stark reality of people's suffering, and the crying need to make the rest of the world remember. In 2001, soon after Union Carbide merged with Dow Chemicals, Sarangi presented a brief note titled "Two humanitarian things the Dow Chemical Company, USA can immediately do to help survivors of Bhopal, India" to the managing director of Dow India in Mumbai. The appeal was to release the unpublished medical information. The response was curious; Dow agreed to send an inventory of published medical research but they had found no unpublished material, and they could not locate anyone in UCC who was aware of any such research. In December 2009, as the Bhopal disaster steps into its twenty-fifth year we get a clear picture of its true legacy. The appeal for medical redressal has acquired greater urgency, and a more or less neglected area of research is now calling for attention. It is in this connection that we need to take a quick look at research done by NGOs, so as to bring to the forefront the more politically loaded issues of women's reproductive health and the effect of the gas on the second generation.

These independent scientific studies were crucial for an understanding of the multisystemic damage caused by the gas leak. The information gathered from these studies and laboratory evidence showed how the gas had caused extensive damage to several systems in the body. It had affected reproductive health by an increase in spontaneous abortions, still birth rate; it had decreased life expectancy by the onset of premature senility; and it had raised the serious possibility of delayed effects due to changes in the immune system, genetic damage, and mutagenic changes in the survivors.[11] The information was brought out in the form of reports that were widely disseminated in the public domain. But limited funding and inadequate tools of research bogged down nongovernment schemes, so they could not replace government studies. To carry out a cross-sectional study of the entire exposed population was out of question for any voluntary effort. So the objectives of the studies were narrowed down to gathering information that would be of direct and immediate use for the survivors, both for strengthening the legal case and for developing a critique of the methodology of processing of claims adopted by the Directorate of Claims. Scientific research was meant to feed into activism, which was clearly the ground for Sriramachari's complaint against voluntarism.

The Bhopal Reader in the two sections aptly titled "Sickness" and "Healing" provides a sensitive analysis of what linked the symptoms of gas exposure to the symptoms of poverty. Unfortunately, the doctors, bureaucrats, and the middle class were not able to unlock the chain of unmitigated suffering where sickness and impeding work capacity caused greater poverty and sickness (126). The absence of statistical evidence and diagnostic protocol went hand in hand with the class bias against the poor, to create conditions that added to the suffering instead of healing. What the NGOs managed to do was dispel the myth about science's disinterestedness. For instance, the methodology for assessing personal injury that was toted by the claims office was based on a scoring system. Each claimant was allotted marks for his/her suffering and this was totaled to arrive at a category. The system had serious flaws, which were never addressed. There was no mechanism for comparing the acute, subacute, and chronic phase of the disease. It created an arbitrary hierarchy that placed different body systems, the nature of investigations on different aspects of morbidity, in random order. Most importantly, it did not consider the possible future outcome of each of the gas-related affects on the body. What doctors have always feared to admit in the case of Bhopal was the grim reality that research had been terminated not for purely administrative reasons, but when conclusive evidence of second-generation damage had begun to emerge. Given the fact that such evidence could have dramatically increased the liability of the corporation, and made the government responsible for long-term rehabilitation, the move on the part of both the industry and the state was systematic clampdown on any kind of sensitive information.

In this section I draw attention to some of the startling findings of research conducted against all odds by groups of dedicated professionals. The role played by radical scientific organizations cannot be underplayed. The earliest research was undertaken in February 1985 by a group of four doctors, and Morcha played a role in helping with the fieldwork.[12] Gynecologists examined 114 women from the 2 most severely affected bastis, J. P. Nagar and Kazi Kemp, and 104 women from the control group. There were widespread cases of leucorrhoea, pelvic inflammatory disease, cervical erosion/endocervicities, excessive menstrual bleeding, and suppression of lactation. A preliminary survey of 3,270 families reported by Daya Varma found that 43 percent of pregnancies did not result in live births; it also showed a substantial increase in spontaneous abortions and neonatal deaths.[13] Varma juxtaposed these studies with animal experiments done by exposing pregnant Swiss mice to 1 or 3 ppm of MIC. The results showed increased number of dead fetuses at birth, with 75 percent of the mice losing their entire litters. Sathyamala draws attention to experimental studies that suggested the possibility of direct maternal toxicity or direct fetal toxicity through transplacental transfer.[14] Disruption of the menstrual cycle suggested hormonal changes in girls. A population based study brought out by The MFC indicated adverse effects on pregnancies conceived after the disaster. The MFC went to the extent of recommending that couples should avoid conception till they were detoxified by sodium thiosulphate therapy. Despite the mounting evidence of damage to women's reproductive health, the government refused to accept the truth for a very long time. The ICMR's 1985 epidemiology study did not even have a provision for recording gynecological disorders. This was largely because gynecological disorders are normally linked up with fertility, and gynecological symptoms are not seen as indicators of morbidity in their own rights. This resulted in an inherent bias, so that gynecological disorders ended up carrying unequal weight as compensation injury.

The denial carried deeper implications. In 1988 the ICMR team that was studying children born after the disaster to exposed mothers came up with findings that suggested delayed physical and mental development. In a letter dated December 1, 1990, Dr. Bhandari, who was then Head of Pediatric, Gandhi Medical College, Bhopal wrote to the DG, ICMR: "Children born to pregnant women exposed to toxic gas have revealed deceleration of growth. Puberty is an important milestone in the growth of an individual. Several chemical and other environmental factors have been documented to have a grossly adverse effect on human growth and development. Since MIC had an initial grossly lethal effect on embryos and fetuses of humans at the time of exposure, there might have been damage to the cell chromatin. Hence it might be worthwhile to observe and study its long-term affects on these children, especially mean adult height pubertal and adolescent growth and cognitive intelligence." In its annual meeting the PAC recommended further study on the children's sexual development and immunological functions till they attained puberty. The findings were significant for they pointed toward teratogenic effects of toxic exposure, but the study was wound up in June 1991.

In 2001, the Sambhavna Trust undertook a "Study of growth pattern of young people born in Bhopal between 1982 and 1986."[15] The findings were grim: children conceived after the disaster to exposed parents were showing tendencies of growth retardation; they were shorter, thinner, lighter, and had smaller heads. This was a pilot study and there was a felt need for a more detailed study using a larger sample. Only then would the hereditary effects of exposure be brought to light. Unfortunately, the medical community adopted a closed-door system; there was no scope for alternative, innovative approach to rehabilitation. When in June 1999, a Hindi magazine called *Meri Saheli* (A Woman's Companion) published an advertisement that showed the continuing gynecological effect of the gas, the principal secretary, MP, actually wrote to the Ministry of Chemicals with a formal complaint against survivor's organizations, for spreading false alarm about the impact of the gas on women. There was widespread paranoia about findings linked to knowledge, which brought in the neglected sector of women and the second-generation children at the center of the medical disaster.

What makes Bhopal such a fascinating case study of the way systems function is that nothing could stop the clamor for alternative research and baseline knowledge. On the one hand, junior gynecologists and midwives at the Sultania Janana Hospital were reporting cases of premature birth, with significant proportion of women losing all or most of their babies. Ironically this was putting pressure on women to bear more children, thus adding the burden of pregnancy on their already deteriorating health. This was the immediate aftermath of the disaster. But has the situation really changed? A pamphlet issued by the ICJB as part of their 2006 padyatra from Bhopal to Delhi titled *We've Come For Justice and We Won't Leave Without It* (February 20—March 27, 2006) suggests that neglect of women's health issues is still rampant. This is how the situation is described in Indira Gandhi Hospital, which is the only hospital in Bhopal set up specifically for women survivors and children. The building was constructed in 1994, the outpatient ward was opened in 1998, and when the Supreme Court-appointed monitoring committee went on a surprise inspection there were no doctors till late, the x-ray room was closed, and there was no one at the counter to take blood samples. The emergency room had an unclean bed and an oxygen cylinder that was not in a running condition. This was the report that was sent to the Supreme Court on October 31, 2005. For a hospital that was dedicated to the women survivors of the disaster, its only function was to deliver babies!

Meanwhile, Dr. Qaiser of Sambhavna Trust showed me a survey that was done by him and the community health workers in the clinic. The survey showed that 43 percent of female teenagers in the age group of thirteen to fifteen had not begun their periods. Approximately 108 babies below the age of two were nursing on breast milk that was found to contain mercury and toxic chemicals. On the Sambhavna Web site www.bhopal.org, I found this chilling summary of the findings of an ongoing study on chromosomal changes among gas-affected people and birth defects in the exposed population, undertaken by Dr. N. Ganesh, a cytogenetic technologist and senior research officer at Jawaharlal Nehru Cancer Hospital and Research Center. According to Ganesh, "So far I have collected information on pregnancy outcome of seventy-five severely exposed mothers. My data shows that fifty-four of their progeny have congenital malformation. These mothers had the history of spontaneous abortion after their exposure to the gas. Malformations among children recorded were cleft palate, bone deformities, Syndactyly, Polydactyly, undecended testis, hydrocephalous, and Down's syndrome." Ganesh added that his study was only indicative of the situation in Bhopal and there was a need for long-term genetic studies.

Silent Voices

Somewhere apart from all the talk about research, treatment, rehabilitation, remediation, compensation, and liability the suffering went on unabated.

I present testimonials without any commentary. The images they evoke are both disturbing and destabilizing. Aziza Bi: "I have three children from before the gas disaster and after the gas I have aborted thrice. Once I was six months pregnant, the second time I was seven months pregnant, and the third time I carried the baby for eight months. They were all born dead. All with black skin like the color of coal and all shrunken in size. The doctors never told me why such a thing was happening to me." Shahida Bi: "A few months after the gas leak I had a son. He was all right. After that I had another child in the hospital. But it was not fully formed. It had no limbs and no eyes and was born dead. I had another child. Its skin looked scalded and only half its head was formed; the other half was like a membrane filled with water. It was born dead."[16]

Unnamed patient from the Sambhavna Clinic records, "When I started menstruating it was quite unbearable and I have been having terrible problems for the last three years. I get periods once in four months. I get irritable, have abdominal pain and I cannot concentrate on anything. For days before my periods I writhe in agony like a fish out of water. I am told not to mention my problems to anybody." Another patient narrates, "My periods started when I was twelve. In last one month I have had periods thrice. Some times they come after three or even six-seven months. My period lasts for fifteen days. I have pain in the limbs, headache, and irritability and do not feel like eating anything. My sister too has similar problems." Aqueela Bi is thirty-five years old and has period two or three times a month while Shahajahan has not had one for eight years. Farihat cannot have children after one malformed delivery followed by a string of miscarriages.[17]

This is what Shakeel's mother has to say about her son who is in his late teens but looks ten years old: "When Shakeel was born he had a boil on his forehead. At three-four months his whole head was covered with boils. His hair used to be sticky with pus. When he was born there were black patches all over his body. At three months he used to blink his eyes and tears flowed often. I was worried he would go blind or something. When he was a few months he had a boil on his upper lips and it split. He could not suckle. He survived mostly on weak tea because we had no money to buy milk." In Oriya Basti lives a young lad born on the night of the disaster and named Jahar Lal (Son of Poison). His father tells me, "He spends his days wandering aimlessly. He suffers from serious mental problems. He was quite normal at first, studying well in a school in the village. Then we brought him here and he started showing symptoms of depression. He runs away from home and has violent fits of anger. Doctors tell me his condition could be delayed effect of gas. But nobody knows for sure."

I end this chapter with some case studies done by The Chingari Trust that is run by Rashida Bi and Champa Devi Shukla and one of its focal areas is medical care for second-generation born children with congenital defects.[18] Here again it is the distraught mother's voices that we get to hear. Muskan's mother: "Muskan is the youngest in our family of eight members. She was born in 2005 in Jawaharlal Nehru Hospital, Bhopal. She did not cry when she was born. When she was two months old her body temperature used to remain high, so that her body felt abnormally hot. The doctors told us the painful truth that our daughter was handicapped. Today she is two years old. She cannot stand nor can she sit properly. If she is made to sit she begins to topple over because her limbs are very weak. She is also mentally challenged. I feel very anxious because Muskan is a girl. She cannot do the basic functions, cannot be toilet trained or be made self-reliant. I am forced to keep her away from larger family gatherings or take her anywhere out of a sense of embarrassment and anxiety. Muskan is also reluctant to go anywhere because too much noise or too many people disturbs her. I have become homebound because she cannot be left behind in the care of anyone else."

Rahil's mother: "Rahil was born in 2004 in Indira Gandhi Hospital, Bhopal. He was a full term baby and cried normally after birth. When he was three/four days old, the doctor advised my husband to take him out in the sun. He did and just after five/six minutes he started having fits. The doctor told us everything was normal and there was no cause to worry. He was given a tablet, which continued for one year. The medicine showed no effect and the fits continued. So we stopped giving him the tablet. We discovered that Rahil was mentally sick. We felt as though a bomb had been blasted on our face. When Rahil was three months old he still had not lifted his head nor had he turned around by himself. When he was six/twelve months old he still did not recognize anybody in the family. Today he is not able to walk, cannot speak, or wear his own clothes, and he cannot indicate when he wants to go to the toilet. He can only eat his food in liquid form. What is going to happen in the future?"

Kushboo's mother: "When I look at her cute face it looks like a rose. My eyes forget to move from her face. But we know that thorns accompany roses. Kushboo is surrounded by problems, she is unable to sit, she is not able pick up her head, she is also mentally sick, and she is unable to understand things. When she was born my husband got angry that I had given birth to a girl child. When she was five/four months old Kushboo caught a fever and had to be taken to Jawaharlal Nehru Hospital and was admitted there. The very next day she was referred to Hamidia Hospital, Bhopal where she remained for six days. At Hamidia Hospital she was not given any medicine but continued the same medicines. We took her to many private doctors and spent nearly Rs 7,000 on her treatment but all in vain. People have even advised me to drop Kushboo in an orphanage, but how can a mother do that to her own dear daughter? All I can do is keep praying for her." Akash's mother: "Akash was born in the year 1999 in Gwalior in a hospital. He cannot speak and is mentally weak. Akash is six years old now but he cannot eat food with his own hands, he cannot change clothes, cannot clean himself, and even if he is hungry he cannot ask for food. He can only move his head to indicate yes or no. One day I decided to experiment. I did not ask him for food for twenty-four hours. He did not indicate even once that he was hungry. I found the situation so intolerable I asked him if he will have food and Akash nodded his head to say yes. I cried a lot that day."

Listening to the testimonials one realizes that in the twenty-five years that have gone by, a situation of no return has been created without possibility of cure or remediation. The question of compensation is, ironically enough, almost redundant. In that case, what is there to retrieve in Bhopal? The campaign for justice has to be seen in this context. In the concluding chapter I shift attention to women "dancing in the streets" as an expression of pain, protest, and victory. It is as though women's body, which has been the site of contestation, used its "visibility" to counter the absence and erasure from official documents. The first padyatra undertaken by the stationery women did not get any media attention. The second padyatra, which took place in 2006 generated media interest when the PM met the survivors. The promise to look into demands went unheeded, so the third padyatra commenced on February 2008 and reached some major milestones in addressing issues in Bhopal. The images of the battle-scarred but victorious survivors were widely disseminated through the visual medium and the Internet. It is women who make their overbearing presence felt in these images. But a new aspect of activism had also entered the picture. Akash, Kushboo, Muskan, and others who are disadvantaged like them, were also present in big numbers. It had taken more than courage for the parents to come all the way to Delhi to participate in the protest action.

Their presence marked an important direction that the struggle for justice had taken. The parents accompanied the children, and it was mostly mothers who talked to the media and voiced their complaints against a system, which had so gravely wronged them. What is interesting is that the demand for a rational system of health care had become the platform for highlighting the need for creating awareness about people's rights. It was mothers, who normally bear the brunt of private grief and the insurmountable difficulties of bringing up children with severe challenges, had stepped forward and placed Bhopal on a global platform where discussions on environment, technology, market resources, and human values had intensified over the years. In the process, marginal voices with its ideological underpinning was beginning to find a place in mainstream politics and the vision for the future. What they were saying, on behalf of their children, was the only truth that mattered. However hard we tried we could hardly afford to forget Bhopal.

CHAPTER 7

"Dancing in the Streets": Protest, Celebration, and Modes of Self-Expression

The sort of people whose names are usually unknown to anyone except their families and neighbours... some played a role on small or local public scenes, the village, the chapel, the union branch, the council... Writing such individuals out of the story would leave no significant trace on the macro-historical narrative. My point is rather that, collectively, if not as individuals, such men and women are major historical actors. What they do and think makes a difference. It can and has changed culture and the shape of history.
—Eric Hobsbawm, *Uncommon People: Resistance, Rebellion and Jazz* (1998).

The sick man is no doubt incapable of working, but if he is placed in a hospital he becomes a double burden for society: the assistance that he is given relates only to himself, and his family is, in turn, left exposed to poverty and disease. The hospital, which creates disease by means of the enclosed, pestilential domain that it constitutes, creates further disease in the social space in which it is placed. This separation, intended to protect, communicates disease and multiplies it to infinity. The care spontaneously given by family and friends will cost nobody anything, and the financial assistance given to the sick man will be to the advantage of the family.
—Michel Foucault, *The Birth of the Clinic: An Archeology of Medical Perception* (1963, English edition 1973).

All those who come and interview me I tell them the same thing. Do not interview me for your personal benefit. Do not refresh my wounds, do not treat my tears as water, do not consider this as a cassette that is playing and repeating...I give these interviews thinking that if our fight can gather strength and my voice goes far and if after watching this someone is being motivated, or has feelings of sympathy in his heart, and he adds his strength to the fight and maybe Bhopal gets justice soon.

—Hazra Bi, Gas Survivor (tape 5).

As the title of this chapter indicates, I address the issues of personality development, identity formation, and self-learning that accompanied the struggle for justice in Bhopal. This brings me to the concluding analysis of oral history, which focuses on the much less documented aspect of historical experience, the subjective domain and individual growth that brings in the cultural facets of the social movement. At the same time, we are analyzing a people's movement in the context of an industrial disaster. The personal plays a functional role in the understanding of larger social/economic/political forces that are operative in society. How was the knowledge base created? More importantly, how did survivor groups use the knowledge? Organizations came up with their own mechanisms for sharing information. Since most of the women survivors lacked education and were barely literate, they had to come up with innovative tools to understand their own role and identity as activists in relation to campaign issues. Activism brought in major changes in the way of looking and doing things. As we listen to the testimonials, we see how women moved away from reliving the experience of suffering to the cognitive understanding of larger issues, particularly the role of government as both protector of its people and ally of corporations, and the question of who ultimately has to take responsibility for rehabilitation. An important question that gets raised again and again is whether grassroots organizations should take the path of confrontation or work in alignment with the state. The testimonials do not offer simple answers, for a great deal of this knowledge is generated within the particular context of the need for mobilization and alliances, and it is specific to the struggle.

The metaphor "dancing in the streets" has been used to suggest the oral nature of this cognitive process and to explain how closely it is tied to expectations, hopes, and beliefs. The visual images that Bhopal has generated have mass appeal. Photographers like Raghu Rai, Pablo Bartholemew, Prakash Hatvalne, and Maude Dorr have captured individual faces that are typical and anonymous. We see the dialectical tension between the individual and the collective that finds expression in the way the cause for justice gets linked with personal needs and empowerment. The images capture both protest and celebration. Interestingly enough, the discourse of rehabilitation and disaster management asks for systems of registration and classification by name, age, gender, and place of residence. It is this specificity that gets pitched against the mammoth anonymity of an industrial disaster. How many dead, how many ill, and how many rendered destitute remain a matter of statistics and official record. The individual is caught in the crossfire between the public and the personal. Therefore, his/her need to speak out is always in the context of monolithic systems of silencing.

In the previous chapters we had seen how oral history provides the analytical tool to unmask the politics of remembering and forgetting that underlies an industrial disaster and its management by the state and the corporation. In this chapter we focus on the interface between individuals and the knowledge base that grew from the needs of the community, and the ways in which this kind of indigenous knowledge fed into the resistance strategies deployed by the movement. Importantly, we witness people's attempt to reverse the process of erasure. I draw on testimonials that are personal in nature; yet they are not meant to be voyeuristic or encourage middle-class complacency. Their power stems from the fact that they are anchored to the framework of democratic thoughts and action, which contributes to the health of a vibrant civil society. A section of women survivors was involved in community-based programmes that nurtured values, which gave direct voice to people in matters that affected their lives. Often these were no more than informal associations led by enterprising women, working within a basti to implement schemes launched by survivor groups. Health camps, community surveys, or simply collecting information for creating data base became part of such collective efforts, mostly executed by women who were in the forefront of different campaigns. Such group activities went a long way in shaping alternative self-help programmes that created awareness, strengthened family ties, and fostered community networks.

We have already seen how in a chemically ridden world, it is the poor and the disadvantaged who suffer the consequences of toxic exposure. We see how the privacy of the body gets invaded, and how the chemical body burden affects the second generation and violates the procreative principle of life. I take up for discussion the creation of a community health clinic and documentation center like Sambhavna, which arose from the need to confront the problems of healing, knowing, and controlling the body. It is interesting to know that Sambhavna was created in the larger context of the total blackout of information on the effects of methyl isocyanate (MIC) and its compounds on the body, the collapse of an overcrowded hospital system, and the onslaught of privatization and corporatization of medical science, which in turn controlled research and its funding. We also need to understand how community activities got linked to the social movement, and how it strengthened the fight for justice. Thus the 2008 padyatra, which is taken up for discussion, was conceptualized on the basis of people's involvement in decision making. At the same time, a major demand was for an Empowered National Commission so that grounds were prepared for conceding demands within the constitutional framework of laws and regulations. An interesting feature of the 2008 action is the involvement of youth, which I believe is an outcome of sustained community level activities. However, a resistance movement directed against a technological disaster also called for high-tech interventions on the part of thinkers and professionals from different walks of life; they contributed to the cause with their expertise and issue-based commitment. Clearly the perception of an "outsider" had changed over the years, and space had been created for wider national and international support.

We have already seen how activism created space for women-centric issues and called for women's participation in large numbers. Women were at the forefront of the march to Delhi; they took part in large numbers in rallies, flash action, hunger strikes, and courting arrests to make their demands visible. What strengthened women' role in the movement was the way in which they represented, in a more visible form, the disadvantages that was already the survivor's lot. Women were twice victimized by systems that promoted economic inequalities, capitalist development, environmental degradation, class, gender, and cultural bias. They provided the vital link between health care and livelihood and showed how the need to strengthen community health was a social, economic, cultural, and political issue. So long as medical rehabilitation in Bhopal ignored the links, there was no possibility of improving the lives of people. Women spoke out on issues that are commonly associated with "shame" and "silence." It is through the politization of the subjective domain and drawing on the traditional role of women as nurturers and healers in the family that the Bhopal movement was able to draw attention to issues of sanitation, clean water supply, alternative therapy, nutrition, and preventive health care. The demand was for resuming research by the Indian Council for Medical Research (ICMR) and making the research findings public. There was also the demand to delink medical care from compensation where women hardly have a voice. In the final analysis, knowledge had to stop serving political ends. Only then could people's right to know get strengthened through the creation of alternative institutional space that promoted both self-development and group solidarity.

As pointed out earlier, oral history throws light on the contentious issue of the unreliability of people's memories and how testimonials can be based on rumors, hearsay, and exaggerations. This becomes more relevant when we are studying an industrial disaster. Therefore, in any form of official reporting the individual voice is carefully eliminated. This chapter tries to reverse the process by showing how people's opinions matter, especially when we are looking at ways in which the community heals itself. Recovery is an arduous and difficult journey, and it has its own stories to tell of people's enterprise, commitment to a cause, and vision for the future. Once again, I bring women to the forefront to show how they brought in their wealth of experience and strong commonsense to shape this vision. Like everything else in Bhopal, this process of learning is accompanied by struggle, so opinions are literally formed in the streets. At the same time, learning has to negotiate the space between the "lived" experience and the "reconstruction" of reality through words. The metaphor of *dancing* shows how words get interlaced with bodies, used as expressive tools for self-expression and resistance. A thin line distinguishes testimonials as affidavits or fact-finding devices and personal memory. The more immediate task at hand is to get across voices that are neglected or never heard. In doing so, oral history helps to probe the reason why certain voices go unheard and to retell forgotten history from an alternative perspective.

"I Will Die Working for the Organization" (tape 11)

The learning process begins with women trying to understand why they joined grassroots organization and what made them take on the responsibility of running the organizations. It brings up larger issues of loyalty to the cause and to fellow workers. Most importantly, it helps to define women-power within the context of the struggle against state power and supremacy of corporations in a globalized world. These are some of the major issues that emerge from the oral testimonials. It is interesting to see how women were able to mediate such important topics through purely visual memories. Memories also evoke nostalgia, and the need to relive and exorcize emotions. There is a lot of self-reflection and analysis. There are doubts and counter questioning. What finally emerges are the years of struggle behind a movement that has seen the ups and downs of small victories, major set backs, hope, and despair. Justice is an elusive term, and in the case of a manmade disaster, compensation can never be enough to bring reprieve for those who have suffered enormous personal tragedies. Benefits have to be shared, so that ones own share becomes fractional and highly inadequate to meet even the most basic needs. Survivors of Bhopal have traveled this long and lonely path, and as they recount their experience we realize that words are inadequate to express the bitterness of their feelings. Cynicism, sweeping statements, backbiting, and rancor comes out in the open. There is a lot of misdirected anger as well, but there is little sophistry. I was touched by the repeated attempt to search for the "truth," as though no amount of telling can translate suffering into real terms.

Some of the women, who had joined Mahila Udyog Sangathan (MUS) right from its inception, talked about the experience of belonging to a grassroots organization. Some felt that women joined organizations based on understanding of issues. What inspires and motivates them can differ, but it is clear that organizational loyalty runs deep. They traced the path of learning and spoke at length about the need to create space for dialogue and collective decision making. The popular opinion was that women had to be given credit for coming together to form organizations. No doubt, fate had played a big role in shaping their lives in entirely different directions. But now that they had entered the public domain there was no going back for most of them. A founder member of MUS, an eloquent speaker (tape 15), went on to link activism to women's sense of solidarity in the face of atrocities that are directed against them. She felt that women are great organizers and remembered with deep nostalgia the early days when the strength of their organization exceeded 17,000 women. "We held meetings on a regular basis where women would talk on important issues. All announcements for dharnas and rallies were made in the meetings. Consensus was sought by show of hands. Pamphlets were printed to publicize events and most announcements were made on loudspeakers in bastis... My motivation comes from issues that make me angry and the anger becomes my strength and inspiration." She is quick to add that "it is the gift of tolerance that allows women to do so many things and fight." Another speaker (tape 11) does not mince words when she says that she is motivated to fight when she sees how "governments perpetrate injustice on the poor." She talks about her initial involvement, "I got to know about MUS from a neighbor. I was told that if I go to Jabbar he would help me. This was in 1985." She was motivated by her pressing needs, but her subsequent involvement, which remains steadfast till this day, comes from inspiration. It is this combination of need and insight that becomes a woman's strength. Most of the women joined because they needed jobs to supplement income in the family, but even after the means of livelihood were snatched away the movement continued. It is the staying power of the struggle that the women talk about with a great deal of pride.

We listen to the women of Pension, who add their own insight to what inspired them to join the movement. "I joined the group because I wanted to help people and expected support in case I had problems. I also felt I would learn something if I attended these meetings and heard what was being spoken" (tape 18 B). Listening to her we realize that the reasons for being part of a group can be deeply personal: "My husband abandoned me after the gas leak for another woman. I never received the compensation money. My husband got his new wife the money in my name and he had all my papers." She goes on to talk about the feeling of being betrayed and cheated as fuelling her motivation to fight. Loss and gain go hand in hand; something that is evident from what a member of Stationery (tape 22) has to say, "The women regard stationery as their home and their household which they are fighting for. All the women have worked together and stayed together as though they are part of a big family." Hazra Bi, who has been with International Campaign for Justice in Bhopal (ICJB), sums up her inspiration for being part of the struggle: "My life changed from the day I accepted the reality of bodies lying in front of me. I did not sit that day. I had come back in search of my son and found my son unconscious. I imagined the plight of other mothers who had gone through the same thing. I got hope, motivation, and anger to fight from that day and I made up my mind to live and work for others" (tape 5).

"Our Struggle Is Supported by Our Own Capacity and Strength" (tape 15)

The women talk about self-reliance, and drawing strength from local concerns and loyalties, that in turn gets identified with their organizations and its particular agenda. The "rootedness" of the Bhopal movement had been its strength and its limitations. Women admit that demands are specific to their needs and what the government must do to rehabilitate them. To the question of what is the need of the hour—compensation or livelihood—a member of MUS is candid enough to say, "money given at one go can help people, for it can be invested in a house. At least we can have a roof over our heads. The poor have many needs. Our organization works to get Below Poverty Line (BPL) for those who are poor, ration cards, admission to hospitals. I like the fact that Jabbar takes up individual cases and many people have got compensation with his assistance" (tape 12). Another member from MUS claims that her group is more grassroots than others: "We not only deal with issues of gas survivors but many other issues that concern the common and needy man. Once we get to know about a particular issue women go to find out more details and to take care of the problem" (tape 16). She feels that the strength of an organization lies in its capacity to mobilize people and that can happen only by extending help and providing support on a day-to-day basis. Another voice (tape 11) takes pride in the fact that MUS has fought for compensation and Rs 200 interim relief before the settlement money could be disbursed. She says that survivors have an urgent need for compensation money, given the high cost of living. She agrees with most other women that no one should underplay the aspirations, needs, and dreams of poor people to improve the quality of their lives. At the same time, she knows that the long-term benefits of compensation in monetary terms are questionable. The speaker goes on to describe the "vicious cycle" in which the poor are trapped. The little compensation money that families got was used to meet basic requirements, like paying off debts, medical bills and getting daughters married. As a result, the education of children got compromised. This in turn meant children were forced to enter the job market. What sort of help can grassroots organizations extend to people in such situations?

In the course of the interviews, another important aspect of the compensation issue came up for discussion. A member of MUS (tape 11) felt that one of the main reasons why participation has decreased over the years is because people have got compensation and they know that nothing else is coming their way. Nobody believes in systemic change. She too shares their cynicism but she believes in the value of struggle. However, not too many people share her enthusiasm. One of the reasons why she feels that MUS has rightly raised the issue of five times compensation is because it would bring back people into the movement. She remembers the time when people used to attend their meetings in large numbers; all they needed to do was make an announcement during their meetings. Today they have to go to bastis repeatedly to gather people. Her fear is that issues raised by her organization can become redundant in the future. "It is not simply a question of numbers. It has more to do with getting people to back the issues you are fighting for," she says. As another member of MUS puts it succinctly, "People do not come for demonstrations because they think they will reap the benefits from others' fights. There are many issues staring us in the face but nobody wants to look" (tape 15).

Sheila Thakur, who is broadly sympathetic to the ICJB, gives her own personal reasons for not being actively involved: "Even today I am ready to join the fight, but since I do not have the capacity to walk around much, I am restrained. There is no boy in the family and the girls have gone to their own homes after marriage. One of my daughters who stays with me and has not married is unwell. Her kidney has got spoilt because she used to do a lot of stitching work with me. She did this continuously for eighteen years before the doctors asked her to stop. We have tried every kind of treatment, allopathic, ayurvedic, but nothing has helped. Doctors said we should get her operated. We showed her in Hamidia where her treatment started. But there too they told us to take her to a private hospital, for which we do not have the money. Now we have stopped her allopathic medicines and give her desi (traditional) care and now she is much better" (tape 6). Hazra Bi has her explanations that are tied with social customs. "A woman," she says "is someone's daughter, wife, and mother, so a woman needs to think, analyze the situation, and then make a decision to participate. If there are people who cannot participate then some are helpless because of their circumstances. In the Muslim community you will see a lot of restrictions" (tape 5). Her own situation is different: "My children have seen the condition at home. My husband abandoned me and I have raised my children single handedly. They understand my difficulties. Encouragement comes when your family has jointly faced difficult times, pain, hunger." Hazra Bi has no complaints against people who stay away. She feels that it is enough that some people can contribute to the movement in a part-time capacity rather than full-time; some come for meetings but not rallies because of personal compulsions. Hazra Bi is able to enter the skins of women who are naturally protective toward their families, "A mother thinks when I am fighting then why should my children join. This is how each woman thinks, my son should earn, my husband should earn and stay away from the fight, for we are already fighting. A woman plays her role of protecting men. This is the truth." But Hazra Bi has hopes for her granddaughter. "I will never let her keep parda. I will bring her up to be open-minded. Even today she performs in Rabindra Bhavan, she passes with first division, and she does well in dancing. I feel really elated that one day she will walk the path I am on" (tape 5).

A member of Pension says quite cavalierly that since she lives alone she does not have to ask anyone's permission. Many people fear the hardship that goes with activism, "but I can get beaten up, arrested because I don't have to worry about family or children back home. I live all alone, but since I have all the women in my group I have no problems. I am getting old but I am not ready to live a confined life at home" (tape 18 B). Another member of Pension echoes her teammates ideas when she says, "I am not scared of the police, court, or prison. After participating in a lot of rallies and demonstrations I have learnt a lot" (tape 18 A). A speaker from MUS (tape 11) feels that the strength she has gathered is of many kinds. Her husband abandoned her but she now feels that the lack of interference works to her advantage. Earlier there was anxiety about getting arrested but once it happens then all fears die. The lessons learnt are wide ranging. Women learn to overcome their shyness and confront the world outside. She has stopped wearing her burkha, so have many others. The reasons can be pragmatic (it is hot and inconvenient) to the question of socialization (a speaker [tape 17] says she does not wear a burkha but her daughter-in-laws have to wear one because her sons insist) to a matter of personal choice. I found it interesting that wearing burkha is never raised as a communal issue or linked to religious practice. At one level, the testimonials show how women can remain mired in outdated notions despite the prolonged and relentless struggle for justice. Sometimes they display prejudice against those who have embraced change, mouthing moral platitudes rather than thinking through issues. At another level, one is taken aback by the maturity displayed by a member of MUS when she says, "Simply registering a group is not enough. What you learn from the movement is what makes a group. The struggle needs to be continuous. And more than anything else social rehabilitation is needed. Women have to break free from traditional customs and the social mindset has to change. For instance, a career-oriented woman is looked at differently in society. I want a solution for that" (tape 15).

Memorable Actions and the Process of Learning

The women bring with them the memories of what they describe as memorable actions. A member of MUS (tape 11) remembers the time when a rally was held with three effigies of prominent state ministers mounted on donkeys. There was another occasion when the women invaded the CM's residence and got to know that he was hiding in the bathroom. Bhopal movement is replete with storytelling, reminiscences, sharing of jokes, and raucous sloganeering. Another member (tape 15) recalls the tenth anniversary protest action in front of the Union Carbide Research Center in Shyamla Hills. Different political parties joined them and the show of strength was impressive. At the same time, such actions proved to be risky. The women faced lathi charge and stone pelting by police and more than twenty-five of them got injured. The speaker admits that for her the memory of such courage and commitment is inspiring. A member of Pension (tape 19) was part of the "jhadoo maro Dow ko" (beat Dow with brooms) agitation in Bombay. For her it was a learning lesson. She understood the reason why the agitation had to be directed against the company. This was Union Carbide Corporation (UCC), which had come back to the country under another name and guise. "We were there to prevent a Bhopal like disaster happening in Bombay," she says with conviction. Actions in Bhopal happened at a regular interval. She remembers the time the women raided the hospital at DIG bungalow because they had got privy to the information that medicines meant for gas victims were being diverted to the open market. "We raided the storeroom and confiscated the medicine boxes," she says. Another voice from Pension (tape 18B) talks of the action when they broke earthen pots in front of the municipal office to protest against irregular water supply. Better still was the time when they took out a procession with rotis in their hand to protest against price rise. On another occasion they tied cloth around their mouth to gag themselves. The women are well aware of the fact that their actions made news on the front pages of local newspapers, with eye-catching photographs! A member of Pension is undeterred by charges of violent action: "The right way is the way that gets work done. We are ready to use violence and face its consequences. We beat and then we get beaten. I have beaten lots of policemen" (tape 20).

A voice from Stationery Union (tape 23) is able to link the ground level action with women power. She has participated in actions where women have displayed enormous strength. She recalls the time when they had broken the police barrier and walked on. They were arrested and taken to the police control room. "They could control us only when they reached the control room," she says with a snigger. No one can tell a story better than Hazra Bi: "When we did the *need udao* (drive away sleep) campaign we had to be out the whole night outside the CM's residence. It was a campaign to spoil the CM's sleep and make his life miserable through the night. It made me very happy that a woman from a poor family, and people running a small organization could challenge the man in power and drive away his sleep. It made me feel very powerful." Here is another incident, which she recounts with great relish: "On a different occasion we went to the Director, Gas Relief's office and we made a lot of noise with metal plates and spoons. We locked the door from inside. The police threw us into their vans and beat up a few of us. Three policemen surrounded me. I just pushed them aside and got into the van. Later in the lock up we had a hearty laugh. They seized our plates and spoons and we said, 'Is this what you have stooped down to?' We demanded our utensils back, and they had to return them. The minute we got them back we started making a racket once again. Some actions bring a lot of joy" (tape 5).

The testimonials offer a clear insight into how activism became a process of learning. A member of Pension explains how her involvement with the movement made her understood the way electoral politics works in a democracy: "I vote every time. An MLA had come to ask for votes in our basti, promising roads, water supply, and electricity. He did nothing after winning, so some of us from Pension gheraoed the corporation office. We did this without telling Namdeo bhai. The final weapon against the government is to vote it out" (tape 19). A speaker from MUS talks about her understanding of wider issues: "We boycott chemicals in our daily life. We have boycotted coke, soaps, toothpaste, liquor, and plastic bags. People use plastic bags to carry hot food, which is very harmful. The poison from the bag leaks into the food. We have protested and shut down liquor shops, have held dharnas against lotteries for they spoil family life" (tape 13).

The testimonials also show how learning can open up areas of conflict. A member of MUS (tape 11) is able to analyze the nature of the conflict that plagues different survivor groups, especially the way demands have changed over the years. According to her, new coalition groups like ICJB brought in the issue of clean up and shifted attention from issues linked to compensation. The speaker voices the tension that is shared by many of her co-workers in MUS; she feels her organization is being sidelined by bigger players that are stealing the show. She is emphatic when she says that a disaster inevitably becomes a money-spinning event with lots of help and relief money pouring in. She feels that a thin line divides international support and getting money from abroad. Another speaker from MUS is in agreement: "I do not trust this kind of international support because wrong kind of people gets highlighted. International support means recognition, awards, and getting written about. So some people get identified with the movement while real people get ignored" (tape 12). Many of the women in MUS express feelings of bitterness and being let down. They complain that they have been used for purposes of propaganda, and once money started pouring in they were left behind.

A lot of accusations are flung at other organizations, often without bothering to verify statements. But this is mainly in the context of what is seen as the "rootedness" of the Bhopal movement. The women of MUS insist that no one should forget their struggle in the initial years, which alone brought in whatever meager compensation was got by the people. But they also agree that in the early days the issues brought groups together and differences were put aside. Talking about differences makes another speaker philosophical: "Each group is doing their own work and god might listen to any one of them. But if all four work together, government will have to listen" (tape 20). A main spokesperson for MUS takes the argument even further as she forcefully reiterates that MUS only takes donations from the survivors: "It gives people a feeling that this is our own struggle. There is a sense of pride and confidence in ones self" (tape 15). It is noteworthy that despite her talk about differences with organizations that take international aid, she constantly qualifies her statements ("It is important to check the background of the donors and most importantly the motives behind donation") and gives the complete picture. Thus she explains that one of the dangers of taking money from the survivors is that anyone who gives donation as membership fee will make demands on the organization. As a result, organizations are compelled to take populist measures. On the issue of groups stopping the government from doing the clean up she is equally perceptive, "The opposition is not against clean up or who does it, but against the way it is being done." Another voice in MUS is candid enough to admit that she is confused on the issue of clean up: "About clean up I feel Dow should do it because it bought UCC. I don't understand the issue very well, but I also feel the government is fully responsible because they gave permission" (tape 12).

Sometimes the women fail to link the government's failure with the antipathy to multinationals. All of them want Anderson punished because it would, in the words of the member of MUS "set an example for all companies across the globe that action can be taken against them in case something like Bhopal is repeated" (tape 15). But she knows that "hang Anderson" is only rhetoric, for the company will never really get punished. Perhaps that is the reason, she feels, the struggle is directed against the government. Women display a canny sense of how industries can bring jobs and wealth to a third world country, but they are equally wary of any notion of development. They all agree that it is the poor who bear the brunt, so only those multinationals that do not harm people are welcome. The case of UCC is instantly sighted to show how such a dream of development and well-being can at best be unreal. At every step, general issues get tied to the particularities of their own situation. In a vital sense all issues in Bhopal are both local and global. What kind of development and for whom is an underlying question that is raised in many of the testimonials. The speaker from MUS is able to trace development to India's colonial past: "On the one hand, we express so much pride in our freedom struggle and the progress India has made since 1947. But life is so difficult for the poor who cannot even afford a decent meal." She is able to draw the roadmap for progress with India winning freedom. But it is the idea of progress that she challenges: "It may look like India is progressing but it is actually enslaved by foreign multinationals. Everything has become so expensive, even water has a price on it. The health of the poor reflects on the kind of development we are heading toward. TB and cancer are so common today. What kind of development is the government boasting of?" (tape 11).

What kind of justice do they envisage for Bhopal? It is a question that makes the women pause and peer into a hazy future. It is interesting to note that according to their calculations a compensation amount of Rs 50,000 to 3 lakhs is fair, for it will help them tide over difficult circumstances. The valuation of human life comes cheap in the context of development for the privileged. Sheila Thakur's definition of justice is more comprehensive: "I see justice as employment for all, proper medical care with no corruption. Also a clean and healthy environment. And since the older generation has already suffered due to the gas, something should be done so that the coming generation does not suffer. Today employment is a top priority, and if there is proper medical care then a person can be healthy and get work" (tape 6). Robust commonsense goes hand in hand with the vision for the future. What makes the vision formidable is that Sheila does not envisage an end for the struggle. What happens after Bhopal gets justice? "Once a human being steps into a particular field then he/she only moves forward and neither gives up or steps back. I feel that none of the women will sit still. Other women are coming forward. Today they are fighting for the rights of gas survivors, tomorrow when the need arises they will join hands with movements and fight for others." It is interesting to observe that at the end of the interview, she is able to link a research project to the future of the movement. When Dharmesh and Tarunima ask her if she is satisfied with the discussion that they have recorded for posterity, her answer is both cutting edge and insightful: "All the questions that you have asked are very well put. It makes me happy to see that youth like you are interested. Can I ask you something? What motivated you to come and work among the Bhopal survivors leaving behind your home and family?"

Community Health Service and the Platform for International Justice

The decade beginning 2000 has in a sense given an entirely new direction to the Bhopal movement. Not all organizations have kept pace with changing times, but a fine balance is maintained between local concerns and Bhopal's contribution to a global debate from a civil society perspective. This alone keeps the issues alive, despite middle-class apathy and state connivance to support corporations. It is in this context that the coalition of groups, national and international, which calls for issue-based support rather than life long loyalty, has evolved as a powerful tool to fight for justice. ICJB created the concept of organizational unity that brings independent local bodies together, under their own banners. It also appoints personnels from outside who are trained in activism and are paid salaries by institutions that sponsor them. An international noncorporate funding that has got FCRA clearance and follows a transparent system of auditing is put in place. The idea is to promote collective action that does not depend on local leadership, except for purposes of mobilization. Clearly, the Bhopal movement is trying to find a solution to the problem of the outsider's intervention that had plagued Morcha, keeping in mind the changing global scenario. It has to go through initial teething problems and follow a trial and error method to tackle the fluidity of the situation. In the rest of the chapter, I look at this phase of activism, keeping in mind its two foundational principles—community work and the platform for international justice. The movement picks up momentum through widespread use of new communication technology that globalization has brought in. Activists are well versed in the use of Internet. It encourages scientific research, and creation of a specialized knowledge base that uses Web sites to make information available to the public. At the same time, it promotes art, music, films, and creative writing to create a rich cultural base to promote people's cause. Its foundational strength lies in sustained community work for purposes of rehabilitation and remediation that goes hand in hand with protest at national and international forums.

To explore the nature of community service, I take up as case study the Sambhavna Clinic, which was set up through the Bhopal Medical Appeal (BMA), as a corrective to all that was wrong with the hospital system in Bhopal. It experimented with alternative treatment. To study the movement for justice, I analyze the 2008 padyatra to show how new methods of protest were envisaged. The Bhopal movement had taken new directions from its early days. The strength of MUS and Pension was to target the government and extract maximum benefits for survivors from welfare schemes that had been put in place following the settlement. With the changing political and economic scenario, this kind of activism had reached a dead end with government trying to manipulate organizations to meet the demands of electoral politics. Although demands were partially conceded to keep the vote banks happy, protest actions had also become almost ritualistic. The 2008 padyatra worked on the basis of a multipronged approach to the fight for justice. It used the Gandhian concept of walking from one city to another, of simultaneous actions in cities across the globe, daily dharna, hunger fast, and mass fax action and petitions to create worldwide solidarity. It involved meeting top leaders, politicians, and government officials to submit the memorandum of demands. The demands ranged from right to information, environmental rights, consumer rights, to the implementation of the precautionary, prevention, and polluter pay's principle within the constitutional framework of laws and regulations. The idea was to compel the state and central governments to make these issues a part of their rhetoric and political agenda.

However, this kind of mainstreaming carries its own inherent risks. We have seen how companies have launched their PR job and reinvented their image. In the global context, governments too have come together to promote notions of sustainable development that allow the environmentalist and the developer to share the same forum and speak a similar language. The key factors are issues of livelihood and the need to eradicate world poverty. There is always the danger of activism getting subsumed by global discourses with demands being tailored to suit the political situation. However, Bhopal has always offered resistance to any such appropriation by its very "rootedness" in local demands of people with very specific needs. Bhopal is a glaring example of everything that went wrong with India's postindependence dreams of industrialization and modernization. It is a reminder that without remediation and restitution there can be no justice. Neither the government nor the corporation can escape liability from the past. An average Bhopali is not convinced by the sop that is dished out to them in the name of environmental sustainability that must go hand in hand with the nation's development. There is the danger that too much talk about the "lessons of Bhopal" renders real suffering into an effete symbol of what can happen in the future. It also implies that nothing much can be done about the present. This kind of cynicism unleashes daily violence in the lives of people who suffer the consequences of an industrial disaster. The padyatra is a clear reminder that Bhopal issues can be resolved only through comprehensive action that includes revised legislations and policies, public debates and opinion building as well as street action. At the same time, none of this is possible without year-round, dedicated community work to cure the sick and offer a healing touch. Resistance on the streets is directly linked to sustained work at the basti level, so that remediation and activism share the same platform.

The Healing Touch

The effort toward remediation began in 1995 with the setting up of a registered charitable trust, The Sambhavna Trust, for providing medical care and improving the health conditions of the survivors. The Bhopal People's Health and Documentation Clinic was set up in September 1996. Situated in Bafna Colony, practically behind the Union Carbide factory, its location in the midst of the severely affected community is important. It stands in sharp contrast to a hospital like BMHRC, which has been the worst example of the corporatization of health care.[1] Sambhavna was set up with the task of undoing a great deal of harm that had already been done. It began with implementing the technology of verbal autopsy since 1996 for monitoring exposure-related mortality in gas-affected areas. Sambhavna provides facilities for Pap smear. It tries to reduce dependence on medicines and encourages patients to stop medicines altogether through ayurvedic methods of purification and yoga. Its approach to treatment is comprehensive, with a holistic orientation toward care, treatment, health education, research, and monitoring facilities.

I spoke to some of the people who run the clinic. I am told the clinic treats a daily average of 200 patients. Dr. Deshpande, who was with Sambhavna since its inception and has only recently left, had laid the foundation for ayurvedic treatment. Two young doctors now run the department. They propagate the use of ayurvedic medicines because it is nontoxin, can be organically grown, and does not use heavy metals. It is part of the "alternative" vision for healing in Bhopal. "The idea is to undo the impact of chemicals on the body," Dr. Jai tells me, "every stage of dispensing medicines is taken care of from growing the plants to formulation to making them. We do the formulation Biju makes them. Initially when I came here I was skeptical of how such a system can run. Now I know that it needs a comprehensive approach to the disease, the medication, and the cure." Almost as an extension of the building is an organic farm that has been meticulously landscaped, creating enough space for people to relax and sit while waiting for their turn to meet the doctors. Each plant carries a placard that provides the botanical and popular name with details of all the benefits. Patients are encouraged to pluck the herbs according to the doctor's prescription and take it home.

The procedure for documenting, recording, and computerizing the details of every patient is highly scientific. Each patient is given a number, date of registration, and a remission chart that records frequency of visits to determine the persistent nature of the disease, and how far treatment has benefited the person. The idea is to encourage patients to come again and again. The purpose is not commercial for treatment is entirely free. To encourage frequent use of facilities the atmosphere of the clinic is made appealing, with colorful posters, pleasing ambiance, and an air of efficiency. Emphasis is on building immune systems and changing lifestyle to increase the general feeling of well-being. At the same time, Sambhavna has a fully functional pathology lab, so that test results are ready at hand. Most importantly treatment is not linked to compensation.

Dr. Devinder Kaur, an allopathic doctor, joined Sambhavna in 2003. She is candid enough to tell me that there is no specific treatment related to MIC. "What I give is broad-based treatment for secondary symptoms. When patients get temporary relief they come back. This is the major drawback of any medical care related to the gas leak. By not giving patients MIC-specific treatment their rights are being denied. I am aware of this, but there is little that one can do. Yet patients have faith in us. I cling on to this faith, and it gives me a sense of purpose." Sambhavna directs attention to educating survivors on preventive and curative measures. It supports research, training programmes, educational, and other academic events. It makes the information accessible to all. But its real strength is in the community health work approach, through which it tries to empower the community to take control of health care of the people. Sambhavna has employed community health workers who carry out door-to-door surveys of 5 communities with a population of 10,000. The idea is to generate a database on demography, health care status, and social and economic conditions of the residents. Health workers help identify people in need of special medical attention to see if the treatment is available in the clinic or elsewhere. They are asked to find out reasons for dropout and whether treatment is continuing from elsewhere. A crucial area in which community health system works well is in the care of tuberculosis. ICMR studies have indicated that TB cases in the affected community are three times more than the national average. Sambhavna health workers identify those with the symptoms, get tests done, and ensure availability of medicines. The effort is also to educate families and dispel common, misguided notions. Emphasis is on follow-up, so as to ensure compliance and proper long-term medication. In many a case, cured patients are used as group leaders to spread awareness.

A lot of importance is given to surveys both as means of making contacts in the community and as means of building local health committees. The results of community health schemes have been very encouraging, and it has grown by involving more and more people. Here if anything else is a model for creating a community-based network with emphasis on health surveillance technology that can be implemented by lay workers in the community. The idea is to make communities self-sufficient. For instance, Nivritta a yoga therapist who links yoga with control of diabetes ran a workshop from December 2000 to mid-September 2002 with a group of twenty-five people who took medicines but did yoga in addition. Their sugar level was tested every fifteen days for four months. Nineteen out of twenty-five people could reduce their drug usage. A lot of emphasis is placed on spreading such information, so that Ramesh at Sambhavna goes to the bastis to persuade people to join programmes whose benefits are clearly underlined. As Biju, the man who makes the medicines said to me, "There is a vision here to spread hope. We combine traditional and western systems of health care to provide sustained relief from chronic conditions. The results have been very encouraging."

A booklet brought out by the Sambhavna Trust titled *Stop the On-going Disaster* makes an earnest plea to eliminate the use of hazardous chemicals from the planet and stop the "slow and silent Bhopals" from happening in our midst. It is a vision that draws its strength from the compassion of ordinary people. It believes that communities need to creatively and collectively intervene to change a situation of despair. How is community level work linked to the formation of an international platform for justice? In the rest of the chapter, we see how the vision becomes multidimensional by taking on the task of bringing justice to people. In doing so it connects communities and people's aspirations across the globe.

Eight Hundred Kilometers on Foot

The 2008 padyatra was a follow-up to the 2006 padyatra, and clearly the inspiration came from the women of the Stationery Union. But the distance covered by the movement in the intervening years has been enormous. Very few people were part of all three events, and the forces that shaped the demands have changed over the years. On April 17, 2006, the Bhopalis called off their hunger-fast because the prime minister (PM) assured a ten-member delegate that their demands regarding supply of clean water, clean-up of the toxic waste, and the setting up of a national commission for medical and economic rehabilitation will be met. The state government also announced the allotment of Rs 100 crores for the construction of a memorial. By 2008 the demands remained unfulfilled with bureaucratic tangles coming in the way. Interestingly enough the 2008 padyatra, which was clearly to protest the inaction following promises made by the Prime Ministers Office (PMO), is a mirror image of the previous event with the reiteration of the same demands. What exactly is happening here? Protest in Bhopal has become part of the yearly calendar, but a close look at the 2008 demands will tell you that this is no empty ritual. This is concerted struggle with a plan.

The demand made in 2006 to hold Union Carbide and Dow Chemicals liable for the continuing disaster had met with a lukewarm response from the PMO. Dr. Manmohan Singh told the delegation of survivors that he was powerless to take any extralegal measures to hold the company accountable. "We have to do business. India has to survive despite these tragedies," he said almost apologetically, and then went on to give the assurance that all options available within the law would be explored. The survivor groups were appalled by the government's admission that no pressure could be brought against an American multinational. "This should set the alarm bells ringing," said Sarangi in a press statement, "It does not make sense to direct our protest on the matter of corporate accountability toward a man who has expressed his powerlessness on this matter." It was in the face of such a Janus-faced approach by the highest authority that the campaign resolved to take direct and legal action against Dow's business, nationally and internationally. As one of the hunger strikers said, "Dow should beware because all our energies will be focused on putting the brakes on Dow's business in India."

It is interesting to observe that over the years, corporate accountability has emerged as an important focal point in the campaign. Why is this so? Talking to women in MUS and Pension indicates that the issue of corporate accountability is only partially understood, and to a large majority of the survivors it is the government that has to take the blame. But in the last decade, which has seen major changes in global politics the question of "whom" to blame has been replaced by reasons "why." The middle-class refrain has been addictive; globalization is inevitable; corporations make profit anyway; and government has to balance profit and people. We have seen how activism in Bhopal has drawn its strength from being consistently antiestablishment by creating ruptures in a lot of mainstream rhetoric. Years of experience have taught the survivors one thing, when the government claims to help people it always comes with a rider. Therefore, victory is met with "cautious optimism." The 2006 padyatra ended with the government "seemingly" conceding to some of the demands made by the survivor groups. But the preparations were already underway for the next phase of the action. A repeat of the padyatra was meant to remind the government that many of its tasks were still incomplete. More importantly, the confrontation between people and monolithic power structures can never really be resolved by quick fix measures and populist resolutions. Activism in Bhopal confronts middle-class rhetoric with the bitter reality that the government is in collusion with the offending corporation, thus making the state the enemy of the people. As campaign strategy the call for corporate accountability is what hurts the government most, by drawing attention to its failure to uphold the principles of democracy.

In a memorandum submitted to the PM on April 21, 2008, with copies to the Ministry of Law and Justice, Commerce and Industry, Chemicals and Fertilizers, and Legal Affairs, and signed by legal practitioners, professionals, academicians, and former judges, the padyatris make it very clear that they were protesting against the government's attempt to "absolve Dow Chemicals of its outstanding liabilities in Bhopal" in the light of "investments promised by Dow." The letter draws attention to the current political imbroglio: "We have learnt from the media reports that the Law Ministry and/or Department of Industrial Promotion and Policy are currently engaged in drafting a note for consideration by the Cabinet. The said note will make an argument for the GOI's proposed declaration of prospective immunity for any matter relating to Bhopal. Notably, the said document will argue for a withdrawal of the application filed by the Ministry Of Chemicals in the MP High Court, seeking Rs 100 crores as advance from Dow to clean up the contamination in Bhopal. Any such prospective immunity to a company that is currently a party in a civil case and has been named a party in a criminal case in the Magistrates court in Bhopal is inappropriate. Matters of liability are not a political decision, but a legal one to be left to courts to decide." Here if anything else was a clear indictment of the government's active role in boosting corporate crime.

The memorandum goes on to explain the nature of the collusion between the government and the corporation. The criminal trial has not been able to progress because UCC is absconding and the government has done very little to enforce its appearance. Meanwhile the toxic waste left behind by UCC has leached into the groundwater that is supplied to 25,000 people. UCC cannot come forward to do the clean up without subjecting itself to the criminal trial. In 2001 Dow took over UCC and has since then maintained that it has acquired the assets without the liability. And what is worse, Dow has even attempted to pass off UCC technology as its own, to avoid questions about Carbide's role as absconder. The nature of corporate crime and its vicious grip on systems becomes apparent. What the memorandum makes very clear is that GOI's proposal to grant prospective immunity to Dow is both unconstitutional and illegal.

The background to the government/corporation nexus was provided in chapter three where we had seen how the US-India CEO Forum, set up in 2005, was talking about the need to "develop a roadmap for increased partnership and co-operation between the Indian and American corporate." The Report of the US-India CEO Forum titled "US-India Strategic Economic Partnership" advocates the setting up of "an independent tribunal formed through the

Arbitration and Conciliation Act 1996 for dispute resolution." The report goes on to state "that specific focus on resolving legal issues such as those impacting Dow/Bhopal tragedy of 1984 would send a strong positive signal to US investors." It is ironical that instead of providing justice for its people, the highest office in the country was trying to refashion the judicial system in a way that could favor corporations. It is against the backdrop of the governments repeated "betrayal" of the people that the padyatra, a 172-day mammoth event, perhaps the longest in the history of the Bhopal movement, was planned.

Importantly, the issues of corporate crime and state negligence in the name of development are a worldwide phenomenon, which is also specific to the Bhopal disaster. The padyatra was meticulously and daringly planned to draw attention to the universality and specificity of the problem. It began with an eight hundred km walk from Bhopal to New Delhi, covering a span of thirty-five km per day to complete the journey in thirty days. Approximately forty gritty men and women made the entire journey, with activists from other solidarity groups and well wishers, joining them at different points. Media was organized with a lot of local level actions planned along the way. The idea was to connect Bhopal to people from other communities that faced danger from reckless corporate activities. The padyatra used a wide range of protest from street action, Satyagraha, nonviolent Gandhian methods of fasting, courting arrest, to creating awareness through exhibitions, film screenings, and organizing media events. The impetus behind such actions was to transform a political action into a movement with social/cultural connotations. I provide vignettes to the days spent on the pavements of Jantar Mantar, New Delhi, the official space for dissent in the heart of the city, and yet imaginatively distant from the seat of power. An interesting feature of the campaign was a blog that was posted on the Bhopal Web site; the daily hits were phenomenally high. The entire campaign was also videotaped, and interesting segments were put on YouTube. The idea was to get professionals and amateurs to capture theme-based images and beam it across continents in a way that could create an instant connectivity with both the issues and the images. I draw upon a lot of material made available on the blog, to show how the campaign worked toward involving the younger generation, by entering into their domain and using the tools of communication that appealed to them.

It is interesting to see how age-old campaign methods were used, but in a powerful innovative way. On April 22, 2008, a Delhi-based organization "Parivartan" (Change) that works on Right to Information (RTI) did a mass campaign asking the PMO for information regarding the status of the survivor's request to meet the PM. The first request for a meeting had been sent before the padyatra began. The idea of using RTI was really to show how the bureaucratic "veil" made the government unapproachable and impenetrable. A lot of the information unearthed through RTI helped to direct action against Dow as well. Thus activists in Pune discovered that the Maharashtra Pollution Control Board had cleared Dow's proposal for an R&D plant on the basis of a three-page proposal. It is interesting to observe that while UCC had got away with secrecy and silence, it is no longer the case with Dow. Today, citizens are far more conscious of the need for transparency and accountability, both key factors in a democracy. On April 25, a die-in action was staged in front of the Agriculture Ministry keeping the target very specific: cancellation of registration of three pesticides Dursban, Nurelle, and Pride made by Dow, following the payment of a bribe to the tune of US $325,000 to the Agriculture ministry officials. The protest was directed against specific government institutions like the Central Bureau of investigation (CBI) that had filed an FIR on August 16, 2007, against the corrupt officials and consultants of Dow's Indian company, but had failed to take any action. Support was gathered from other local organizations, like the Delhi-based Lokraj Sangathan, which invited a group of survivors to visit Sanjay Colony near Okhla Phase II, to share their experience of the struggle for democratic space for the poor. The multipronged nature of these actions was meant to draw attention to the wide implications of the government/corporation nexus.

The most grueling task for the campaigners was lobbying with the government. Here is a snippet from the blog that describes the process: "It is difficult to realize how tough it is to get an appointment with the elected representatives in the government. Hours of telephoning, faxing, and paper work can give you some five or ten minutes of hearing. They never commit. They never refuse. They just listen. You are never sure whether they have really heard. So few of us are doing the paperwork, constantly filing the documents, photocopying them, making proper sets, and assuring that we have everything at hand to cut through the red tape. We file every news-clip on Bhopal; it takes us two to three hours to scrutinize all the papers. We are left wondering what it would take to have Bhopal covered by high circulation newspapers. A newspaper with the highest circulation in Delhi launches the 'Lead India' campaign, but fails to acknowledge one of the oldest movements against corporate crime, led by ordinary people." Delhi-based group Kriti lent films for screening on the roadside. There were musical evenings, and choreography lessons were organized by theater groups for staging a street-play. Popular culture found expression in protest, fulfilling its age-old task of changing society.

It is interesting to see how youth participation was featured in two contrasting images, both powerful and a reminder of the chasm that separates India's phenomenal progress from the plight of those who get left behind. The Bhopali kids carried out a school outreach programme with interactive sessions, in which students from some of the most mainstream, elite schools of Delhi, met children who were less fortunate than them. Workshops were conducted and students were asked to put down their thoughts on paper. One child raised five bullet-point questions: "Do we live in a democracy? Why are people sacrificed for profit? Why no action has been taken despite twenty-four years of the tragedy?

Why does government continue to do business with Dow and UCC when they are refusing to take responsibility for Bhopal?" The Bhopal campaign had managed to enter the middle-class fortress and address issues that could not be learnt by rote as part of the curriculum. The second image was even more powerful. On April 29, 2008 a press conference was held where parents of five children born with congenital defects addressed the media, holding the children in their lap. The journalists who had gathered there looked visibly shaken by the entire experience. Here was a clarion call to the rest of the nation to take stock of what was happening to the future generation in Bhopal.

The reality was indeed grim. This time the media covered the event with photographs of mothers and the deformed children splashed on the front pages of the newspapers. The parents carried a memorandum that highlighted the systemic failure to rehabilitate the second-generation victims of the disaster. Right from the beginning, the government had known about the possibility of children being born with congenital physical and mental disorder, and yet research was prematurely stopped. The state government provided assistance for heart surgery to twenty-seven children under a programme called SPARC (Special Assistance to At Risk Children), but the scheme was abruptly terminated in 1997 siting financial constraints as the reason. The Supreme Court had passed an order in 1991, directing the central government to give medical insurance to 100,000 children born to gas-exposed parents; nothing has been done so far. Today, there are no facilities for detection, treatment, and rehabilitation of children born with congenital disorders. What these five parents were asking for, on behalf of others, was a monthly assistance of Rs 1,000 to take care of the medical expenses. Kesar Bai held twelve-year-old Suraj in her arms as she explained the situation: "My husband is a laborer. We have no money to spend on our son. I get free medical treatment for my breathing difficulties because I am a gas victim. My child does not get any help." Suraj was born brain damaged and cannot sit or talk.

Youth Perspective

On April 9, 2008, thirty-six Bhopal survivors were arrested for staging a die-in in front of the PMO; it included eleven-year-old Yasmin, nineteen-year-old Imran, and six-year-old Nagma. The children were manhandled and slapped; Imran was beaten up with a belt and thrown into lockup. The children said they caught the name of the policeman who was behind this operation. Mahendra Singh is said to have yelled, "Tear the clothes of these bitches." Children's testimonials are startlingly frank, wise, and deeply moving. In a freewheeling conversation they recounted their experience of coming face to face with police repression.[2] Did Nagma ever panic? "Yes, when I was lying in front of the PMO with a sheet over myself. During the die-in I was worried how the police would react. Earlier

Imran bhai had said that the policemen carried guns and they could shoot me. I was thinking of the worst lying on the gravel and a sheet over my face." Yasmin has her own experience to tell: "The cops kept us inside the bus. We said it was too hot inside the bus. One of the policemen taunted us and said why don't you jump out of the window. We decided to start jumping out of the window. Most windows had bars. Only Nagma was small enough to pass through the bars. So we told Nagma why don't you jump out as the policemen are daring us? We supported her upper body and she pushed her feet and legs between the bars and was out of the bus. The women cops were screaming, 'Those kids are jumping out!' After that they got hold of Nagma and made her sit near the door of the bus." While inside the jail, Sarita was able to work out a list of reasons why they would refuse to be released: "If we have to accept that we have done wrong and promise not to do it again, then it is unacceptable. We have not committed any crime. We have been sitting on dharna for so long, and the government has paid no heed, and that is why we had to do this action. If they ask us to present ourselves in court when we are required, it is not acceptable. Warren Anderson has never appeared in court. The government has not done anything against the crimes of Dow Chemicals, why should they take action for our small acts of disobedience. And if they say we cannot carry out such actions without permission, then that too is unacceptable for government allows protest only in those spaces where actions would be ineffective." Yasmin believes that if she had to plan out another die-in she would make sure that more people can sneak in and there is a larger contingent for shouting slogans.

The children enjoyed the songs they chanted to annoy the policemen. Here are a few samples: "Monsieur Jacque's loves and lusts/killed a bitch under the bus the puppies all chased the bus/all will be well/all will be well." The next one was sung to the tune of a popular film song: "One day you will die a dog's death/people will say there goes one who lived on ill-gotten wealth." But children's imagination is rarely violent. When Amir was asked if he believes in violent actions, this is what he had to say: "If there is a village in which the landlord is exploiting the poor people or a factory where the owner is exploiting workers, it is not correct to kill off the landlord or the factory owner. We should allow the person to change his ways. We should make them see that all their landed property or factories are actually acquired through the labor of poor people. If they still do not change their ways even then we should not kill them. We should punish them by taking away their properties and distributing them among people who are really in need."

When it comes to the question of why Dow refuses to pay for the clean up the children know the reason. "It would set an example for companies all over the world and they would go bankrupt," says Yasmin. Young Abhishek is able to link corporatization with colonization: "They have more money than they can count. There is no way they can spend all this money on themselves. Yet they will keep collecting more and more money. They dream of ruling the world and of becoming the richest people in the world. The corporations want to rule the world." In the face of such powerful opponents can they ever hope to win the struggle? Sarita's answer is unflinching: "We will keep fighting. Justice will come eventually. We never lose hope. Defeat motivates us to fight harder. People who have been fighting for so many years motivate us. The young ones have to take the fight forward." Abhishek chips in: "From the time we have started the padyatra Dow must be worried that the Bhopalis would drive them away from India." The children chuckle on hearing such a prophecy. Living on the pavement for 172 days is part of the long and arduous journey toward freedom that began long before they were born.

Vision for the Future

The 2008 padyatra also brought to the fore the need to frame a comprehensive vision for the future. It was as though, survivors had learnt their lesson from years of protest that simply conceding to demands does not count as victory. Though Prithviraj Chavan came on May 29 to the dharna, on behalf of the PMO, and made a statement that conveyed the government's in-principal agreement to an Empowered Commission on Bhopal, the news was seen as only a big step forward. As one of the organizers puts it, "It has been a long road. Elation followed by a feeling of being let down is a familiar pattern in Bhopal. We have learnt our lesson. Each time we win an agreement it comes with more guarantees. It has more teeth. Cynicism only means better preparation, better follow up for the beginning of another long struggle. Going by our experience every little detail has to be examined, every deadline has to be enforced. This is only a prologue to the struggle ahead." This preparedness, of taking things one step at a time and exploring all the pros and cons, creates the foundation for change that is envisaged by those who are at the helm of the struggle. The vision has two basic guiding principles, the need for remediation and holding the offender accountable. Neither one of them can be sacrificed on the grounds of political expediency. To that extent the vision is larger than merely the event of 1984. The disaster was preceded and followed by events with worldwide implications; therefore, justice will remain both complex and elusive in Bhopal. Tulsa Bai, who has been sitting at the dharna site for the 172 days, sums it up for me with her native wisdom: "By the time our demands will be met, many will get old, others will die, and who knows if our children and grandchildren will live to see the day! But what to do, nyai (justice) does not come easily."

Bhopal offers a unique example of a vision that grows from community struggle, which has been scripted by people who are actively part of the struggle. The vision is by no means complete. It will change and grow in the future. It is equally significant that the vision is clearly defined in an open letter to the PM, which is a collective document drafted on behalf of all the Bhopal-based organizations that are part of the international coalition. Its strength lies in the fact that it is available for interpretation and comments in the public domain. The final frontier of secrecy and behind doors policymaking has been pierced. I have been witness to its writing on the pavement, with group leaders typing away on their laptops, with children busy making posters, women singing protest songs, and boys and girls standing at the street junction and distributing pamphlets to the passerby.

The letter dated May 31, 2008, is addressed to the PM. It begins by thanking the government for its "commitment to speedily work out the modalities for setting up of the Commission." It then goes on to put forward suggestions for better implementation, thus initiating the survivors into the decision-making process that is so vital to a democracy. The demands belong to the survivor's organizations, and they use their collective voice to ask the PM to ensure that the commission is empowered through an Act of Parliament. To carry out its task of rehabilitation, the commission needs certain power for summoning and enforcing attendance of persons, of inspecting documents through the discovery process, and of requisitioning public records from courts or any office. The commission also needs secured corpus fund of Rs 2,000 crores to function for the next thirty years. This is in the light of the fact that one is talking about rehabilitation for the next generation of Bhopal victims. Rehabilitation demands that the MP government takes proactive steps to complete its numerous projects. The most important task is to supply clean water to communities affected by contaminated ground water. The payment of "user fee" means the project will only benefit those who can pay the money; therefore, a fee waiver is the other necessary step. The government has promised that ICMR will resume research. The survivors put forward their own mandate—link research with treatment protocol, and broaden the scope of research by including effects of water contamination with toxic gas exposure. But the most important demand is to ask the government to strengthen the law to takes its course and bring the culprits to book. The demands to extradite Anderson, to deregister the pesticides Dursban, Nurelle, and Pride and to revoke the license granted to Reliance to import UCC's Unipol technology are all legally mandated. The extradition has been pending for the last sixteen years and is only waiting for speedy implementation. The de-registering of illegally registered pesticides manufactured by Dow ought to be done suo motu by the government. For revoking the permission given to Reliance, the government only has to follow the 1992 directives of the Bhopal District Court regarding confiscation of UCC's properties in India. The Ministry of Industries and Commerce had permitted Reliance to purchase the property by overriding objections by Ministry of Chemicals. Here is a case of the government going against its role as prosecutor in a criminal case. Last but not the least, the survivors ask the government to pursue the application in the MP High Court, seeking Rs 100 crores from Dow as advance to clean up the toxic waste and contaminated ground water.

The vision can only be realized with people claiming their rights through voices raised in protest. Each step forward in the realization of the vision is celebrated in abandon, with distribution of sweets, splashing of colors, drum beats, and dancing in the streets. On August 8, 2008, Chemical Minister Mr. Ram Vilas Paswan came to the dharna site and made the following announcement—government will go ahead with the Empowered National Commission; it will not withdraw the application filed in the High Court for depositing Rs 100 crores as advance payment for environmental remediation of the plant site; Ratan Tata's offer to set up a Site Remediation Fund was not acceptable to the government as it was a conditional offer to absolve Dow Chemicals from liability. I joined in the celebration as the Bhopalis greeted each other with tears and hugs. Then they began dismantling the tents and packing their belongings, ready to take the night train back to Bhopal. Yasmin was grinning from ear to ear. "We are going home," she said joyously, "I am so happy! I will miss this place. But who knows when we will be back?" I too make my way back to my safe nest, ready to type out the history of a journey, which is far from over. I am reminded of the lines from one of Nida Fazli's verse.[3] The Bhopalis have their favorites; this is one of them: "The journey is long and arduous/Can you muster the courage to keep walking/There are thousands already walking against you/Can you still find space to reach your destination?"

Notes

Introduction

1. For a colonial history of Bhopal, see Shaharyar M. Khan, *The Begums of Bhopal: A Dynasty of Women Rulers in Raj India* (London and New York: I B Tauris, 2000).
2. See Satinath Sarangi, "The Movement in Bhopal and Its Lessons," in *The Movement in Bhopal and Its Lessons: Environmental Victims.* Ed. Christopher Williams (London: Earthscan, 1988), 101.
3. Suroopa Mukherjee, *Bhopal Gas Tragedy a Book for Young People.* 2nd ed. (Chennai: Tulika, 2005).
4. A very useful compendium on oral history is *The Oral History Reader,* ed. Robert Perks and Alistair Thomson, 2nd ed. (London: Routledge; Taylor & Francis Group, 2006). *The Oral History Reader* is particularly important for it introduces writings from diverse cultures and national contexts. The "Introduction to Second Edition" reiterates the point that "literature of oral history is increasingly cross-disciplinary, borrowing and blending from the many intellectual and professional contexts that consider memory, orality and the interview" (xii).
5. Oral history became a popular form with Alex Haley's bestseller *Autobiography of Malcolm X* (London: Penguin Books, 1965).
6. In 1948 Alan Nevins, a Columbia University historian, established the Columbia Oral History Research Office. In 1967 American oral historians founded the Oral History Association, and in 1969 British oral historians founded the Oral History Society. There is now an International Oral History Association, which is devoted to promoting oral history theory and practices.
7. See Paul Thompson, *The Voice of the Past: Oral History,* 3rd ed. (Oxford: Oxford University Press, 2000). He played a key role in forming the British Oral History Society. He highlighted oral history for its capacity to transform historical content by bringing recognition to groups that were formerly ignored. He also drew attention to people exploring and making their own history.
8. Raphael Samuel was the cofounder of the journal *Past and Present* in 1952 and pioneered the study of working-class history. Also see E. P. Thompson, *The Making of the English Working Class* (London: Victor Gollancz, 1963), Christopher Hill, *The World Turned Upside Down: Radical Ideas during the English Revolution* (London: Penguin Books, 1976), and Eric Hobsbawm, *Uncommon People: Resistance, Rebellion and Jazz* (London: Abacus, 1998).

9. See Richard Candida-Smith, *Art and Performance of Memory: Sounds and Gestures of Recollection* (London: Routledge, 2003). Luisa Passerini has provided valuable insight on the role of subjectivity in history in *Fascism in Popular Memory: The Cultural Experience of the Turin Working Class* (Cambridge: Cambridge University Press, 1987). Passerini draws attention to the unconscious meanings of experience, and the gaps and silences in the way memory works. This brings oral history closest to literature.
10. Folklore has close links with literature. It includes the entire body of expressive culture—music, dance, legends, proverbs, and popular beliefs. It is also the set of practices through which these expressive genres are shared. Historically, folklore deals with oral narratives such as fairy tales and mythology, but in modern times it has developed links with social sciences and is no longer strictly oral communication.
11. See the issue on *The Public Life of History in Public Culture: Society for Transnational Cultural Studies*, vol. 20, no. 1 (Winter 2008). Especially useful are the two essays: Neeladri Bhattacharya, "Predicaments of Secular Histories" and Bain Attwood, "In the Age of Testimony: The Stolen Generation Narrative, 'Distance' and Public History."
12. Oral historians have developed their own handbooks that provide practical guidelines on oral history methodology. Recently, a number of Web sites has been designed to provide online guidance. It helps research students to adopt reliable methods for conducting interviews, transcribing, and making data available through Internet.
13. It is post-eighties that emphasis was put on the political scope of oral history. Attention was directed toward social issues linked to advocacy and conflict resolution. To get the perspective of feminist oral historians, see Sherna Berger Gluck and Daphne Patai, *Women's Words: The Feminist Practice of Oral History* (New York: Routledge, 1991).
14. Of special interest here is a survey conducted by Bhopal Group for Information and Action (BGIA) in New Gandhi Nagar, Shakti Nagar, and Taj Mahal Colony on November 3–15, 1991. Another survey was conducted by the Center for Community Health and Social Medicine, Jawaharlal Nehru University, New Delhi in December 1989. Its report titled *Against All Odds* focused on the health status of women. Questions were raised about the importance of such voluntary efforts that would be of direct and immediate use for strengthening the case of the gas-affected victims. The idea was to develop a critique of the methodology of processing of claims that would then feed into activism.

I The Killer Factory: A Disaster Waiting to Happen

1. For a brief history of the company see David Bembo, Ward Morehouse, and Lucinda Wykle, *Abuse of Power: Social Performance of Multinational Corporation: The Case of Union Carbide* (New York: New Horizon Press, 1990), 12–20.
2. Kim Fortun in her book *Advocacy after Bhopal: Environmentalism after Bhopal* (Chicago and London: University of Chicago Press, 2001) shows how UCC's profit graph was kept in check by reversals in global agricultural output, by bringing

down yield from 3 to 1percent of annual food production. She argues that rise in food costs, decline in per capita availability, and the need to rely on surplus stocks to meet the increasing demand were directly linked to the ecological side effects of new technology promoted by giant chemical companies like Monsanto, DuPont, and Union Carbide. It had two important side effects. Human health was subject to cost-benefit analysis. A phase of environmentalism was initiated at the community level, which opposed the siting of chemical treatment and disposal facilities in the United States. It was time to search for newer pastures (xiii–xvii). The two quotations at the beginning of the chapter are cited in her book.
3. Weir argues that Nazi scientists devised the first generation of insecticides—parathion—as an agent for chemical warfare. At the end of the war a burgeoning chemical industry was left without a market. It was then that attention was diverted to the extermination of pests for better yield of crops. In 1979 the *United Nation's Environment Programme* stated that half a million people were poisoned every year by pesticides, and the number of deaths had been increasing at the rate of 5 percent per year. A pernicious side effect of all this was the dumping of nonregulated and banned items in developing countries (11).
4. Gupta shows how UCC and India, both wanted to enter the competitive arena where pesticides had become big business, with worldwide sales touching $13 billion mark by 1984. It resulted in a sharp increase in the domestic use of chemical fertilizers and pesticides per unit of cropped areas, which grew from 5 kg per hectare in fifties to 32 kg at the beginning of the eighties (New Delhi: Ajanta, 1991), 54.
5. See www.studentforbhopal.com for infamous quotes from American corporate bosses and Indian officials and politicians.
6. Leubuscher shows how the simple test of weighing social against economic interests, which courts use, is seen as outrageously unworkable when it is applied to corporations as a norm for determining legal duty. Susan Leubuscher, "How Green Was My Fig Leave: Grandiose International Standards Cannot Save the World," *The Little Magazine, Globalization and Its Contents*, vol. V, no. 4&5 (2004), 79.
7. Abstracts of the unpublished papers are available in CD form as issued by IIT, Kanpur in 2004.
8. See Bridget Hanna, Ward Morehouse, and Satinath Sarangi, ed. *The Bhopal Reader* (New York: Apex Press and Goa: Other India Press, 2004), 19.
9. Cited in Arvind Rajagopal, "And the Poor Gets Gassed: Multinational Aided Development and the State—The Case of Bhopal," *Berkeley Journal of Sociology*, vol. 32 (1987).
10. I have drawn from court papers compiled by Prof. Upendra Baxi in two invaluable books: *Inconvenient Forum and Convenient Catastrophe: The Bhopal Case* (Bombay: N. M. Tripathi, 1986) and *Valiant Victims and Lethal Litigations: The Bhopal Case* (Bombay: N. M. Tripathi, 1990).

2 Monstrous Memories: "Reliving" the Night of the Disaster

1. The archival sources are drawn from pamphlets brought out by Bhopal Group for Information and Action (BGIA) in 1986 and 1990. They were researched in a pain

staking way in hostile conditions and were freely distributed so that the material could be widely disseminated. A lot of this material is now available on the net at the www.bhopal.net, www.studentsforbhopal.net, and the Bhopal Memory Project at Bard University. The live interviews are drawn from the research work that I have undertaken in Bhopal since 2003. I have worked on specific areas of interest and a lot of the research findings have found shape in published articles and essays. Some of the testimonials are taken from informal conversations with people, mostly recorded as personal notes. In chapters that look at activism, I have used material that is taken from the QMU, Edinburgh research project (August 2007 to September 2008) on the Ethnology of Bhopal Campaigners for Justice. The different sources of the testimonials have been duly acknowledged.
2. In later chapters, I will juxtapose testimonials with official documents and show how structures that were put in place for the rehabilitation programme end up becoming the systems of oppression. I will also refer to pamphlets and propaganda literature brought out by the state government from 1986 onward. This will particularly be relevant for discussions on economic and medical rehabilitation.
3. See Anil Agarwal, Juliet Memfield, and Rajesh Tandon, *No Place to Run: Local Realities and Global Issues of the Bhopal Disaster* (Highlander Center and Society for Participatory Research in Asia, 1985), 1.
4. Indra Sinha's moving account of Sunil soon after his death "Life and Death of a Mad Bhopali Child" is posted on www.bhopal.net. Sunil was found hanging in his room last year. He had left an elaborate note where he did not blame anyone for his death. But he made it a point to wear a black T-shirt, which said "No More Bhopals."
5. It is worth taking a look at a pamphlet brought out by the state government on the occasion of the first anniversary of the tragedy titled *Disaster and Its Aftermath: Life Asserting Itself* (1986). The tone is commemorative and almost self-congratulatory. Again and again we are told that despite the horror of what happened, life is getting back to normal, and the onus for this is largely on the survivor's themselves. "Bhopal mourns its dead and tends the large number of people who are still suffering from the after-affects of the poisonous gas. There is however a resurgence of confidence and faith. The injured are adjusting themselves to the situation and are trying manfully to start life anew." As a propaganda material, the language is cautious and avoids putting the blame on anyone. The night is described as "fateful" with the underlying message that nothing could have averted the situation. The attempt is to deny human agency as far as possible.
6. See Suroopa Mukherjee, "MIC- Night's Children." Ghosts. *The Little Magazine*, vol. IV, no. 4 (2003).
7. Kim Fortun puts it succinctly when she says that Bhopal was targeted for industrial development because it was backward, and yet its connection by rail and road with all major ports made it nodal in a complex global system. So the world came into Bhopal, but on the night of the disaster the residents had no way out (Ibid., xiv).
8. David Weir, *The Bhopal Syndrome: Pesticide Manufacturing in the Third World* (Penang: International Organization of Consumers Union, 1985), v.
9. Paul Shrivastava, "Long Term Recovery from the Bhopal Crisis," in James R. Mitchell ed., *The Long Road to Recovery: Community Response to Industrial Disaster* (Tokyo, New York, Paris: United Nations University Press, 1996), 122.

10. The question of fate has often come up in the discussions I have had with the survivors. I find the case of Sazda Banu truly ironical. In 1981 her husband Asraf Mian who worked in the Union Carbide factory was killed by a phosgene leak while on duty. On December 3, she came to Bhopal with her two children and her trauma began from the railway station. It is worth listening to her story: "On December 3rd 1984 I arrived at Bhopal by the Lucknow Bombay Express from Kanpur. The train stopped at the platform at 1.30 a.m. I started coughing. My two children were with me. One was 5 and the other was 4. We were all coughing, after which I don't remember anything. Someone carried me to the hospital from where I was later dropped at my brother's house. My children were abandoned at the platform. At 7 a.m. I asked for my children. Then my brother went to the station to look for them and brought them back. At 9 am my elder son expired. After my husband died I got no compensation. My in-laws sent me out of the house after my husband died. My husband died on December 25th 1981. This also happened because of the manager's mistake. His duty time was over and he was asked to open a valve. The valve had not been opened or even touched for 3 years, and there was phosgene gas inside. My husband asked him three times if there was gas inside. Three times the manager said, no. After the valve leaked, my husband was kept in the factory dispensary and later taken to the hospital. I have not got anything yet" (BGIA, 1986). I have often discussed the case of Sazda Banu with the other women asking them whether it was fate that brought her back to Bhopal on December 3. Almost all of them see it less as fate and more of what Union Carbide represents, a "killer factory" that failed to take heed of the kind of danger that was in store for everybody. "Everybody talks of fate," said Champa Devi, "because they refuse to make the connections that would put the blame where it really belongs."
11. Veena Das has a chapter on Bhopal titled "Suffering, Legitimacy and Healing: The Bhopal Case" in her book, *Critical Events: An Anthropological Perspective on Contemporary India* (New Delhi: Oxford University Press, 1995), 138.
12. William Bogard, *The Bhopal Tragedy: Language, Logic and Politics in the Production of a Hazard* (London: Westview Press, 1989), 34.
13. Suroopa Mukherjee, "A Woman of Substance: An Encounter with Rashida Bi" in *The Ecologist Asia*, vol. 11, no. 4 (2003), 12.

3 Bhopal Lives On: The Many Faces of the Continuing Disaster

1. See *Clouds of Injustice: Bhopal Disaster 20 Years On* (Oxford: Amnesty International, 2004), 59.
2. UCC's *Annual Report* (2003) clearly stated that "The Corporation's business activities comprise components of Dow's global businesses rather than stand alone operations." The report can be accessed at www.unioncarbide.com.
3. Article V of the Merger Agreement states, "there are no civil, criminal or administrative actions, suit claims, hearings, investigations on proceedings pending or, to the actual knowledge of its executive officers, threatened against it or any of its shareholders." Amnesty International (2004), 55.

4. See H. Rajan Sharma, "Bhopal Gas Tragedy: Veil of Deception," *Frontline* (March 26, 2008).
5. See Brent Fisse and John Braithwaite, *Corporations, Crime and Accountability* (Cambridge: Cambridge University Press, 1993). Fisse and Braithwaite argue for an accountability model that literally holds "an axe over the head of a corporation that has committed the actus reus of a criminal offence. This may almost literally be an axe that ultimately can deliver the sanction of corporate capital punishment—liquidation, withdrawal of license or charter of the firm to operate. The private justice system of the firm is then put to work under the shadow of that axe" (15). Bhopal is a case in point that no such private justice system is either in place or reliable.
6. "Bhoposhima: Crime without Punishment," V. R. Krishna Iyer, *Economic and Political Weekly* (EPW), (November 3, 1991).
7. *Twelfth Report* of Committee of Government Assurances [2003–2004] (Lok Sabha Secretariat, New Delhi), 57.
8. *Infochange Agenda*, Issue 1 (December 2004), 32–35.
9. See "Corporate Science," Peter Montague, www.thetruthaboutdow.org. Also see Marc S. Reisch, "Suits and Lab Coats: Industry Draws on Academic Know-How to Help Develop Specialty Chemicals and Other New Materials," *Chemical & Engineering News*, vol. 85, no. 47 (November 19, 2007), 15–20. Reisch writes, "Dow said it would make a gift of $10 million over five years to launch the Sustainable Products & Solutions Program within the Haas School of Business at the University of California, Berkley. Berkeley says the program will operate in partnership with the school's College of Chemistry. It will also tap faculty across the campus to fund basic research in chemistry, environmental policy, and the interface between the two disciplines."
10. Satinath Sarangi, in an unpublished article, "Health Effects of Exposure to Chemicals" gives us some startling facts. "The world production of organic chemicals has increased 500 folds in the last 60 years and continues to increase at an exponential rate doubling every 7 years. Between 50,000 to 100,000 chemicals are now in common use." He wrote this in 1997 so the numbers would have compounded accordingly now. In another book titled *Silent Invaders, Pesticides, Livelihoods and Woman's Health* (New Delhi: Orient Longman, 2003) Miriam Jacobs and Barbara Dinham have shown how billions of kilogram of toxic chemicals are deliberately added to the global environment every year. More than 1,000 active ingredient chemicals and 1,200 other ingredients (inerts) are formulated into thousands of different pesticide products. Pesticide contamination affects air, water, soil, food, domestic animals, wildlife, pets, humans, breast milk, and the developing fetus.
11. In 1990, Citizen's Environmental Laboratory in Boston identified highly toxic materials (dichlorobenzenes and polynuclear aromatic hydrocarbons) in the soil and water surrounding the factory. In 1996 State Research Laboratory of Public Health Engineering Department reported serious chemical contamination in samples taken from 11 tube-wells in the area. In 1999 Greenpeace International conducted a study that reliably identified 73 organic compounds that go back to the production process. In its report *The Bhopal Legacy*, Greenpeace confirmed the presence of PAH associated with crude oil or petroleum pollution. Two

organochlorine compounds found in the samples are both formed as by-products in a range of industrial processes that involve chlorination. Mercury was used around the plant as a sealant, while high levels of chromium and nickel confirms the fact that most of the processing equipment and storage facilities were made of stainless steel and alloys of nickel. High levels of copper, zinc, and lead were the result of widespread usage and corrosion. Copper is an excellent electrical conductor and would have been used in electrical wires and cables. Its alloys were used for welding, and lead was used for water distribution or in containers for storing corrosive liquids like acids.

12. See *Corporate Crimes: The Need for an International Instrumentation on Corporate Accountability and Liability* (Amsterdam: Greenpeace, August 2002).
13. See Nityanand Jayaraman, "Environment India: Union Carbide Must Clean Bhopal Mess," *Inter Press Service* (September 1, 2006).
14. See *Johannesburg Memorandum for the World Summit on Sustainable Development* (August 2002, Heinrich Boll Foundation).
15. See Sonu Jain, "25 years on, Govt wakes up to Bhopal waste but cannot find anyone to clean it up," *Indian Express* (June 15, 2008).
16. All materials are taken from the PMO papers retrieved by BGIA through the Right to Information Act. The papers are available on the www.bhopal.net.
17. See Sudha Ramachandran, "Delhi forgets Bhopal and fights for Dow," *South Asia* (November 2, 2007).
18. A Rap sheet on the "Ugly face of Tata" is widely distributed on www.bhopal.net.
19. It is equally well known that Dow Chemical is shielding Union Carbide from its status as an absconder, even while facilitating its business in India. Between 1994 and 2005, Union Carbide has managed to sell more than $20 million worth of products through a host of intermediaries, including Dow Chemical. Payments up to Rs 8.8 million were reported to have been made by De-Nocil, the then subsidiary of Dow Chemicals, for getting various regulatory clearances for Dow's pesticides business in India during 1996 and 2001.
20. See Sonu Jain, "Dow to US Watchdog: We Bribed Indian Officials for Clearances," *Indian* Express (February 24, 2007). Also see Aasha Khosa, "CBI to send letter rogatory to US in case against Dow subsidiary," *Business Standard* (May 2, 2008).
21. Arundhati Roy in conversation with Shoma Chaudhuri, www.tehelka.com (March 26, 2007).

4 Women as Bread Earners: Shattered Lives and the Relentless Struggle for Survival

1. For a comprehensive definition of disaster see John I. Clarke, ed., *Population and Disaster* (Oxford: Basil Blackwell, 1989), 7–11.
2. A phrase coined by Shiv Vishwanathan and Harsh Sethi in their innovative Social science Fiction titled "Bhopal: A Report from the Future" in the *Lokayan Bulletin*, vol. 7, no. 3 (1989), 54.
3. Taken from a booklet brought out by the Chingari Trust in 2007 titled "The Struggle to Stay Alive," 2. Rashida Bi won the Goldman Environment Award in

2004. The trust was set up with the prize money, and today it works for rehabilitation of second-generation children of gas-affected parents, born with congenital birth defects. Rashida Bi told me that her inspiration to help children comes from the moment of total helplessness when her son died in the wards of Sultania Zanana Hospital.
4. See S. Ravi Rajan, "Rehabilitation and Voluntarism in Bhopal," *Lokayan Bulletin*, vol. 6, no. 1/ 2 (1988), 7.
5. Cited in *777: The Newsletter of the Bhopal Medical Appeal* (Spring 2004).
6. See Suroopa Mukherjee, "MIC- Night's Children." Ghosts. *The Little Magazine*, vol. IV, no. 4 (2003).
7. See Vijaya Ramaswamy, ed., *Researching Indian Women* (New Delhi: Manohar, 2003), 229–316. Also see U. Ramaswamy, et al., ed., *Reconstructing Gender towards Collaboration* (Bangalore: Books for Change, 2000), 1–12.
8. Various aspects of women in the contemporary employment scenario has been discussed by Shiela Rowbotham and Stephanie Linkcoyle, ed. *Women Resist Globalization: Mobilizing for Rights* (London: Zed Books, 2001); Malini Bhattacharya, ed. *Globalization: Perspective in Women's Studies* (Jadavpur University: School of Women's Studies, 2004); Nirmala Bannerjee, ed. *Indian Women in Changing Industrial Scenario* (New Delhi: Sage, 1991).
9. For a fuller discussion on how the government changed parameters in an arbitrary way, see Brojendra Nath Bannerjee, *Environmental Pollution and Bhopal Killings* (Delhi: Gian Publishing House, 1987), 104.
10. See *Unfolding the Betrayal of the Bhopal Gas Tragedy* (Delhi: B. R. Publishing Corporation, 2008), 193.
11. For an extensive account of the meeting with bureaucrats by student members of "We for Bhopal" see *Closer to Reality, Reporting Bhopal Twenty-Three Years after the Gas Tragedy* (2004), 51–59.
12. Avasthi and Srivastava discuss the electrical industry where women mostly did armature winding for electrical fans, but with technical improvements wage rates went up and jobs were taken over by men. A similar shift happened in pharmaceuticals and toiletries, which had been women-dominated jobs. Avasthi and Srivastava, ed. *Modernity, Feminism and Women Empowerment* (New Delhi: Rawat Publications, 2001), 205.

5 "We Are Flames Not Flowers": The Inception of Activism

1. The testimonials are drawn from *Bhopal We Will Never Forget* (BGIA: 1986 and 1987) and *Voices from Bhopal* (BGIA: n.d.).
2. Anil Sadgopal is a retired Professor from Delhi University and has done pioneering work on education. Satinath Sarangi is a metallurgical engineer from Banaras Hindu University, founder of BGIA and Management Trustee of Sambhavna Clinic in Bhopal.
3. The interviews were conducted by Dharmesh Shah and Tarunima Sen. The pilot phase of the study on *Ethnography of Bhopal Survivor's Movement* developed contact with the various campaign groups within the movement. Research methods were

refined, drawing on Freirean pedagogical methodology and using video technology as a means of generating dialogue between the research team and the experiences of the survivor activists. The use of participant observations was a key factor. I am grateful to the project for giving me permission to quote from the interviews. Tape numbers are used to indicate the source.
4. For a detailed discussion see Paul Shrivastava, "Long Term Recovery from the Bhopal Crisis," in James Mitchell, ed., *The Long Road to Recovery: Community Responses to Industrial Disaster* (New York: United Nations University Press, 1996), 137.
5. See S. Ravi Ranjan, "Rehabilitation and Voluntarism in Bhopal" in *Lokayan Bulletin,* vol. 6, no. 1/ 2 (1988), 24.
6. The BMA also brings out its newsletter *777: The Newsletter of the Bhopal Medical Appeal,* which is the print version of the appeal for fund. Like the BGIA newsletters its purpose is to spread awareness, but the tone is more propagandist and meant for encouraging volunteers from different walks of life.
7. See Suroopa Mukherjee, "Anger and Denial on the Streets of Bhopal," in *Infochange Agenda, Industrial Pollution: 20 years after the world's worst industrial disaster* (Issue 1, December 2004). This article has been reprinted in *The Bhopal Reader.*

6 "No More Bhopals": Women's Right to Knowledge and Control of Their Bodies

1. For a succinct analysis of all the contingent factors see Ramana Dhara, "Health Effects of the Bhopal Gas Leak: A Review," *New Solutions* (Spring 1994), 42.
2. It is important to clarify at this initial stage that research in the crucial area of medical rehabilitation proved to be difficult. While doctors who had retired and had distanced themselves from the gas tragedy were forthcoming in granting me interviews, ICMR was far more cautious when it came to giving me the go-ahead to use data from their published material. As one of them said candidly, "We have our jobs to protect." However, I was assured that I had the freedom to quote from published material and I could give the reference in the bibliography. There was a catch. Public domain had to be strictly adhered to and I was not free to use material from any report that was only meant for internal circulation. I have adhered to their stipulations, and all the data that I have gathered are from secondary sources or from references made by doctors in the course of their oral testimonies. The yearly reports remained internal, as part of the administrative task of keeping a record of the progress made by the research that was being carried out. Some working manuals were published for doctors; two such manuals were brought out in 1986 and 1989, and a separate manual of mental health care was brought out in 1987 in collaboration with NIMHANS, Bangalore. Thus from 1984 to 1994 the only published material that was meant for public consumption was a special supplement titled Scientific Studies on Bhopal Gas Victims, Part A, which was brought out in *The Indian Journal of Medical Research* (vol. 86, 1987). The articles were based on the research findings of doctors involved in various projects. Part B was not published. In 1994 ICMR wound up the projects without publicly providing any reasons.

3. See *Evaluation of Some Aspects of Medical Treatment of Bhopal Gas Victims*. Bhopal and Indore: BGIA and Socially Active Medicos, 1990. Even as ICMR was carrying on with its research projects, which were shrouded in secrecy, proactive groups stepped in to conduct surveys and write reports that were freely circulated. As one of the doctors said to me, the situation was conflict ridden and often did not help the victims.
4. See C. Sathyamala, "The Medical Profession and the Bhopal Tragedy," *Lokayan Bulletin* (vol. 6, no. 1/ 2, 1988). Sathyamala's article "Reproductive Health Consequences of Bhopal Gas Leak: Fertility and Gynaecological Disorders," *Economic and Political Weekly* 14. Also see *Economic and Political Weekly* (January 6, 1996), 43.
5. See S. Sriramachari, "The Bhopal Gas Tragedy: An Environmental Disaster," *Current Science,* vol. 86, no. 7 (April 10, 2004), 906–907.
6. Theo Colburn, Dianne Dumanoski, and John P Myers, *Our Stolen Future: Are We Threatening Our Fertility, Intelligence, and Survival?* (New York, London: Plume Book, 1997).
7. See article on "Early observations on lung function study," *Scientific Studies on Bhopal* (New Delhi: ICMR, 1987), 75.
8. Comprehensive analysis of the medical crisis has been provided by Thelma Narayan, "Health Impact of Bhopal Disaster: An Epidemiological Disaster," parts 1 and 2. *Economic and Political Weekly* (August 18, 1990): (August 25, 1990) and Rajiv Lochan. "Health Damage Due to Bhopal Gas Disaster: Review of Medical Research." *Economic and Political Weekly* (May 25, 1991).
9. Post-Bhopal many institutions worldwide undertook animal experiments on inhalational toxicology of MIC. In the "Epidemiological and Experimental Studies on the Effects of MIC on the Course of Pregnancy," *Environmental Health Perspectives,* vol. 72 (1987), Daya Varma refers to a vital experimental study that was carried out on the effects of MIC on pregnant mice, at the Graduate School of Public Health, University of Pittsburgh in September 1985.
10. This is what Sriramachari and Heeresh Chandra had to say in one of their articles "The Lessons of Bhopal Toxic MIC Gas Disaster Scope for Expanding Global Biomonitoring and Environmental Specimen Banking," in answer to the vital question of whether MIC crossed the placental barrier, "We failed in our attempts to demonstrate S-carbamoylation because of our inability to prepare reference standard of S-carbamoylated cysteine, and we had no access to a mass speedometer with chemical ionization of detection systems. It is worth recording here that by employing such a technique in 1991, Bailey and Slatter successfully demonstrated the distribution or ferrying of MIC through out the tissues." *Chemosphere,* vol. 34, no. 9/10 (1997), 2244.
11. See *Against All Odds: Continuing effects of the Toxic Gases on the Health Status of the Surviving Population in Bhopal, Preliminary Report of a Medical Study carried out Five Years after the Disaster,* Coordinated by C. Sathyamala, Nishith Vohra, and K. Satish (New Delhi, The Center for Community Health and Social Medicine, 1989).
12. Rani Bang and Mira Sadgopal, "Effects of the Bhopal Disaster on the Women's Health: An Epidemic of Gynaecological Diseases" (1985). Pesticide News No. 46, December 1999.

13. See "Epidemiological and Experimental Studies on the Effects of MIC on the Course of Pregnancy," *Environment Health Perspective*, vol. 72 (1987), 151–155.
14. "Reproductive Health Consequences of Bhopal Gas Leak: Fertility and Gynaecological Disorders, *Economic and Political Weekly* (January 6, 1996), 44.
15. The findings of the research were published in *JAMA* (vol. 290, no. 14 [October 8, 2003]). It pointed to the fact that in the absence of research and surveillance, it was likely that thousands of children suffering from birth defects are not recognized as being affected by the disaster, leave alone compensated for it.
16. Drawn from BGIA Newsletter (1990).
17. From *777: The Newsletter of the Bhopal Medical Appeal* (Spring 2004).
18. For more details on the Chingari Trust, see www.chingaritrust.org.

7 "Dancing in the Streets": Protest, Celebration, and Modes of Self-Expression

1. Though BMHRC is a research center, there is total absence of epidemiological and clinical research. A 500-bed hospital, which is specially set up to serve gas survivors, does not have any system to monitor the health status of gas victims undergoing treatment. To give an example, there is a general dearth of information regarding the continuing exposure-related mortality, but BMHRC does not have a system for monitoring exposure-related mortality. There is no information on treatment protocol, so BMHRC continues with the indiscriminate use of harmful, unnecessary drugs. A joint study done by BGIA and Socially Active Medicos (Indore) shows that 27 percent of drugs used are harmful and 13 percent are banned in other countries. The Medical Commission on Bhopal has highlighted the indiscriminate use of steroids, antibiotics, psychotropic, and symptomatic drugs in government hospitals in Bhopal. BMHRC has done nothing to improve the situation. And finally, BMHRC has done very little to draw attention to gas-induced gynecological problems.
2. Provided by Sarangi to be freely shared with friends and well-wishers.
3. Born on October 12, 1938, in the city of Delhi, Nida Fazli (Muqtida Hasan Nida Fazli) did his schooling from Gwalior. His father was an Urdu poet himself. During the Partition of India his parents migrated to Pakistan, but young Nida Fazli decided to stay in India. His best known works are *Mor Naach, Ham Qadam*, and *Safar Me Dhoop To Hogi*.

Bibliography

Agarwal, Anil, Juliet Merrifield, and Rajesh Tandon. *No Place to Run: Local Realities and Global Issues of the Bhopal Disaster.* Highlander Center and Society for Participatory Research in Asia, 1985.

Amnesty International. *Clouds of Injustice: Bhopal Disaster 20 Years On.* Oxford: Amnesty International, 2004.

———. *The U N Human Rights Norms for Business: Towards Legal Accountability.* London: Amnesty International, 2004.

Andersson, N, M. Kerr Muir, V. Mehra, and A. G. Salmon. "Exposure and Response to Methyl Isocyanate: Results of a Community Based Survey in Bhopal." *British Journal of Industrial Medicine.* Vol. 45 (1988).

Ariyabandu, Madhavi Malalgoda, and Maithree Wickramasinghe. *Gender Dimensions in Disaster Management: A Guide to South Asia.* India edition. New Delhi: Zubaan, 2005.

Ashwin, Abinav, Abhishek Shinde, John Daniel Mithran, and Avishek Prasad. *Corporate Criminal Liability: An International Comparative Study.* Research Paper for Greenpeace. Bangalore: National Law School of India, n.d.

Asian Regional Exchange for New Alternatives—An Interdisciplinary Programme of Asian Studies and Research Cooperation. *Bhopal—Industrial Genocide?* Hongkong: Arena Press, 1985.

Attwood, Bain, Dipesh Chakrabarty, and Claudio Lomnitz. Guest ed. *Public Culture: Society for Transnational Cultural Studies.* Vol. 20, No. 1 (Winter 2008).

Avashia, B., M. C. Battigelli, W. K. C. Morgan, and R. B. Reger. "Effects of Prolonged Low Exposure to Methyl Isocyanate." *JOEM.* Vol. 38, No. 6 (June 1996).

Avasthi, Abha, and A. K. Srivastava, ed. *Modernity, Feminism and Women Empowerment.* Jaipur: Rawat, 2001.

Bajpai, S., N. Jain, H. P. K. Warrier, and J. P. Gupta. *Bhopal Gas Tragedy and Its Effects on Process Safety.* International Conference at IIT, Kanpur. Souvenir Book and Abstracts. December 1–3, 2004.

Banerjee, Brojendra Nath. *Environmental Pollution and Bhopal Killings.* Delhi: Gian, 1987.

Banerjee, Nirmala, ed. *Indian Women in a Changing Industrial Scenario.* Indo-Dutch Studies on Development Alternatives-5. New Delhi: Sage, 1991.

Basu, Amit Ranjan. *Bhopal Gas Disaster and Mental Disorder: Narratives from the Survivors.* New Delhi: Fact Finding Mission on Bhopal, n.d.

Baxi, Upendra. *Inconvenient Forum and Convenient Catastrophe: The Bhopal Case.* The Indian Law Institute. Bombay: N. M. Tripathi, 1986.

Baxi, Upendra. "Bhopal: Litigation and Social Reality." *Lokayan Bulletin.* Vol. 6, No. 1/2 (1995).
———. *The Future of Human Rights.* New Delhi, Oxford University Press, 2002.
Baxi, Upendra, and Amita Dhanda. *Valiant victims and Lethal Litigations: The Bhopal Case.* The Indian Law Institute. Bombay: N. M. Tripathi, 1990.
Beckman, Karen. *Vanishing Women: Magic, Film and Feminism.* Durham, NC: Duke University Press, 2003.
Benthall, Jonathan. *Disaster, Relief and the Media.* London: I. B. Tauris, 1993.
Bergman, David. *The Perfect Crime? How Companies Can Get Away with Manslaughter in the Workplace.* London: West Midlands Health and Safety Advise Centre, n.d.
Bhargava, Pushpa M. "The Bhopal Tragedy: A Middle Word." *Economic and Political Weekly.* Vol. XX, No. 22 (June 1, 1985).
Bhattacharya, Malini, ed. *Perspectives in Women's Studies: Globalization.* School of Women's Studies, Jadavpur University. New Delhi: Tulika Books, 2004.
Bhopal Gas Tragedy Relief and Rehabilitation Department, M P. *Bhopal Disaster and Its Aftermath: Life Is Reasserting Itself* (December 3, 1986).
———. *Report on Relief and Rehabilitation* (December 3, 1995).
———. *Report on Relief and Rehabilitation* (December 3, 1998).
———. *Report on Relief and Rehabilitation* (December 3, 2002).
———. *Report on Relief and Rehabilitation* (December 3, 2005).
———. *Report on Relief and Rehabilitation* (December 3, 2006).
———. *In Memoriam* (December 3, 2007).
Bhopal Group for Action and Information (BGIA). *Voices from Bhopal.* Bhopal: BGIA, n.d.
———. *Evaluation of Some Aspects of Medical Treatment of Bhopal Gas Victims.* Bhopal and Indore: BGIA and Socially Active Medicos, 1990.
———. *Compensation Disbursement: Problems and Possibilities.* A Report of a Survey Conducted in Three Gas Affected Bastis of Bhopal (January 1991).
———. *Bhopal Lives '84–'94: Anniversary Notes.* New Delhi: Bhopal Gas Peedit Sangharsh Sahayog Samiti (BGPSSS) and BGIA, 1994.
Bhopal Medical Appeal. "We Are All Helping Build the New Clinic." *777: The Newsletter of the BMA* (Spring 2004).
———. "Twenty Years Since That Night, Bhopal 1984–2004." *777: The Newsletter of the BMA* (Spring 2004).
———. "For more than 120,000 Bhopalis That Night Has Never Ended." *777: The Newsletter of the BMA* (Autumn 2004).
———. "Bhopal's Damaged Children: How Many More?" *777: The Newsletter of the BMA* (Autumn 2007).
———. "Saira's Story: When Love is Not Enough." *777: The Newsletter of the BMA* (December 2008).
Bhopal Survivors' Movement Study. *Bhopal Survivor's Speak: Emergent Voices from a People's Movement.* Edinburgh: Word Power Books, 2009.
———. Data archive. Queen Margaret University, http://edata.qmu.ac.uk.
Bhushan, Bharat, and Arun Subramaniam. "Bhopal: What Really Happened?" *Business India* (February 25–March 10, 1985).

Bidwai, Praful. "Prevent a Third Bhopal Tragedy." *Mint. The Wall Street Journal* (April 2, 2008).

———. "Nano from Gujarat: Legitimizing Moditva." *Rediff News* (October 20, 2008).

Blake, P. G., and S. Ijadi-Maghsoodi. "Kinetic and Mechanism of the Thermal Decomposition of Methyl Isocyanate." *International Journal of Chemical Kinetics.* Vol. 14 (1982).

Bogard, William. *The Bhopal Tragedy: Language, Logic and Politics in the Production of a Hazard.* London: Westview Press, 1989.

Bomann-Larsen, Lene, and Oddny Wiggen, ed. *Responsibility in World Business: Managing Harmful Side-effects of Corporate Activity.* Tokyo: United Nations University Press, 2004.

Buch, M. N. *Environmental Consciousness and Urban Planning.* Tracts for the Times/2. New Delhi: Orient Longman, 1993.

Bucher, John R. "Methyl Isocyanate: A Review of Health Effects Research Since Bhopal." *Fundamental and Applied Toxicology.* Vol. 9 (1987).

Buckingham-Hatfield, Susan. *Gender and Environment.* London: Routledge; Taylor & Francis Group, 2000.

Callender, Thomas J. Restricted Circulation. Medical Health: Case History with Findings. November 1994.

Candida-Smith, Richard. *Art and Performance of Memory: Sounds and Gestures of Recollection.* London: Routledge, 2003.

Carson, Rachel. *Silent Spring.* London: Penguin Books, 1962.

Cassels, Jamie. *The Uncertain Promise of Law: Lessons from Bhopal.* Toronto: University of Toronto Press, 1993.

Chandoke, Neera. "Global Civil Society and Global Justice." *Economic and Political Weekly* (July 21, 2007).

Chishti, Anees. *Dateline Bhopal: A Newsman's Diary of the Gas Disaster.* New Delhi: Concept, 1986.

Chauhan, P. S. *Bhopal Tragedy: Social Legal Implications.* Jaipur: Rawat, 1996.

Chavez, Hugo. *The South Also Exists.* New Delhi: Leftword, 2005.

Chomsky, Noam. *Profit over People: Neo-Liberalism and the Global Order.* New York: Seven Stories Press, 1999.

Chouhan, T. R., and others. *Bhopal: The Inside Story, Carbide Workers Speak out on the World's Worst Industrial Disaster.* 2nd updated ed. Goa: Other India Press; New York: Apex Press, 2004.

Clarke, John I., and others, ed. *Population and Disaster.* Cambridge, MA: Basil Blackwell, 1989.

Clinard, Marshall B., and Peter C. Yeager. *Corporate Crime.* London: Free Press, 1980.

———. *Corporate Crime.* Rev. Ed. New Brunswick, NJ: Transaction, 2006.

Colburn, Theo, Dianne Dumanoski, and John Perterson Myers. *Our Stolen Future: Are We Threatening Our Fertility, Intelligence and Survival?—A Scientific Detective Story.* New York: Plume, 1997.

Dagani, Ron. "Data on MIC's Toxicity Are Scant, Leave Much to Be Learned." Bhopal Report. *C&EN*, Washington (February 11, 1985).

Das, Veena. *Critical Events: An Anthropological Perspective on Contemporary India.* Delhi: Oxford University Press, 1995.
Daunderer, Max. "The Consequences of the Poisonings at Bhopal." *Medical Corps Intervention* (3/1986).
Delamore, Eugenia C., Natania Meeker, and Jean F. O'Barr, ed. *Women Imagine Change: A Global Anthology of Women's Resistance. From 600 B. C. E. to Present.* New York: Routledge, n.d.
Delhi Committee on Bhopal Gas Tragedy. *Repression and Apathy on Bhopal.* Delhi: Lokayan, 1985.
Dembo, David, Clarence J. Dias, Ayesha Kadwani, and Ward Morehouse. *Nothing to Lose But Our Lives: Empowerment to Oppose Industrial Hazards in a Transnational World.* Hong Kong: Arena, 1987.
Dembo, David, Ward Morehouse, and Lucinda Wykle. *Abuse of Power: Social Performance of Multinational Corporations, The Case of Union Carbide.* New York: New Horizons Press, 1990.
Dhara, Ramana. "Health Effects of the Bhopal Gas Leak." *New Solutions.* Vol. 35 (Spring 1994).
Dias, Tony. "The Disaster and Its Aftermath: The Hiroshima of the Chemical Industry." Working paper, Conference on Environmental and Economic Rationality, n.d.
Doyle, Jack. *Trespass against Us: Dow Chemical and the Toxic Century.* Monroe: Common Courage Press, 2004.
Eckerman, Ingrid. *The Bhopal Saga: Causes and Consequences of the World's Largest Industrial Disaster.* Hyderabad: Universities Press, 2005.
Everest, Larry. *Behind the Poison Cloud: Union Carbide's Bhopal Massacre.* Hyderabad: Sangam Books, 1985.
Feffer, John, ed. *Living in Hope: People Challenging Globalization.* London: Zed Books, 2002.
Fisse, Brent, and John Braithwaite. *Corporations, Crime and Accountability.* Cambridge: Cambridge University Press, 1993.
Fortun, Kim. *Advocacy after Bhopal: Environmentalism, Disaster, New Global Orders.* Chicago: Chicago University Press, 2001.
Foucault, Michel. *The Birth of the Clinic: An Archeology of Medical Perception.* Tr. A. M. Sheridan. London: Tavistock, 1973.
Gill, Barry K., ed. *Globalization and the Politics of Resistance.* New York: St. Martin's Press, 2000.
Gittelsohn, Joel, Margaret E. Bentley, Pertti J. Pelto, Moni Nag, and Saroj Pachauri. *Listening to Women Talk about Their Health Issues and Evidence from India.* New Delhi: Har-Anand, 1994.
Gluck, Sherna Berger, and Daphne Patai. *Women's Words: The Feminist Practice of Oral History.* New York: Routledge, 1991.
Goel, Aruna. *Organization and Structure of Women Development and Empowerment.* New Delhi: Deep & Deep, 2004.
Grazia, Alfred De. *A Cloud over Bhopal: Causes, Consequences and Constructive Solutions.* Bombay: Kalos Foundation, 1985.
Greenpeace. *The Bhopal Legacy: Toxic Contamination at the Former Union Carbide Factory Site, Bhopal, India, 15 Years after the Bhopal Accident* (November 1999).

———. *Corporate Crimes: The Need For An International Instrument on Corporate Accountability and Liability*. Johannesburg: Earth Summit, 2002.

Grimshaw, Patricia, Katie Holmes, and Marilyn Lake, ed. *Women's Rights and Human Rights: International Historical Perspectives*. Basingtonstoke and New York: Palgrave Macmillan, 2001.

Guha Ramachandra. *Environmentalism: A Global History*. Delhi: Oxford University Press, 2000.

Guillette, Elizabeth A. "An Anthropological Interpretation of Endocrine Disruption in Children." In *Environmental Endocrine Disruptors: An Evolutionary and Comparative Perspective*. Ed. E. A. Guillette and D. A. Crain. New York: Taylor and Francis, 2000. 322–338.

Gupta, Ashis. *Ecological Nightmares and the Management Dilemma: The Case of Bhopal*. Delhi: Ajanta, 1991.

Hanna, Bridget, Ward Morehouse, and Satinath Sarangi, ed. *The Bhopal Reader: Remembering Twenty Years of the World's Worst Industrial Disaster*. Goa: Other India Press; New York: Apex Press, 2004.

Hawkinson, Jon. *The Cyanide Controversy: A Toxicological Report of the Bhopal Gas Disaster*. San Francisco: The Bhopal Project, 1986.

Hazarika, Sanjoy. *Bhopal: The Lessons of a Tragedy*. New Delhi: Penguin Books, 1987.

Heinrich Boll Foundation. *The Jo'burg Memo: Fairness in a Fragile World*. 2nd ed. Berlin: Heinrich Boll Foundation, 2002.

Hobsbawm, Eric. *Uncommon People: Resistance, Rebellion and Jazz*. London: Abacus, 1999.

Indian Council of Medical Research. *Scientific Studies on Bhopal Gas Victims. Part A. The Indian Journal of Medical Research*. New Delhi, 1987.

———. *Health Effects of the Toxic Gas Leak from the Union Carbide Methyl Isocyanate Plant in Bhopal: Technical Report on Population Based Long-term Epidemiological Studies (1985–1994)*. New Delhi, n.d.

Indo-German Environment Programme. Technical Proposal for the Final and Complete Remediation of the Abandoned Factory Site of Union Carbide at Bhopal India. Restricted Circulation. Submitted to M P State Pollution Control Board, March 2006.

International Campaign for Justice in Bhopal. *We've Come for Justice and We Won't Leave Without It* (February 20–March 27, 2006).

International Confederation of Free Trade Unions, International Federation of Chemical Energy, and General Workers Union. "The Report of the ICFTU—ICEF Mission to Study the Causes and Effects of MIC Gas Leak at the Union Carbide Plant in Bhopal, India" (paper presented at the International Labor Organization's Annual Conference in June, 1985).

International Institute of Concern for Public Health, Canada, and Ministry of Concern for Public Health, USA. "Twelve Years After Bhopal—An Editorial Reflection." *International Perspectives in Public Health*. Vols. 11 & 12 (1996).

Ives, Jane H., ed. *Transnational Corporations and Environmental Control Issues: The Export of Hazards*. Boston: Routledge and Kegan Paul, 1985.

Iyer, V. R. Krishna. "Bhoposhima: Crime without Punishment. Case for Crisis Management Jurisprudence." *Economic and Political Weekly* (November 23, 1991).

Jacobs, Miriam, and Barbara Dinham, ed. *Silent Invaders: Pesticides, Livelihoods and Women's Health.* New Delhi: Orient Longman, 2004.

Jain, Sonu. "Dow to US Watchdog: We Bribed Indian Officials for Clearances." *Indian Express* (February 24, 2007).

Jana Swasthya Kendra. *Proposal for Health Activities for Bhopal Gas Victims for the Next Four Months: Progress Report.* Bhopal: Jana Swasthya Kendra, 1985.

Jayaprakash, N. D. "Perilous Litigation: The Leak Disaster Case." *Economic and Political Weekly* (December 22, 1990).

———.*Contempt of People: Ramifications of the Bhopal Gas Leak Disaster Case.* New Delhi: Delhi Science Forum, October 1992.

Jayaraman, Nityanand. Guest, ed. *No More Bhopals. The Ecologist Asia.* Vol. 7, No. 6 (November/December 1999).

———. Guest ed., *Industrial Pollution: 20 Years After the World's Worst Disaster Many More Bhopals Are Waiting to Happen. Why Has So Little Changed? Agenda Infochange*, Issue 1 (December 2004).

Jones, Tara. *Corporate Killing: Bhopals Will Happen.* London: Free Association Press, 1988.

Karliner, Joshua. *The Corporate Planet: Ecology and Politics in the Age of Globalization.* San Franciso: Seirra Club Books, 1997.

Karnad, Raghu. "Air, Water, Earth and the Sins of the Powerful." *Tehelka.* Vol. 5, No. 13 (April 5, 2008).

Keefer, Philip, and Stuti Khemani. "Why Do the Poor Receive Poor Services?" *Economic and Political Weekly.* Vol. XXXIX, No. 9 (February 28–March 5, 2004).

Kendon, Adam. *Gesture: Visible Action as Utterance.* Cambridge: Cambridge University Press, 2004.

Keswani, Rajkumar. "Bhopal, Sitting on the Edge of a Volcano." *Rapat Weekly, Issue 2, Bhopal,* (October 1, 1982).

———. "Bhopal Gas Disaster." *Free Press Journal* (December 16, 1984).

Khan, Shaharyar M. *The Begums of Bhopal: A Dynasty of Women Rulers in Raj India.* London: I. B. Tauris, 2000.

Koplan, Jeffrey P., Henry Falk, and Gareth Green. "Public Health Lessons from the Bhopal Gas Disaster." *Journal of the American Medical Association.* Vol. 264, No. 21 (December 5, 1990).

Kothari, Ashish. *Understanding Biodiversity: Life, Sustainability and Equity.* Tracts for the Times/ 11. New Delhi: Orient Longman, 1997.

Kothari, Rajni. *Transformation and Survival: In Search of a Humane World Order.* Delhi: Ajanta, 1988.

———. *Politics and People: In Search of a Humane India.* Vol. I. Delhi: Ajanta, 1989.

———.*Politics and People: In Search of a Humane India.* Vol. II. Delhi: Ajanta, 1989.

Kothari, Smitu, and Rajni Bakshi Ed., *Lokayan Bulletin.* Vol. 7, No. 3 (May–June 1989).

Kripalani, Manjeet. "Dow Chemical: Liable for Bhopal?" *Business Week* (May 28, 2008).

Lapierre, Dominique, and Javier Moro. *It Was Five Past Midnight in Bhopal.* New Delhi: Full Circle, 2001.

Lepkowski, Wil. "Union Carbide-Bhopal Saga Continues as Criminal Proceedings Begin in India." *C&EN, Washington* (March 16, 1992).

Lochan, Rajiv. "Health Damage Due to Bhopal Gas Disaster: Review of Medical Research." *Economic and Political Weekly* (May 25, 1991).
Lok Sabha Secretariat, New Delhi. Committee of Government Assurances (2003–2004) Twelfth Report. Limited circulation. Presented to Lok Sabha on February 27, 2003.
Lord, Albert Bates. *The Singer of Tales*. Cambridge, MA: Harvard University Press, 1960.
Low, Alaine, and Soraya Tremayne, ed. *Sacred Custodians of the Earth? Women, Spirituality and the Environment*. New York: Berghahn Books, 2001.
Malik, Vinay, R. S. Tiwari, and H. M. Mishra. *Socio- Economic Impact of Disbursement of Interim Relief to Gas Affected Families of Bhopal*. Bhopal: Academy of Administration, 1991.
Mankekar, Purnima. *Screening Culture, Viewing Politics*. New Delhi: Oxford University Press, 2000.
Martinez-Alier, Joan. *The Environmentalism of the Poor: A Study of Ecological Conflicts and Valuation*. New Delhi: Oxford University Press, 2004.
Mathur, Kanchan. "Body as Space, Body as Site: Bodily Integrity and Women's Empowerment in India." *Economic and Political Weekly*. Vol. XLIII, No. 17 (April 25–May 2, 2008).
McNeill, David. *Gesture and Thought*. Chicago: Chicago University Press, 2005.
Medico Friends Circle. *The Bhopal Aftermath: An Epidemiological and Socio-Medical Survey*. Vadodara: Medico Friends Circle, 1985.
———. *Distorted Lives: Women's Reproductive Health and Bhopal Disaster*. Pune: Medico Friends Circle, 1990.
Mehta, Pushpa S. Anant S. Mehta; Sunder J. Mehta, MD, and Arjun B. Makhijani. "Bhopal Tragedy's Health Effects." *Journal of the American Medical Association*, Vol. 264, No. 21 (December 5, 1990).
Mehta, Suketu. "Bhopal Lives: Twelve Years Later." *The Indian Magazine*. Vol. 17 (December 1996).
Menon, Meena. "Bhopal: Poisoned Lives." Bhopal Revisited. *The Hindu Survey of the Environment* (2003).
Milman, Parry. *The Making of Homeric Verse: The Collected Papers of Milman Parry*. Ed. James Parry. Oxford: Oxford University Press, 1971.
Mitchell, James K., ed. *The Long Road to Recovery: Community Responses to Industrial Disaster*. Indian ed. Delhi: Bookwell, 1998.
Mohanty, Amarnath. "Affirmative Action in India: An Alternative Perspective." *Economic and Political Weekly*. Vol. XLII, No. 30 (July 28–August 3, 2007).
Morehouse, Ward, and M. Arun Subramaniam. *The Bhopal Tragedy: What Really Happened and What It Means for American Workers and Communities at Risk*. New York: Apex Press, 1986.
Morris, Chris. "Commission for Bhopal Grievances." *BBC News* (May 29, 2008).
Mukherjee, Suroopa. "Lethal Documents: An Anatomy of the Bhopal Crisis." In *India in the Age of Globalization: Contemporary Discourses and Texts*. Ed. Suman Gupta, Tapan Basu, and Subarno Chattarji. New Delhi: Nehru Memorial Museum and Library, 2003. 233–252.
———. "MIC-Night's Children." Ghosts. *The Little Magazine*, Vol. IV, No. 4 (2003).

Mukherjee, Suroopa. "Dancing in the Streets: Narratives of Resistance in Bhopal Eighteen Years after the Gas Tragedy." *IIC Quarterly* (Summer 2003).

———. "A Woman of Substance: An Encounter with Rashida Bee." *The Ecologist Asia. Corporate Crime: Popular Resistance in a Globalized World.* Vol. 11, No. 1 (October–December 2003).

———. "Anger and Denial on the Streets of Bhopal." *Agenda Infochange*, No. 1 (December 2004).

———. Bhopal Gas Tragedy: The Worst Industrial Disaster in Human History, A Book for Young People. 2nd ed., Chennai: Tulika, 2005.

———. "Anger and Denial on the Streets of Bhopal." In *The Bhopal Reader*. Ed. Bridget, Morehouse, and Sarangi. Originally published in *Agenda Infochange*, ibid., 2005. 118–124.

Muralidhar, S. *Unsettling Truths, Untold Tales: The Bhopal Gas Victims' Twenty Years of Courtroom Struggles for Justice.* New Delhi: Fact Finding Mission on Bhopal, n.d.

Muralidharan, Sukumar. "Bhopal after 12 Years: Industrial Accidents and Corporate Liability." *Frontline* (December 27, 1996).

Murthy, R. Srinivasa. *Mental Health Impact of Bhopal Gas Disaster.* New Delhi: Fact Finding Mission on Bhopal, n.d.

Narayan, Thelma. "Health Impact of Bhopal Disaster: An Epidemiological Disaster," parts 1 and 2. *Economic and Political Weekly* (August 18, 1990); (August 25, 1990).

National Dialogue-Women, Health and Development. (November 23–25, 2006). *Towards Women's Rights and Responsibilities.* Pune: MASUM.

———. *The Indian Women's Health Charter.* Pune: MASUM, March 8, 2007.

National Environmental Engineering Research Institute (NEERI). Process Package for Disposal of Sep Contents At UCIL Bhopal. Restricted Circulation. November 1992.

Neeraj. *Globalization and Recolonisation?* 2nd ed. Pune: Alka Joshi, 2006.

Pandey, Shashi Ranjan. *Community Action for Social Justice: Grassroots Organizations in India.* New Delhi: Sage, 1991.

Pandit, Tooshar. "Killer Gas, Callous Carbide." *Sunday* (December 16–22, 1984).

Parasuraman, S., and Unnikrishnan P. V., ed. *India Disasters Report: Towards a Policy Initiative.* New Delhi: Oxford University Press, 2000.

Pearce, Frank, and Laureen Snider, ed. *Corporate Crime: Contemporary Debates.* Toronto: University of Toronto Press, 1995.

Perks, Robert, and Alistair Thomson, ed. *The Oral History Reader.* 2nd ed. London: Routledge Taylor & Francis Group, 2006.

Permanent People's Tribunal. *On Industrial and Environmental Hazards and Human Rights: The Bhopal Session.* October 19–24, 1992.

———. *Findings and Judgements.* 1992.

Planning Commission. Report of the task Force on Governance, Transparency, Participation, and Environmental Impact Assessment in the Environment and Forest Sector for XI Five Year Plan, December 2006.

Prasad, Archana. *Against Ecological Romanticism: Verrier Elwin and the Making of an Anti-Modern Tribal Identity.* New Delhi: Three Essays Collective, 2003.

———. *Environmentalism and the Left: Contemporary Debates and Future Agendas in Tribal Areas.* New Delhi: Leftword Books, 2004.

Raj, Ashok. *Wither Bhopal Workers? A Report on Their Occupational Dislocation and Assessment of the Efforts towards Economic Rehabilitation*. New Delhi: Fact Finding Mission on Bhopal, n.d.

Rajagopal, Arvind. "And the Poor Gets Gassed: Multinational Aided Development and the State—The Case of Bhopal." *Berkeley Journal of Sociology*. Vol. 32 (1987).

Ramaswamy, Uma, Bhanumathy Vasudevan, Anuradha Prasad, Gagan Sethi, and Sulagna Sengupta. *Reconstructing Gender towards Collaboration*. Bangalore: Books for Change, 2000.

Ramaswamy, Vijaya, ed. *Re-searching Indian Women*. Delhi: Manohar, 2003.

Rao, G. J., A. K. Saraf, and V. K. Sharma. "Bhopal Gas Disaster: Unidentified Compounds in the Residue of the MIC Tank 610." *Indian Academy of Forensic Sciences*. Vol. 30, No. 1 (1991).

Ray, Shashwat Gupta. "Warkaris on Warpath." *Sakaal Times* (October 7, 2008).

Rowbotham, Sheila, and Stephanie Linkogle, ed. *Women Resist Globalization: Mobilizing for Livelihood and Rights*. London: Zed Books, 2001.

Roy, Arundhati. "Power Politics: The Reincarnation of Rumpelstilskin." *Outlook*. (November 27, 2000).

———. "Instant- Mix Imperial Democracy: Buy One Get One Free." *Outlook*. (May 26, 2003).

Roy, Dunu. "The Neutralization of Bhopal" (paper presented at National Convention: Lessons from Bhopal—Environment, Science and Democratic Rights, February 17–18, 1985).

Sadgopal, Anil, and Sujit K. Das. *A Preliminary Report of Concern Regarding Persistence of Toxins in the Bodies of Bhopal Gas Victims*. Hoshangabad: Kishore Bharati Group, 1987.

———. *Interim Report on Sodium Thiosulphate Therapy of the Bhopal Gas Victims*. Hoshangabad: Kishore Bharati Group, 1988.

———.*Final Report on Medical Relief and Rehabilitation of Bhopal Gas Victims*. Hoshangabad: Kishore Bharati Group, 1988.

Saksena, Anu. *Gender and Human Rights: Status of Women Workers in India*. New Delhi: Shipra, 2004.

Sambhavna Trust. *Research Studies on Neurological Morbidities Related to the December '84 Union Carbide Gas Disaster at Bhopal*. Bhopal: Peoples Health and Documentation Clinic. (March 1997).

———. *Ten Years of Possibilities*. Private Circulation. Bhopal: Sambhavna Trust, 2006.

Sarangi, Satinath. "Bhopal Gas Victims: Dismal Dispersal of Compensation." *Economic and Political Weekly* (December 23, 1995).

———. "The Movement in Bhopal and Its Lessons." In *The Movement in Bhopal and Its Lessons: Environmental Victims*. Ed. Christopher Williams. London: Earthscan, 1998.

———."Bhopal Gas Tragedy." *India Disaster Report: Towards a Policy Initiative*. Ed. S. Parasuram, P. V. Unnikrishnan. New Delhi: Oxford University Press, 2000. 334–340.

———. "Crimes of Bhopal: Holding Corporations Accountable." *Samar* 16 (Fall–Winter 2003).

Sarkar, Sravani. "Gas Tragedy Widows: A Forgotten Lot." *Hindustan Times* (July 3, 2003).

Satyamala, G. "The Medical Profession and the Bhopal Tragedy." *Lokayan Bulletin.* Vol. 6, No. 1 /6 (1988).

———. "Reproductive Health Consequences of Bhopal Gas Leak: Fertility and Gynaecological Disorders." *Economic and Political Weekly* (January 6, 1996).

Satyamala, G, Nishith Vohra and K. Sathish. "Health Status of the Bhopal Survivors." *Lokayan Bulletin.* Vol. 7, No. 5, 1989.

———. *Against All Odds: Continuing Effects of the Toxic Gases on the Health Status of the Surviving Population in Bhopal.* New Delhi: The Centre for Community Health and Social Medicine, Jawaharlal Nehru University, 1989.

Schafer, Kristin S., Margaret Reeves, Skip Spitzer, and Susan Kegley. *Chemical Trespass: Pesticides in Our Bodies and Corporate Liability.* Pesticide Action Network North America, 2004.

Schlesinger, Jacob M., and Thaddeus Herrick. "Chemical Manufacturers Elude Crackdown on Toxic Materials." *Wall Street Journal* (May 21, 2003).

Sen, A. K. "It's Dow or Die: Did Union Carbide's Liability end with a $470 Million Settlement?" *Outlook* (May 27, 2002).

Sengupta, Arjun, K. P. Kannan, and G. Ravindran. "India's Common People: Who Are They, How Many Are They and How Do They Live?" *Economic and Political Weekly.* Vol. XLIII, No. 11 (March 15–21, 2008).

Sengupta, Somini. "Decades Later Toxic Sludge Torments Bhopal." *New York Times* (July 7, 2008).

Shaini, K. S. "Parasites of Disaster: The Other Tragedy Is What's Being Done in the Name of Bhopal." *Outlook* (December 16, 2002).

———. "No Takers for Bhopal Toxic Waste." *BBC News/World* (September 30, 2008).

Sharma, H. Rajan. "Bhopal Gas Tragedy: Veil of Deception." *Frontline* (March 26, 2006).

Sheoin, Tomas Mac. *The Report on Union Carbide Corporation (UCC).* New Delhi: The Fact Finding Mission on Bhopal, n.d.

Shiva, Vandana. *Staying Alive: Women, Ecology and Survival in India.* New Delhi: Kali for Women, 1988.

Shrivastava, Paul. *Bhopal: Anatomy of a Crisis.* London: Paul Chapman, 1992.

Singh, M. P., and S. Ghosh. "Bhopal Gas Tragedy: Model Simulation of the Dispersion Scenario." *Journal of Hazardous Material.* Vol. 17, Elsevier Science Publishers, 1987.

Singh, Moti. *Unfolding the Betrayal of the Bhopal Gas Tragedy.* Delhi: B. R. Publishing Corporation, 2008.

Singh, Tejbir, and Harsh Sethi Ed., *Elusive Justice: A Symposium on the Bhopal Gas Disaster after Twenty Years. Seminar* 544 (December 2004).

Sriramachari, S. (1989). "Background Paper on Pathology—Collection, Processing and Storage of Pathological Material for Immediate Analysis and Later Study of Toxicological Effects and Their Long-Term Implications." In *Methods for Assessing and Reducing Injury from Chemical Accidents.* Ed. Philippe Bourdeau and Garesth Green. N. p: John Wiley & Sons. 223–233.

———. "Bhopal Gas Tragedy: An Environmental Disaster." *Current Science.* Vol. 86, No. 7 (April 10, 2004).
Sriramachari, S., and Heeresh Chandra. "The Lessons of Bhopal: Toxic MIC Gas Disaster Scope for Expanding Global Biomonitoring and Environmental Specimen Banking." *Chemosphere.* Vol. 34, Nos. 9/10 (1997).
Srishti. *Surviving Bhopal: Toxic Present—Toxic Future. A Report on Human and Environmental Chemical Contamination around the Bhopal Disaster Site.* New Delhi: Fact Finding Mission on Bhopal, 2002.
Stanton, Paul, and Armin Rosencranz. "A Blanket Spread too Thin: Compensation for Bhopal Victims." *Economic and Political Weekly* (July 1994).
Stiglitz, Joseph. *Globalization and Its Discontents.* New Delhi: Penguin Books, 2002.
Subramaniam, Arun. "The Catastrophe at Bhopal." *Business India* (December 17–30, 1984).
———. "Bhopal: The Dangers of Diagnostic Delay." *Business India* (August 12–25, 1985).
———. "Bhopal Litigation: Carbide's Defense." *Business India* (December 15–18, 1986).
Subramaniam, Arun, Javed Gaya, and Rusi Engineer. "Beyond Bhopal: The Policy Issues." *Business India* (December 2–15, 1985).
Sufrin, Sidney C. *Its Setting, Responsibility and Challenge.* New Delhi: Ajanta, 1985.
The Dow Chemical Company Annual Report. *The Way Forward.* 2002.
The International Medical Appeal for Bhopal. "Thousands of Our Children Were No So Lucky. They Survived." *Guardian* (December 3, 1994).
The TLM Team. *Globalization and Its Contents. The Little Magazine.* Vol. V, Nos. 4 & 5 (2004).
Thomson, Paul. *The Voice of the Past: Oral History.* 3rd ed. Oxford: Oxford University Press, 2000.
Thorat, Meenakshi. "Gender Budgeting in Disaster Relief." *Economic and Political Weekly.* Vol. XLIII, No. 17 (April 25–May 2, 2008).
Trivedi, Shashikant. "H C to Decide on Dow Chem Plant Waste Today." *Business Standard* (July 3, 2008).
Union Carbide Corporation. *Research Compendium Prepared for Communities Concerned about Corporations.* N. p., 1994.
———. *Bhopal Methyl Isocyanate Incident Investigation Team Report.* March 1985.
Varma, Daya. "Epidemiological and Experimental Studies on the Effects of Methyl Isocyanate on the Course of Pregnancy." *Environmental Health Perspectives.* Vol. 72 (1987).
Vishwanathan, Shiv. "Reflections on the Transfer of Technology." *Lokayan Bulletin.* Vol. 6, No. 1 /2 (1988).
Vishwanathan, Shiv, and Harsh Sethi. "Bhopal: A Report from the Future." *Lokayan Bulletin.* Vol. 7, No. 3 (1989).
Vivek, P. S. *The Struggle of Man against Power: Revelation of 1984 Bhopal Tragedy.* Bombay: Himalaya, 1990.
We for Bhopal. *Closer to Reality: Reporting Bhopal Twenty Years after the Gas Tragedy.* New Delhi: We for Bhopal, 2004.

Weir, David. *The Bhopal Syndrome: Pesticide Manufacturing and the Third World.* Penang: International Organization of Consumer's Union, 1985.

Wilkins, Lee. *Shared Vulnerability: The Media and American Perceptions of the Bhopal Disaster.* Contributions to the Study of Mass Media and Communications, No. 8. New York: Greenwood Press, 1987.

Whitaker, Mark, et al. "It Was Like Breathing Fire…" *Newsweek* (December 17, 1984).

Index

Agent Orange case, 84, 134
Ahmedabad, 139
Akash, 156, 157
Ali, Mustaq, 105
Aluoi Valley, 134
Aluwalia, Montek Singh, 77
Alvares, Claude, 55, 56
Anderson, Warren, 19, 22, 62, 64, 65, 66, 106, 120, 181, 183
Arbitration and Conciliation Act 1996, 178
Arthur D. Little & Co, 70
Auschwitz, 49

Bai, Basanta, 50
Bai, Bhagwati, 115, 116
Bai, Gomti, 104
Bai, Kamala, 87
Bai, Nanni, 86
Bai, Narayani, 55, 81, 104
Bai, Parvati, 86
Bai, Sumati, 105
Banerjee, Nalok (Dr), 143, 145
Bano, Sajida, 72
Bartholemew, Pablo, 160
Bhandari, N. R, 144, 153
Bhopal, *passim*
   BGDRC (Bhopal Gas Disaster Research Center), 140, 142, 143, 144, 145, 149
   BGIA (Bhopal Group of Information and Action), 44, 45, 49, 50, 52, 53, 55, 63, 70, 99, 101, 107, 112, 126, 140, 141, 142
   BGPMSKS (Bhopal Gas Peedit Mahila Stationery Karamchari Sangh), 103
   BGPMUS (Bhopal Gas Peedit Mahila Udyog Sangathan), 103
   BMA (Bhopal Medical Appeal), 124, 151, 172
   BMHRC (Bhopal Memorial Hospital and Research Center), 67, 146, 173
   BTGD (Bhopal Toxic Gas Disease), 140, 141
   co-ordination committee on, 79
   district court of, 34, 66, 183
   gas relief cell, 75, 85, 87, 91, 94
   gas tragedy of, 19, 27, 32, 42, 69, 70, 71, 81, 91, 137, 138, 147
   ICJB (International Campaign for Justice in Bhopal), 118, 122, 123, 129, 154, 164, 166, 169, 171
   many faces of continuing disaster; lives on, 61–80
      absconders from law, 64–67
      corporate inheritance, 63–64
      environmental degradation and legal wrangle, 70–73
      environmental issues and political action, 73–76
      quick fix solutions, 78–80
      road map to the second settlement, 76–78
      voluntary codes and responsible care, 67–70
   municipal corporation of, 79, 140
Bee, Razia, 49, 50, 52
Bi, Aziza, 155
Bi, Bano, 44, 47, 50, 53, 54, 55, 73, 96, 99
Bi, Bhoori, 53
Bi, Haseena, 72, 74
Bi, Hazra, 17, 47, 48, 55, 96, 98, 99, 160, 164, 166, 168
Bi, Jubeida, 96
Bi, Rashida, 49, 51, 56, 59, 84, 85, 114, 115, 117, 118, 119, 123, 155
Bi, Sabra, 95
Bi, Shahida, 155
Bi, Zubeda, 49
BJP (Bharatiya Janta Party), 120, 128
Bogard, William, 22, 26, 58
Bombay (later Mumbai), 18, 33, 111, 120, 122, 151, 168
BPL (Below Poverty Line), 165
Brazil, 37

Calcutta, 18, 20, 67
Canada, 138
Carson, Rachel, 71, 131, 135
CBI (Central Bureau of investigation), 38, 64, 65, 78, 179
Chandra, Heeresh (Dr), 147, 149

Chavan, Prithviraj, 182
Chidambaram, P, 77
Chouhan, T. R, 17, 24, 25, 26
CIA (Central Investigation Agency), 113
Communist Party Marxist (CPM), 111
Communist Party of India (CPI), 111
Congress party, 39, 105, 110, 111
    Gandhi, Rajiv, 39, 111, 115, 116, 117
CSIR (Council of Scientific and Industrial Research), 30, 64, 65

Danbury, 17, 19, 28, 37
Dancing in Streets: Protest, Celebration, and Modes of Self-Expression, 159–184
    community health service and platform for international justice, 171–173
    eight hundred kilometers on foot, 175–180
    healing touch, 173–175
    I will die working for organization, 163–165
    memorable actions and process of learning, 167–171
    our struggle is supported by our own capacity and strength, 165–167
    vision for future, 182–184
    youth perspective, 180–182
Das, Veena, 54, 84
Deo, M. S, 36
Devi, Mohini, 126
Dinham, Barbara, 134
Dorr, Maude, 160
Dow Chemical Company, 61, 63, 67, 68, 69, 75, 76, 77, 78, 118, 120, 134, 151, 168, 170, 176, 177, 178, 179, 180, 181, 182, 183, 184
    see also UCC
Dwivedi, M. P. (Dr), 142, 149

Edwards, Tim, 57
Eveready, 20

Fazli, Nida, 184
FIR (First Information Report), 62, 179

Gandhi, Indira, 39, 122
Gandhi Medical College, 138, 143, 144, 148, 149, 150, 153
Gandhi Peace Foundation, 107
Gandhi, Rajiv, 39, 111, 115, 116, 117
    see also Congress Party
Ganesh, N. (Dr), 57
Germany, 138
GOI (Government of India), 21, 22, 23, 34, 35, 64, 65, 68, 73, 74, 75, 76, 77, 144
Grazia, Alfred De, 48

Gujarat, 76
Gupta, Ashis, 21

Hamidia Hospital, 49, 54, 57, 88, 132, 133, 138, 140, 142, 166
Handa, A. K. (Dr), 149
Hatvalne, Prakash, 160
Hazard (Hazardous), 20, 21, 22, 25, 26, 27, 28, 29, 32, 35, 37, 55, 59, 64, 69, 70, 71, 75, 101,112, 133, 134, 135, 136, 175
Hindus, 114
Hiroshima, 49, 56, 61

ICMR (Indian Council of Medical Research), 73, 88, 132, 133, 136, 137, 138, 139, 140, 141, 143, 144, 145, 146, 147, 148, 149, 150, 153, 162, 174, 183
IIT (Indian Institute of Technology), 27
ILO (International Labor Organization), 138
India, 17, 18, 20, 21, 22, 24, 32, 33, 34, 35, 37, 38, 39, 56, 62, 64, 66, 67, 68, 73, 76, 78, 94, 109, 111, 112, 116, 117, 124, 142, 144, 151, 170, 176, 177, 179, 182, 183
Indonesia, 37
Indore, 52, 76, 114
Iyer, V. R. Krishna (Justice), 65

Jadav, Ramnarayan, 46
Janata Dal (JD), 111, 127
    Singh, V. P., 111
Japan, 56
Jones, Tara, 19, 22, 24, 111

Kanpur, 27
Karnik, Sadhana, 107
Kaur, Devinder (Dr), 174
Keswani, Rajkumar, 27
Khan, Irfan, 121, 122, 123
Khan, Jabbar, 121, 122, 123, 128, 164, 165
Khan, Nawab, 121, 122, 123
Khan, Shahnawaz, 27
Kheer, Tanwant Singh, 94
Killer Factory: Disaster Waiting to Happen, 17–39
    containing crisis, 30–31
    December 3, 1984, 37–39
    development models, perception of hazards, and risk calculations, 20–23
    final betrayal, 35–37
    inside factory, 24–26
    lethal litigation, 34–35
    monolithic entity, 31–33
    question of "who" paid price, 29–30
    slow Bhopals and routine accidents, 23–24
    voices in wilderness, 26–29

KSSP (Kerala Shastra Sahitya Parishad), 109
Kushboo, 156, 157

Liveris, Andrew, 76
London, 30, 67

MacLeod Russell (India) Limited, 67
Madhya Pradesh, 18, 19, 22, 27, 61, 67, 72, 74, 75, 76, 78, 79, 87, 93, 94, 107, 111, 114, 117, 128, 140, 143, 145, 146, 149, 150, 153, 177, 183, 184
   High Court of, 74, 75, 76, 118, 177, 184
   MPPCB (Madhya Pradesh Pollution Control Board), 75
Maharashtra Pollution Control Board, 178
Mahashakti Seva Kendra, 94
Mahindra, Keshub, 66
Melius, James, 133
MFC (Medico Friend Circle), 141, 152, 153
MIC (methyl isocyanate), *passim*, 18, 20, 21, 24, 25, 26, 28, 31, 33, 34, 35, 37, 38, 39, 54, 55, 57, 71, 72, 132, 133, 134, 135, 139, 140, 147, 148, 149, 150, 151, 152, 153, 161, 174
Misra, N. P. (Dr), 138, 139
Monstrous Memories: "Reliving" Night of Disaster, 41–59
   "I learnt biggest lesson of my life," 58–59
   "I saw it…an insidious white cloud," 44–47
   "it seemed like end of world," 47–49
   "it was a stampede of living and dead," 49–51
   "nobody knows if trauma will end," 54–57
   "there was no time for any emotions," 51–54
Morcha, 106, 107, 108, 109, 110, 112, 113, 120, 121, 122, 123, 124, 125, 126, 152, 171
Moxon, Andy, 57
Mukund, J, 27, 28
Murthy, Srinivasa R, 141
MUS (Mahila Udyog Sangathan), 121, 122, 123, 124, 126, 127, 163, 164, 165, 166, 167, 169, 170, 172, 176
Muskan, 156, 157
Muslims, 114
Myrtle Grove Trailer Park, 69

Nagda, Kailash, 112
National Carbon Company (India) Ltd, 18
NEERI (National Environmental Engineering Research Institute), 70, 72
New Delhi (Delhi), 64, 70, 107, 115, 120, 127, 141, 146, 162, 178, 179
   oleum gas leak, 64
   parivartan, 178
New York, 23, 37, 65, 72, 73, 74, 75

Nigam, V.G, 145
No More Bhopals: Women's Right to Knowledge and Control of Bodies, 131–157
   bureaucratic approach, 139–143
   evoking collective guilt and stereotypes, 136–139
   further testimonials from doctors, 143–146
   future research in Bhopal, 146–149
   nature of conflict, 149–151
   nature of gender discrimination, 134–136
   silent voices, 154–157
   true legacy of disaster, 151–154

Oleum Gas leak, *see* New Delhi

PAC (Project Advisory Committee), 142, 143, 145, 153
Pachuari, Suresh, 116
Padyatra, 157, 173, 175, 176, 178, 182
   first, 157
   second, 157
   third, 157
Pandey, Rachna (Dr), 145
Parivartan, 178
   see also New Delhi
Parveen, Shehnaz, 97
Paswan, Ram Vilas, 184
Pathak, Prashant (Dr), 145
Pesticides, 18, 20, 21, 71, 77, 124, 134, 135, 179, 183
   carbaryl, 18
   DDT, 71
   Dursban, 77, 179, 183
   Nurelle, 179, 183
   Pride, 179, 183
   Sevin, 18, 26, 28, 70
   Temik, 18
Pragati Selai Udyog, 97

Rai, Raghu, 160
Ramachandran, P.K. (Dr), 147
Ramalingaswamy, V. (Dr), 138
Ramanathan, Usha, 66
Reliance, 183
Roy, Arundhati, 78
RTI (Right to Information), 137, 178
RVVH (Relief Valve Vent Header), 38

Sadgopal, Anil, 108, 109
Sambhavna Trust, 56, 124, 137, 153, 154, 155, 172, 173, 174, 175
Sarangi, Satinath, 70, 101, 107, 112, 113, 121, 151, 176
SEP (Solar Evaporation Ponds), 71

SEWA (Self-Employed Women's Association), 111
Sharma, O. P. (Dr), 149
Sharma, Parvesh, 99
Sharma, Rajan, 63
Sharma, Shankar Dayal (Dr), 117
Sharma, Vimla, 117
Shinde, Jeevan, 45, 51
Shukla, Champa Devi, 42, 43, 44, 46, 51, 52, 58, 114, 115, 117, 119, 120, 123, 155
Singh, Alok Pratap, 109
Singh, Bhupal, 91
Singh, Manmohan (Dr), 176
Singh, Santosh, 105
Singh, V. P, 111
  see also Janata Dal
Singh, Yashwir, 74
SPARC (Special Assistance to At Risk Children), 180
Sriramachari, S. (Dr), 137, 146, 147, 149, 151
Stationery Union, 105, 113, 114, 115, 118, 119, 120, 168, 175
Sultan, Aziza, 44, 45, 46, 56
Sunil, 46, 47, 48, 51, 87
Supreme Court, 34, 35, 36, 62, 64, 66, 67, 79, 108, 127, 146, 149, 154, 180

Tata, Ratan, 76, 77, 184
Texas, 19, 63
Thakur, Sheela, 81, 97, 99, 166, 170, 171
TISS (Tata Institute of Social Sciences), 91
Trivedi, H. H. (Dr), 139

UCC (Union Carbide Corporation), *passim*, 17, 18, 19, 21, 22, 23, 24, 30, 31, 33, 34, 35, 36, 37, 38, 39, 62, 63, 66, 67, 69, 70, 72, 73, 75, 78, 79, 110, 111, 113, 133, 138, 139, 148, 150, 151, 168, 170, 177, 179, 180
  Dow Chemical Company, 61, 63, 67, 68, 69, 75, 76, 77, 78, 118, 120, 134, 151, 168, 170, 176, 177, 178, 179, 180, 181, 182, 183, 184
  UCKS (Union Carbide Karamchari Sangh), 28

UCWU (Union Carbide Workers' Union), 28
UCIL (Union Carbide India Ltd), 17, 18, 20, 21, 24, 27, 33, 34, 35, 37, 39, 62, 65, 67, 71, 78, 112
  agricultural products division of, 18, 23, 33
UK (United Kingdom), 57, 65, 124, 138
USA (United States of America) (United States), 18, 30, 31, 32, 63, 65, 68, 69, 74, 76, 77, 78, 87, 113, 118, 138, 144, 177, 178

Varadarajan, S. (Dr), 30, 64
Vietnam, 134
  war of, 68, 84
Vishwakarma, Sharda, 46
Vohra, Motilal, 109, 115, 144

Waterman, Ruth, 42
We Are Flames Not Flowers: Inception of Activism, 101–129
  community activism and daily hardships, 104–105
  formation of grassroots organization, 121–125
  local concerns versus macro level issues, 125–129
  march for justice, 113–117
  organized opposition and vested interest, 110–113
  protest and battle for survival, 106–110
  stepping out of workplace, 117–121
Weir, David, 49
Women as Bread Earners: Shattered Lives and Relentless Struggle for Survival, 81–100
  alternative knowledge base, 85–88
  gender perspective, 88–90
  inside work-sheds, 95–99
  interim relief, 90–91
  long-term action plan, 91–94
  nature of disasters, 83–85
  voluntarism and empowerment, 99–100
World War II, 18

YouTube, 178